THORNHAM and the WAVENEY VALLEY

An historic landscape explored

THORNHAM
and the
WAVENEY VALLEY

An historic
landscape explored

John Fairclough and Mike Hardy

To John, 8th Lord Henniker (1916-2004)
A man of vision whose faith in us made it all possible.

ISBN 0 9544456 7 8

Designed and Published by
Heritage Marketing and Publications Ltd
Hill Farm. Great Dunham, King's Lynn, Norfolk, PE32 2LP
Tel: 01760 755645 Fax: 01760 755316
e-mail: sales@heritagemp.com

An extensive range of new and selected out-of-print books on
archaeological and historical subjects is available on the
Heritage Marketing and Publications website at:
http://www.heritagemp.com

Contents

List of Colour Plates (Between pages 96 and 97)

1. A view across the Waveney Valley
2. The Dove Valley at Stoke Ash
3. The Hundreds and Liberties in relation to the river systems
4. Roman Tiles
5. Cow Pasture Lane, part of an ancient long distance route
6. Roman pottery: an early piece of samian imported from France
7. Roman glass from Thornham
8. Anglo-Saxon girdle hangers
9. Anglo-Saxon coins
10. Major holdings at the time of the Domesday Survey
11. Wall painting of St Edmund in Thornham Parva church
12. Grims Ditch near Thornham Parva church
13. Greshaw Green and South Elmham Hall
14. Seventeenth century beadwork plate showing Thornham Hall
15. Thornham Hall in the seventeenth century
16. Thornham Hall in the nineteenth century
17. John, first Lord Henniker
18. John, eighth Lord Henniker
19. Elaborate decoration inside Flixton Hall
20. The Duke of Chandos' yacht
21. A table decoration by John Perkins
22. The Walled Garden at Thornham Hall today
23. The Gardens at Thornham Hall in the nineteenth century
24. Thornham Hall today

Acknowledgements

The authors are grateful to the Henniker family for allowing them access to the estate and encouraging their research both in the field and among the family records. The fieldwork would not have been possible without the support of many farmers and landowners in the Thornham area and elsewhere in North East Suffolk. Members of the Thornham Estate Research Group have spent many hours in the field in all sorts of conditions helping us to find the evidence. Staff of the Suffolk Archaeological Service, Suffolk Record Office and Ipswich Museums provided valuable assistance. Stephen Schwarz has prepared the illustrations for publication.

We are grateful to the Henniker family, Ipswich Borough Council Museums and Galleries, Suffolk Record Office, West Stow Anglo-Saxon Village, Bob Malster and Bob Carr for help with illustrations.

Abbreviations used in notes

BAR	British Archaeological Reports
EAA	East Anglian Archaeology, a series published by the Scole Committee for East Anglian Archaeology
PSIAH	Proceedings of the Suffolk Institute of Archaeology & History
RCHM	Royal Commission on Historical Monuments
SCC	Suffolk County Council
SROB	Suffolk Record Office, Bury St Edmunds branch
SROI	Suffolk Record Office, Ipswich branch
UEA	University of East Anglia
VCH	Victoria County History

FOREWORD

I have always been interested in landscape, but until I came to live at Thornham nearly 30 years ago, and found myself living and working in a landscape that had documented history in boxes and files scattered about the place, I had not really understood that the history of landscape is bound up with the history of the men and women who lived and worked in that landscape. The political, economic and social changes that have occurred over time formed what we see today and the landscape archaelogist must delve deep to start understanding how people have lived on a piece of land since the hunter gatherers stopped wandering, and started to clear the wild wood for fuel, building and crop growing.

The documents we found when cleaning and tidying the Estate office and various buildings. We sent most of them to lpswich to join the large collection deposited there in the 1930s when Thornham Hall was dismantled. Some we kept here to enjoy and to help us fill in the gaps in our knowledge of the Henniker family and their lives at Thornham.

I also began to assemble in magpie fashion, an uncoordinated collection of papers and references, and to read the masters of their subject: Norman Scarfe , W.G. Hoskins, Ronald Blythe, Tom Williamson, and, inevitably, I ended up at one of Mike Hardy's courses on Landscape Archaelogy. The rest came naturally, my husband suggested that Mike should do a survey of the Estate, and that idea was expanded later to include the Waveney Valley. This book is the result of years of study and research; not to mention walking, by both John Fairclough and Mike Hardy, who have brought together all the strands and unconsidered trifles and, with their scholarship, have made them into a fascinating picture of Thornham and the Waveney Valley. And in small part, the Henniker family. I am just sad that my husband died before the book was finished.

Julia, Lady Henniker

Chapter 1

Introduction to the Landscape

Explain the story of the Thornham Estate! Why did we accept this challenge? It was intriguing to ask whether the estate really did extend to 33,000 acres of Suffolk in the nineteenth century. Did Elizabeth I and Charles II really stay here? We knew it had produced prehistoric pots and Roman remains, but was it the home of a Roman called Faustinus? It seemed even less likely that one owner was descended from an Englishman who was elected 'King of the Romans'. In the past it was home to politicians, courtiers, statesmen and city merchants, but now it is a quiet backwater of rural Suffolk. In the eighteenth century it belonged to a family connected with some of the wealthiest merchants in the City of London. Now it is both a working farm and a Centre for Learning, proving it can keep up with changes demanded by modern

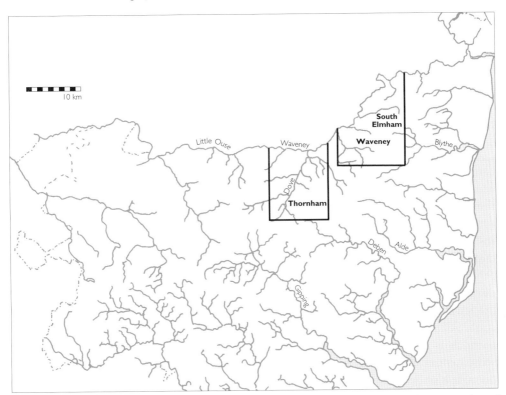

Figure 1.1 *Thornham and South Elmham in relation to the rivers. This shows the complex pattern formed by the streams in our area.*

life. We had permission to walk all the fields and explore the earthworks preserved in woodlands. Could we explain deep ponds some of which did not appear to be moats? Could we discover how the house acquired and lost valuable collections of paintings and porcelain? We couldn't resist the opportunity to try to read the story of this landscape and its people.

Thornham lies in the valley of the river Dove which runs into the Waveney. Already we had a great deal of evidence about the history of the South Elmham group of parishes further down the Waveney valley, south of Bungay. This has come from many years of field walking and documentary research by Mike Hardy. As we developed our work at Thornham we realised that in many ways the Thornham parishes look north towards the river Waveney which now marks the boundary between Suffolk and Norfolk, and they show many similarities with the landscape history of the Elmhams, as well as some intriguing differences. It soon became clear that there was scope to develop the comparisons between these two areas of rural Suffolk. This led to a greater understanding of both. The result is this book revealing the development of two landscapes, travelling far back through their long history and giving an insight into their past.

To most people Thornham Magna and Parva are just names on signs opposite the turnings to Eye, and the main landmark is the White Horse public house on an isolated crossroads in Stoke Ash. However detailed research is revealing that not only does the estate have an interesting and complex recent history, but this area was a centre of activity as early as the New Stone Age, some 6000 years ago. There are signs of increasing human activity through the Bronze and Iron Ages. Under the Roman Empire, about 1800 years ago, this part of the countryside has a special interest because we have documentary evidence of the name of a landowner. It was very probably part of the Estate of Faustinus, called Villa Faustini in an imperial directory of roads. In the Middle Ages ownership of some of it changed between the great abbey of Bury St. Edmunds and the local Priory of Eye, one of whose monks lived here as a hermit. Why did he choose this spot? Why was his chapel dedicated to St. Eadburga? It helped when we found out who Eadburga was.

The estate centred on the hall and park in Thornham Magna now has about 2000 acres with 1386 acres under the plough but at one time it extended to more than 10,000 acres. It has not attracted much notice from historians being located in the apparently remote rural centre of East Anglia, although it adjoins one of the region's main trunk routes. This account of the estate's history draws on documentary evidence for the history of the villages, manors and farms in local and national records. It uses the maps and plans prepared for the estate's owners at various dates as well as the nineteenth century tithe and Ordnance Survey maps. There are records of archaeological finds during the last two centuries which have been brought together. We have examined the surviving earthworks, particularly moats, some protected from destruction and concealed from modern eyes by the extensive woodlands. Thorough field walking of as much as possible of the available farmland has added evidence about the centres of settlement at different periods and the nature of the activities carried on in some of them. It is only by combining all these different types of evidence that we can build up an accurate picture of the changing landscape of the area, and reconstruct the story of its inhabitants as they used local resources and responded to influences from far afield.

At no stage should we think of these people as isolated from the national scene. We can see signs of contact with the outside world as early as the metalworkers of the Bronze Age and potters of the Iron Age. Then came soldiers and travellers in Roman times and the monks of the Middle Ages communicating with their mother house in France and the papal administration in Rome. The wider interests of those who owned the estate in more recent times presumably meant they valued its strategic location on the road from Norwich to Ipswich and onward to London.

Why has this area attracted settlement? The answer seems to lie, at least partly, in its location, that factor beloved of estate agents! Thornham sits on good agricultural land on the edge of the wet lands around the headwaters of tributaries of the River Waveney. It is drained by its major tributary the Dove, which flows through Eye. The actual source of the Waveney in Lopham and Redgrave Fens is only 6 miles away and from here it flows, growing rapidly in size, past Scole, only 4 miles away on the A140 where it would be navigable by small barges, to Bungay. There at one time it became a commercial navigation and used to enter the sea through the Great Estuary at Yarmouth until an artificial outlet to the North Sea, then known as the German Ocean, was created through Lowestoft in the nineteenth century. The Waveney is said to have been named after the 'quaking bogs' of fenland in the valley through which it meanders[1] but it is a substantial waterway with sufficient stretches of solid bank to accommodate quays and staithes. Ships entered the lower reaches of the river from the sea, then traders could transfer goods to, and from, barges to carry their business far inland. Today we tend to forget how important water transport was right up until the railways were built in the nineteenth century. Our area has always had access to the outside world along the River Waveney but also by substantial roads. What is now the A140 from Ipswich to Norwich and two straight roads either side of the Elmham parishes have been in use since they were constructed by the Romans, who ignored the long distance tracks already cutting through our countryside. The new Roman roads were only the major highways, the trunk roads of their day, so most of the older routes remained in use. Some stretches of these ancient tracks are still in use and relate to prehistoric field systems of which some elements are visible today. These tracks, surviving now as minor roads, bridleways or footpaths, appear to be some of the earliest evidence for the management of our landscape. People must have used them over many generations to move domesticated animals between pastures and to markets, to transport agricultural produce and enable itinerant traders as well as local residents to move easily between settlements. The long tracks running almost parallel through the Elmham parishes, and the neighbouring Ilketshalls, are not straight enough to be the work of Roman surveyors, although one appears to have been improved by Roman engineers to become part of the road known as Stone Street. Their appearance, and the associated field systems that survived into the nineteenth century, have been compared by Oliver Rackham[2] to the Dartmoor reaves which were in use in the Bronze Age. It may well be that these Suffolk tracks also survive from planned divisions of the landscape at an equally early date. People were farming the land and travelling long distances by that time and there has always been a tendency to keep existing roads and boundaries unless there are pressing reasons to change them. So our area had productive farm land and good communications by water and by road.

Some elements of the road system and field patterns have survived from very early days. We can see evidence in part but not all of the area for the later creation of some large open fields, managed in typical medieval strips. However in our region sufficient individual small fields survived to preserve the older pattern which is visible on our earliest maps. Later those few open fields were divided into smaller units, many of which were more recently destroyed in the creation of massive fields for the modern fashion of devoting large areas to a single crop of cereals, rape or beet. In a medieval fashion visible throughout our region greens were created with artisans living on their edge, but some of these have since become large arable fields. We have been able to unravel some of the sequence of changes that created the landscape as we see it today. Such changes are still happening and more evidence turns up about past changes, so this account can only be a snapshot of what we know at the moment.

Much of the land is glacial boulder clay which today grows good crops of grain and sugar beet but has also at times supported large dairy herds. The valleys of the Dove and its tributaries, like the broader stretch of the Waveney, with their gently sloping sides offer rich soil refreshed by flood waters from the river. These can be managed as grazing meadows. On the higher ground is the chalky boulder clay, known as Lowestoft Till, left behind by the melting ice of a great Ice Age glacier that extended as far south as the Thames valley. As the climate warmed the ice melted leaving our area covered by a thick mantle of heavy clay containing chalk and flints from the Cretaceous rocks that are now deeply buried here. It also holds a variety of stones ranging from large sarsen boulders to small pebbles of granite, sandstone and almost every type of rock. Some of these must have travelled considerable distances in the ice before it melted, and are

Figure 1.2 *Fossils of creatures that lived in the sea found at Thornham. These include ammonites (top right), gryphaea, sea urchins (bottom right) and belemnites (bottom left).*

generally referred to as erratics because they have wandered so far from their natural origins. The composition and density of the clay varies and some deposits have been used to make pottery and bricks. Deep digging through the clay occasionally reveals below it shelly crag which was laid down as a sea bed in the Pleistocene period about two million years ago and shows our area was then under the edge of a great sea, wider on both sides than the present North Sea. Deep below this is the chalk rock, containing layers of flint, which was formed in the Cretaceous period about ninety million years ago. Other evidence of the geological forces that created this setting comes from fossil remains: we have picked up pieces of twenty three fossil ammonites, several of which are large and unusually well preserved. A vertebra from the backbone of a large prehistoric animal and a great variety of fossilised ancient oysters (gryphaea), squid (belemnites) and sea urchins have been found among the stones and rounded pebbles from the debris left behind by melting glaciers when the Ice Ages shaped this landscape with its valleys. This was always an area of valuable woodland which is reflected in local place names that refer to thorn, ash, oak, willow and wattle and there are still extensive woods, now more valuable for their shooting rights than the supply of building timber and brushwood fuel.

Some clearly visible features of the landscape are clues to activities in the past, but more can be revealed by close examination of the fields. For a number of years, with the help of the Thornham Estate Research Group and many individuals, we have field walked methodically over 29,000 acres on the Thornham Estate and in the Waveney valley. Disciplined field walking is a useful archaeological technique for collecting material disturbed by ploughing or other farming activities. We walk across whole fields, even very large ones, generally crossing them in straight lines at regular intervals. We pick up all objects visible on the surface that appear to be man made, whatever their

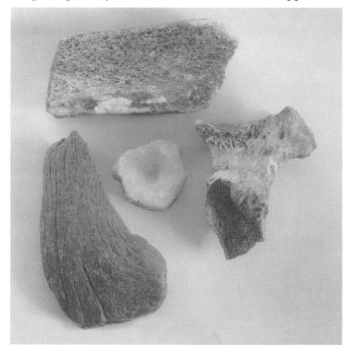

Figure 1.3 *Fossils of animals that lived on land found at Thornham.*

age or material, and note any particular concentrations of material. Areas that produce a lot of material need to be recorded and inspected later in more detail, but the initial aim is to see the pattern of finds across the whole field. Most fields are walked several times under different conditions to see what has been revealed by different methods of cultivation or by the effects of the weather. By following a systematic pattern in walking over ploughed fields and recording all the objects that are collected – fragments of pottery, worked flints, pieces of corroded metal – we can decide where people were living and working. This material disturbed by the plough can belong to any period in the past and we use all of it to see changes over the centuries. It has a special value at times when we have no written records, so that a few pieces of hand-made pottery from the years after the end of Roman government in Britain about AD 410 can be more significant than large quantities of mass produced Roman pottery. Much less pottery, or material of any sort, survives from those so-called Dark Ages and our discovery of a few Early Saxon objects indicates that people did continue living here and almost certainly farmed much of the land even though possibly not so intensively. At least we can argue against the old claim that most of our land was totally abandoned. On the contrary we suggest that its occupants contributed to the great wealth and international trading links of the king of East Anglia who was buried with his treasures at Sutton Hoo, and of his successors who supported Christian abbots and bishops prepared to travel to and from Rome itself. When we use this material evidence we cast light on the life of people in the period that is only a 'Dark Age' because historians have very few contemporary written records to study.

In some cases the failure to find any evidence, sometimes called negative archaeology, is an important factor. It can suggest that we are looking at an area that was formerly parkland or woodland. It might have been used as pasture before being ploughed up quite recently. It still helps us to understand the development of the landscape. This is also the case if we find only a thin scatter of material as this usually represents manuring scatter. When the material from the muck heap in the farmyard was spread on the fields because of all the organic waste it contained there was also a certain amount of broken pottery, animal bones and general household refuse that went with it. This can tell us something about activity in the nearby farmstead and provide significant dating evidence. We can also discover greater concentrations of refuse centred on the middens of the houses, that is where they dumped the household rubbish in the days before Local Authorities organised refuse collections. These were always close to the actual houses, so if we walk the fields several times in different years and under various conditions we can build up a picture of where people had their houses, where they dumped their rubbish and which fields were receiving farmyard manure. This tells us about the edges of settlements and the extent of arable cultivation at different periods. It all depends on careful observation and meticulous recording, to ensure that our conclusions are valid.

We augment the information from field walking by the systematic use of metal detectors, which can be a great help provided that all finds are carefully plotted on maps and we do not dig below the plough soil. Below the reach of the plough material from the past can survive undisturbed, so this must only be examined in a controlled excavation that distinguishes the different layers which enable us to see the relationship between material of different periods, technically referred to as the stratigraphy. We have an obligation to report all our finds to the landowners and to ensure they are recorded on the county council database, the Historic Environment Record. This is often referred to by its previous name the Sites & Monuments Record (SMR) and is maintained by the Archaeological Service of Suffolk County Council at Bury St Edmunds. Examination of the record of earlier finds included in the SMR enables us to benefit from the work done by previous generations of archaeologists, both amateur and professional. Unfortunately study of aerial photographs of the Thornham area has added little to our knowledge, probably because of the intensive farming activities in medieval and modern times on land which is largely boulder clay. In the Waveney Valley area they are more informative and in particular show many ring ditches, most of which are likely to be Bronze Age burial sites. We are making some use of geophysical techniques that make it possible to locate buried features without excavation, and a resistivity survey in Stoke Ash appears to be confirming the original line of the Roman road where the modern A140 takes a slightly different line. We plan to confirm this finding by extending the survey and by small test excavations on the apparent line of the road.

Tools made from flint are among our more frequent finds. Flint occurs naturally in our region, both as broken pieces in the surface drift deposits of clay with flints that form much of our soil and in layers deposited in the chalk that underlies the whole area. It is this flint in the chalk that was being mined at Grimes Graves in Norfolk some 6000 years ago when people dug as much as 40 feet down through the chalk to extract the best quality flint for making tools. Flint in its original form is generally grey and translucent but it can take on all sorts of colours from chemicals in the ground. In its natural deposit in the chalk it develops a hard outer coating known as the cortex, which makes it look like an opaque white stone. Flint nodules can take many shapes, sometimes because the flint has formed from the fossilised remains of ancient sea creatures, but often showing complex patterns of no obvious origin. When broken and left in the ground its surface acquires a patina derived from its surroundings. Later breaks will reveal the original interior colour. The speed at which it acquires a patina seems unpredictable, so is not a reliable guide to whether a break is ancient or modern. The structure of flint is very similar to that of glass so it can be broken to produce a sharp edge. A skilled flint knapper can use this to create complex and efficient cutting, chopping and boring tools. In ancient times they used hard pebbles as 'hammerstones' to strike flakes from the core of the flint nodule, and then did more detailed flaking with the aid of tools made from deer antler which can remove flakes of flint with great accuracy. The earliest flint tools that we find were made long ago in the Old Stone Age but some of the finest flint tools were produced by skilled workers in the New Stone Age, Beaker period and Early Bronze Age. Inferior but practical rough cutting blades were struck during the Roman period, no doubt in much the same way that modern workers out in the fields still strike a sharp flint blade if they do not have a steel knife to hand. Blocks of flint can be knapped to produce a square face and this was much used in the Middle Ages to produce decoration in the stonework of churches, sometimes creating elaborate flushwork panels containing letters or symbols. Rough flints were used to build strong walls and these made strong structures provided they were carefully

Figure 1.4 *Burnt flints are found frequently when field walking.*

selected and set in a strong mortar. In more recent times metal tools were used to produce gun flints in huge numbers as long as flint lock weapons were in general use. When field walking it is easy to be deceived by the many different colours and shapes in which natural and worked flints can be found. It takes practice to recognise them and then to distinguish between those broken naturally by frost action or accidentally struck by a farm machine and the tools or the waste products left by the making of tools. Making a single tool resulted in a huge number of waste flakes, some of which could themselves be made into tools, but most were left where they fell. This waste itself indicates places where people were making tools.

One common feature throughout the Waveney Valley is the presence of large spreads of burnt flints which are broken in a crackled fashion that is quite distinct from the deliberate striking of flakes that marks human workmanship. They do not show the random fractures created by weathering, particularly frost, and by chance blows from farm machinery. These are not the product of natural processes which can create many different varieties of flint that confuse casual observers. They are not related to the manufacture of flint tools. The burnt flints appear in different varieties: those exposed to dry heat are generally red or reddish brown in colour, but wet heat produces a blue or blue and white/ light grey colour. Mike Hardy has carried out a series of controlled firings of flint to reproduce the different varieties (see Appendix 1 for details). Really blue/ grey burnt flints are only created when the hot flints are totally immersed in water, so we can be confident that piles of blue crackled flints mark places where people have boiled water by heating flints on a fire then tipping them into a container of water which will boil instantly. This process was used when people did not have ceramic pots or metal bowls that could stand direct exposure to a hot fire. Such pot boiler flints can be dated when they are associated with pottery or worked flints. In some cases they include the waste flint cores discarded when making tools from flakes of flint and then included in the pot boiling material. This means that we can confidently date some of these spreads to the New Stone Age, but other groups show this method of boiling water being used much later. Red flints created by dry heat may be part of the hearth or fireplace made on a beaten earth floor which incorporated flints in its clay in which case they are likely to be associated with contemporary finds that can be dated. This combination can be a valuable indicator of possible house sites although it needs to be tested by excavation to confirm the presence of a floor. However heaps of dry burnt flints can be the result of improving farm land using a process, popular in the nineteenth century, of burning mounds of clay to make its structure more fertile. A book of the mid nineteenth century[3] says this process of clod-burning was particularly prevalent in the parishes between Stradbroke and Framlingham to improve the turnip crop, but it was clearly practised more widely. The evidence from the Waveney valley presented in Appendix 1 shows a significant number of concentrations of burnt flints associated with prehistoric material suggesting they were being used as pot-boilers, so we are seeing how some people were boiling their food. However a much larger number, particularly in the adjacent parishes of Mendham and Metfield, are products of nineteenth-century agricultural improvements and the results of this more modern activity can be recognised on some of the fields at Thornham. It is conspicuous in some fields on Wood Hall Farm in Stoke Ash. They remind us that in looking for and interpreting evidence on the fields we have to bear in mind all the different activities that have gone on here over many centuries.

Thornham is on the southern edge of the Waveney valley which now forms the boundary between Norfolk and Suffolk. That administrative division already existed when the Domesday Book was compiled in the eleventh century, but the people of this valley form a community that does not belong entirely to either county, for even those on the Suffolk side tend to look towards Norwich more often than to Ipswich. This was presumably part of the ancient territory of the great Iceni of northern East Anglia rather than the southern Trinovantes, but being at the interface between them may always have had an individual identity. Perhaps we should be thinking about 'the people of the Waveney valley' just as even more clearly defined to the south east of them were 'the people of the Blyth valley', in the area that became the Hundred of Blything. Even in the Domesday Record of 1086 a number of holdings overlap the River Waveney suggesting that they survived from a time when it did not mark a rigid boundary. We certainly need to consider developments at Thornham in relation to what was happening along the Waveney valley. Fortunately Mike Hardy has carried out detailed field walking surveys in the Waveney parishes of the South Elmhams, Mendham and Flixton[4]. All parts of the South Elmham parishes have easy access to water with only one small area as much as a mile away from a stream, but the high water table means that even here ponds would provide enough water for a settlement. In these parishes the highest recorded point is at 56 metres in Metfield while much of central Metfield and St. James lie on the 50 metre contour. This high land would have supported natural woodland and finds of Neolithic axeheads suggest people started to clear it as early as the New Stone Age, but traces of it may survive in the high percentage of woodland species, including elm, hazel and some chestnut, growing in local hedges.

Mike has examined all the accessible land in that part of the valley to collect any evidence of human activity exposed by ploughing, including fragments of broken pottery, worked flints and metal objects. These have been recorded on detailed plans to show concentrations of material typical of living sites and the more general spread of small abraded fragments resulting from the spreading of manure across arable fields. He has also collected information from those who use metal detectors to find coins, brooches, buckles and various other objects. Adding records of casual finds made over the years and putting this information together with the interpretation of crop marks on aerial photographs he has built up a picture of the changing pattern of settlement which he has tested in places by the excavation of small areas. The same methods of investigation and recording have been used in the Thornham area so the results can be compared directly. We are seeing similarities and differences between the activities of people in these different parts of the Waveney valley. Extensive professional excavations ahead of gravel extraction at Flixton and in advance of housing and road construction at Carlton Colville have provided more detailed information about limited areas which prove to have complex histories. Systematic study of all the available evidence enables us to build a picture of how people lived and worked in our area, although inevitably it leaves some questions unanswered, at least for the moment. It seems that from early times until the last century the average size of individual farms was about 50 to 60 acres, with fields generally being between two and six acres. Many of these farms belonged to one of the great estates that controlled much of the land in this area.

Once we reach Norman and later times things can become easier because increasing numbers of written documents survive to give us names and precise dates. Many of these are preserved in the Suffolk Record Offices, but others are in private hands. The search has also led us to the Public Record Office, now officially The National Archive, at Kew and the British Library at St Pancras. Rarely are the contents of early documents straightforward and they can present serious challenges when we have to interpret their significance and compare them with the archaeological evidence from the ground. However using this combination of evidence we find farms, generally of about 50 acres, being worked by yeomen who might own their land as freeholders or more often are tenants of a larger manor. We can also see how greens were created, apparently on the edge of the land farmed by existing settlements. These greens are open areas where certain people acquired the common right to pasture animals on terms fixed by the manorial courts. Round the outside edge of the open green they built houses with small enclosures of land, presumably used to grow vegetables and provide compact paddocks for domestic livestock. Many of them seem to have been artisans or craftsmen keeping a few animals to augment the income earned through their skills: they were not attempting to become yeoman farmers but remind us that there was a market for manufactured artefacts from shoes and buckles to ploughs and household furniture. Thus new communities grew up a short distance from existing villages or hamlets and some of these are still called …… Green, others are known as tyes or commons. We can also trace some elements in the development of the manufacture and trading of pottery in the area on a commercial scale.

Of course to some extent the activities in a particular area were dictated by the natural features. We find arable fields and enclosed meadows on the best agricultural land, while dry heath provided rough grazing and brushwood or turf for fuel. Some of the wetter land sustained managed woodland to supply timber for building and underwood for fuel, while really wet fenland, such as Palgrave, Redgrave and Lopham fens, might support wildfowl which could be caught for food, with pools for fish. Some of the really wet areas were managed strategically: for example Eye castle, which was the centre of an important Honour, was shielded from medieval attackers by large areas of water in addition to its immediate defensive earthworks. All these uses of the land have left their mark on the modern landscape if we understand how to read them. As we get nearer to the present we find increasing numbers of buildings survive, not only the stone churches but also some substantial timber framed houses and barns. Understanding of carpentry techniques, and the use of tree ring studies to provide absolute dates (dendrochronology), show some of them have been standing for much longer than we used to think. These remind us that buildings survive as long as a good roof and sound footings protect them from the effects of the weather, but quite small changes in the climate can affect which crops grow well and how big a population the land can support. The evidence for this is not so easy to find and much of it is disputed but we need to bear it in mind, along with the impact of natural disasters such as the great plague of the Black Death in the fourteenth century. Such factors affect the relationship between the owners of large estates and their tenants, as when the decline in population after the Black Death raised the cost of labour. They might be expected to change the way land was managed. We can look for signs of these changes, but must beware of assuming everybody reacted in the same way.

When considering the buildings in which people lived, worked and worshipped, we need to take into account the materials available to the builders. East Anglia lacks suitable stone for the squared blocks of ashlar and detailed mouldings produced by skilled stone masons. Such stone had to be imported by water from other parts of the country or from abroad. However to exploit local resources great skills were developed in using flint as a building material. Selected flints were laid in courses to face walls, bedding rougher flints in mortar for the core of thicker walls and knapping good quality flint to produce flat faces that could be used in decorative panels of flushwork. Many large buildings were constructed with solid timber frames in which the wall panels were filled with wattle and daub and the roof covered with thatch. We see that this use of timber was an ancient tradition and we can be sure that local carpenters acquired great skills in cutting and joining timbers to produce strong structures. However there was always the incentive to make better use of the local clays than as the daub applied to wattling or as 'clay lump', which was simply large blocks of clay allowed to dry naturally and then used in the fashion of modern breeze blocks. As early as Roman times people were making a variety of building, flooring and roofing tiles by firing clay to a high temperature in kilns. There is still much debate about the earliest date at which medieval builders started to use bricks, similar in shape to modern ones. The presence of suitable brickearths in many parts of our region and the skills of kiln construction developed by potters certainly provided the opportunity. We find kilns for making bricks and tiles in several locations, but the evidence for dating the earliest of these remains elusive. More recently the bricks used by the Hennikers when rebuilding Thornham Hall in the nineteenth century were made specially on the estate.

Craftsmen of past generations have left their mark in some unusual places. The tower of Ilketshall St Lawrence church has a lead covering and the men who laid it have left a remarkable collection of graffiti. There are outlines of pointed shoes of sixteenth century design and the portrayal of an incident that might represent a hanging. Etched into the lead is the outline of a person with a noose around his neck and on the other end of the rope is a sack of cereals perhaps used in suspending the body (or perhaps it related to his offence). There is also the outline of a gallows. Could the workman see a real gallows from his high vantage point? Hanging bodies would be a familiar sight as the record of the burial of Dorothy Carver on 26 September 1593 tells us that she was 'wife of George Carver, hanged on Gallows Hill, Homersfield on a gibbet for bringing to death by poison his said wife and his mother in law also Millesene Bennet'.

When we find different types of object they highlight changes of emphasis in farming activities. Numerous pieces of millstones show that cereal crops were being processed, while a number of bronze bells that were worn by livestock let out to graze mark the keeping of animals. The latter remind us of written records telling us that for many years this was part of a major dairying region producing large quantities of butter and cheese. We say 'changes of emphasis' because for most of the history of human activity in our region it was an area of mixed farming where the manure from numbers of livestock was spread over arable fields that produced cereal crops. Domesday Book records that in 1086 throughout our area arable land was being worked with ploughs pulled by teams of oxen, although if the plough was totally wooden without even a metal share nothing of it will survive. It is tempting to assume that all medieval farmers worked in the same way but those in East Anglia clearly did not always follow the fashion that seems to have been standard in much of the Midlands. Edward Martin has pointed out that in Suffolk just as we do not see consistent use of the open field system typical of medieval farming in much of the midland region, we also see a different method of ploughing. The midland open fields were ploughed in long strips creating the pattern

Figure 1.5 *Oak Farm, Metfield: an early timber framed building. One of the oldest in the parish, still standing in its moated enclosure on the edge of Metfield Common, it is typical of the yeoman class using large quantities of oak in its structure. See page 142.*

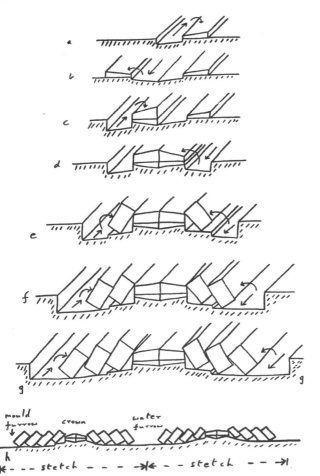

Figure 1.6 *Stetch ploughing: how the pattern of furrows was created from the turning of the central furrow to the completion of the water furrow that helped drainage.*

of ridge and furrow, sometimes still visible where such fields were converted to pasture. In Suffolk it seems that as early as the Middle Ages the method of ploughing was the same as that documented in the nineteenth century, in which the size and number of fields was variable and the ploughing was done in blocks called stetches. A stetch was a block of furrows between three and eighteen yards wide, depending on the nature of the soil, ploughed as a unit with open furrows to drain the water being left only in the strip between stetches. The ploughman left a broad strip of headland at the ends of the field to allow space to turn his team, but completed the field by ploughing right round the headlands. Even the strips in those common fields that were used seem to have been worked as stetches. The division of fields in Thornham suggests that a few large fields were divided into strips, many of which were consolidated into larger blocks before the end of the Middle Ages, although a few strips do appear on later maps. However it seems that some of the land was always divided into individual small fields, which might even have formed part of the pre-Roman landscape. This mixed situation appears typical of Suffolk where few villages practised the text-book three field system of the Midlands. Even the common open fields that did exist were largely converted to individual fields before the days of formal enclosure acts. Detailed work in Walsham le Willows[5] has revealed a similar situation.

We can see the effects of some developments in the tools used by farmers. Apart from the occasional rusty remnant of an iron plough share and less obvious broken iron attachments little survives of the ordinary labourer's equipment. The occasional lost sharpening stone reminds us of the need to stop regularly and sharpen the blade of the scythe or sickle when harvesting was done with hand tools. However the introduction of steam ploughing engines in the later part of the nineteenth century led to the removal of some long established field boundaries in order to create the long stretches needed for the economical operation of these large machines. We suspect that some finds of coal and coal ash at certain points on the headlands might mark their presence. More recently the combine harvesters and ever bigger multi-furrow ploughs have led to opening up of even larger areas, creating open prairie fields on parts of the estate.

The fragments of millstones recovered during field walking testify to the processing of grain, but do not tell us what type of mill was being used. Small millstones might well have been used as handmills in the home, but we know that at least as early as Roman times water power was being used to power machinery. Evidence of a Roman waterwheel was found at Scole during excavations prior to the construction of the bypass. Some mills might also have depended on donkeys to turn them, another application familiar in the Roman Empire. The introduction of windmills is said to have been later than 1100, although it is now suggested that they might have been an East Anglian invention[6] so we cannot be sure. As the earliest examples are thought to have been very small structures supported on a single large post set in the ground, we should not expect to find the more substantial evidence left by the later more elaborate postmills or the brick tower mills of more recent times. However it is generally assumed that the mills referred to in the Domesday Book of 1086 were powered by water. Examples are recorded in the Waveney Valley at South Elmham and Homersfield with two in Mendham, and the last two parishes still have watermills standing at the present day. In the Thornham area the only mill recorded in Domesday Book was at Braiseworth, no doubt on the River Dove which marks the eastern boundary of the parish.

Archaeological evidence tells us that the Thornhams were a significant focus of human activity from at least as early as the New Stone Age until the early Middle Ages. At least from Iron Age times some of the occupation was too concentrated for farming activity and suggests a commercial market centre that had an administrative function. It seems that they lost this role shortly before the Norman conquest of 1066 when Robert Malet, the new Norman lord of the area, chose a strategic location for his castle on the island of Eye, two miles away on the other side of the main road. This was a good site because it was surrounded by water, most of which has since been removed by later drainage schemes, so it was easier to create a fortress that was simple to defend, and it had better access by boat than places higher up the Dove. This was important for a successful market, but even more so for bringing building materials and supplies to the castle. Being less than two miles from the main road from Ipswich to Norwich, now the A140, across open country Eye castle could still dominate this strategic highway. Malet had extensive lands which became the Honour of Eye and having imposed his authority by building a motte and bailey castle on this new site, he developed the market town. This had probably been established in the first place by his predecessor Edric of Laxfield, who also owned the growing private port of Dunwich. Domesday Book records the early stages of this new centre with 25 burgesses in Malet's town of Eye and the complaint that the Bishop's long established market at Hoxne, some two miles away on the other side, had lost its trade to the new market at the castle gate. Malet established his authority in territory between the great holdings of the abbey of St. Edmund at Bury to the west, which held land in Thornham, and the holdings of the bishopric at Hoxne to which the mighty bishop Herbert de Losinga attached importance in his rivalry with Bury abbey. When he moved his see from Thetford to Norwich in 1094 he retained the bishopric's interest in both Hoxne and South Elmham. Further down the Waveney Roger Bigod was master of Bungay where his castle dominated the river. Once Eye became the commercial and administrative centre, reducing the status of Thornham as well as that of Hoxne, it is significant that Bury abbey later leased its valuable hermitage in Thornham to the new priory established by Malet at Eye. However Bury insisted on continued acknowledgement of its lordship over the property.

It is clear that in the early Middle Ages the Waveney valley was a focus of religious activity. The places named Flixton were called after East Anglia's first bishop, St. Felix, while Homersfield is linked to the later bishop Humberht[7]. Mendham is recorded as a minster community as early as bishop Theodred's will in AD 951. Best known is the association of Hoxne with the bishopric, being described as its seat in Suffolk in the Domesday Book. It was retained by later Bishops of Norwich who apparently changed its connection with the earlier martyred East Anglian king St. Ethelbert to link it to the later martyrdom of St. Edmund. The administrative hundred centred on Hoxne was generally referred to as the Bishop's Hundred and was so described as early as Domesday Book in 1086[8]. We shall examine in detail the religious connections at Thornham itself including the presence of a hermitage at a chapel with the unusual dedication to St. Eadburga. This focuses attention on the churches and particularly that of Thornham Parva with its wall paintings, including part of a medieval version of the story of the martyred king of East Anglia, St. Edmund. The recent find of the medieval seal matrix for the Deanery of Hartismere reminds us that we are in the centre of the administrative Hundred of Hartismere. It extended north to the Waveney and included Mendlesham to the south, having its boundary on the edge of the parishes that look towards the River Gipping. This conforms to the way that many of the Hundred divisions relate to the catchments of rivers so that Hartismere takes in land that drains into the Waveney and its tributary the Dove, while to its south the Hundred of Bosmere and Claydon feeds the River Gipping and its tributaries (Plate 3). The hundreds of Suffolk existed before the compilation of Domesday Book and are probably based on very much older regional units as they relate so closely to the geography of the river systems. The southern boundary of Hartismere Hundred was marked by a massive ditched lane that was probably of great antiquity in defining this regional unit. It is recorded in plate 17 of the first edition of Norman Scarfe's 'Suffolk Landscape' (1972) and its loss is noted on page 83 of his third edition (2002), reminding us how vulnerable these features of our historic environment really are.

After the Dissolution of the monasteries local gentry were able to enlarge their substantial land holdings and we can see the owners of Thornham increasing the estate of the Wiseman and Bokenham families which passed by marriage to the Killigrews who were influential courtiers of Charles II. The only transfer of this estate by sale was when Sir John Major added it to his property in Worlingworth. His daughters introduced it to the peerage as one married the future first Lord Henniker and the other the second Duke of Chandos. Major and Henniker were wealthy entrepreneurial merchants involved in the timber trade with Russia including the importation of masts for naval ships. The Hennikers have been lords of the manor from the eighteenth century to the present day. We can see changes in agriculture from mixed but predominantly dairy farming to an almost totally arable landscape, while woodland has been reduced and transformed from being a source of timber and fuel to become ornamental plantations and coverts for game birds. As the main residence Thornham Hall has changed from Elizabethan mansion to modern pavilion. In the following chapters we explore all these changes in more detail and find evidence of independent attitudes among the people we study. As you will see there are few easy answers but many fascinating stories.

Notes

1   Gelling, M, and Cole, A, 1984 *Place-Names in the Landscape*, Stamford, 60.
2   Rackham, O, 1986 *The History of the Countryside*, London, 156.
3   Raynbird, W and Raynbird, H, 1849 *On the Agriculture of Suffolk*, London, 57.
4   'Mendham & Metfield', *PSIAH* **36** (1985), 47–8; South Elmham St. Cross & St. James, *PSIAH* **36** (1986), 147–150; South Elmham St. Margaret, All Saints & St. Nicholas, *PSIAH* **36** (1987), 232–5; South Elmham St. Michael & St. Peter, *PSIAH* **36** (1988), 315–7; Flixton, *PSIAH* **37** (1989), 66–9; see also John Ridgard, South Elmham Minster, *PSIAH* **36**, 196.
5   West, S, and McLaughlin, A, 1998 *Towards a Landscape History of Walsham le Willows*, EAA, **85**.
6   See discussion in EAA, Occasional Paper **11** (2003) on the Boreham windmill.
7   Scarfe, N, 1986 *Suffolk in the Middle Ages*, Woodbridge, 25–28.
8   Rumble, A (ed) 1986 *Domesday Book, Suffolk*, Chichester, e.g. entry 1.92.

Chapter 2

The First People in the Landscape

It is always difficult to comprehend the time-scale of the earliest evidence of man. It covers such a vast period of time: how can we relate to 500,000 years ago? That is the age of Homo Erectus, our earliest stage of man, when we have the first indications of people moving over a landscape still being shaped and developed towards the countryside we see today. At that time a land bridge linked us to Europe. As many thousands of years passed new ideas and ways of life were emerging. We call this period of time Palaeolithic, the Old Stone Age, which refers to the use of stone for shaping into simple tools and weapons. The Palaeolithic Age itself is divided into three periods: the Lower, Middle and Upper phases.

Our understanding of early people comes from many sources and we have to look at distant places to discover how they affected our local landscape. The study of ancient human bones enables us to understand their lifestyle and stature. We can build up a picture of how and where they lived. From their teeth we know the type of food they ate and we can determine the age of an individual. We know that more than two and a half million years ago the earliest stone tools were used in Ethiopia and East and Southern Africa, being simple flakes and flaked pebbles. The first humans steadily improved in stature and changed their way of life. In Britain the first indication of human beings comes from finds at Boxgrove in West Sussex and is dateable to about 500,000 BC. From Swanscombe in Kent comes evidence of the next stage in the development of man with three pieces of skull, the first being found in 1935 and additional material in 1936 and 1955. These have been dated to about 400,000 BC, the time of Homo Heidelbergensis. Additional information comes from twenty human teeth found at Pont Newydd cave in North Wales which were dated to 210,000 BC. The people we call Neanderthals, who are believed to have populated Europe and Western Asia from 130,000 to 30,000 BC, give us definite clues to the links with present day Europeans. We learn more about Homo Sapiens Sapiens from Cro Magnon man who was named after the rock shelter in South-West France discovered in 1868. All this evidence gives us a clearer understanding of how the landscape, animals and flint tools changed and developed in our own area. As more evidence emerges our ideas and thoughts become clearer, adding to our understanding of the present landscape. This puts into perspective the finds from the Waveney valley and those discovered along the course of the River Dove at Stoke Ash and Thornham Magna.

The Palaeolithic was a time when the way of life followed a pattern of hunting and gathering, as the principle food sources were hunted along the main river valleys. The wild animals were not only a source of food but also provided skins for clothes and bones to make needles and other implements. Additional food was found along the edge of the woodland, including wild fruits, nuts and edible roots. From the evidence of bones and teeth we know that the southern elephant, Etruscan rhinoceros, hippopotamus, hyena, deer, horse and vole were hunted. Pollen samples, remains of trees, bones of wood mice and bank voles indicate areas of woodland and marsh where alder trees grew as well as pond weed, sedge, water-lilies, mares-tail and many other flowering plants. The family groups of men, women and children were governed by the seasonal movements of wild animals. We can assume that wood and hides were used to make shelters similar to leather tents, although of course no evidence survives. The people themselves were short in stature but very muscular and had a short lifespan when compared to the present day.

In geological terms our area experienced the cold phase of the Anglian Glaciation which covered it with a thick ice sheet more than 400,000 years ago. The melting of this ice created our present system of river valleys, and introduced the warm phase of the Hoxnian Interglacial. This takes its name from the important site at Hoxne in the Waveney Valley which revealed evidence of the Pre or Early Temperate Environment dominated by birch and pine trees. Here the great age of the earliest tools made by man was recognised as early as 1797 by John Frere, squire of Roydon Hall and MP for Norwich. He found flint hand-axes in a brickyard at a depth of about twelve feet on a site that had been the shore of a lake at Hoxne, and sediments which settled in this lake have also been discovered at South Elmham St Michael. Frere was the first to recognise the immense antiquity of mankind. More recently John Wymer has dated two separate flint working industries at Hoxne to about 350,000 years ago and about 315,000 years ago[1]. Here people were making Acheulian[2] hand-axes about nine inches long from local flint during regular visits to this area beside the fresh water of the river and lake, where they could catch fish and hunt animals grazing on the flood plain or in the nearby scrub and forest. These hand-axes were hand held chopping tools that were very suitable for butchering animal carcasses and perhaps for digging up edible roots. Evidence at Hoxne indicates their use in adzing, boring and scraping wood as well as wedging and whittling. There was also evidence of plant gathering, meat cutting, bone boring and the cutting of hides where the use of a flat wooden base meant a more accurate cut could be achieved. Other tools made from flint were clearly designed to clean the animal skins that could be used to make clothes and perhaps leather tents,

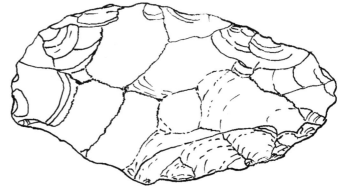

Figure 2.1 *Palaeolithic handaxe found at Flixton showing the marks of the complex pattern of flakes removed to create this general purpose cutting tool.*

because we cannot think of people living in caves in this region. The animal bones and teeth found here show the presence of straight tusked elephant, red deer, wolf, bison, pig, horse, beaver, otter, vole, macaque monkey, birds and fish. Pollen analysis shows the diet also included wild fruits, nuts and edible plants. Well over 300 find spots of Acheulian material have been recorded in Norfolk and Suffolk. These include finds in the Dove valley at Thornham Magna and hand axes have also been found in the Waveney Valley at Shotford Heath, Homersfield and Weybread, where an ovate axe was found. During this time the temperature was occasionally higher than that of the present day, but it was followed by the cold Wolstonian phase of about 200,000 years ago. Gravel workings in the Waveney valley in the 1950s revealed the bones of many prehistoric animals including bear, mammoth and woolly rhinoceros which could roam freely over our countryside during this cold phase. Similar evidence has been found at Thorndon close to the river Dove.

It has always been considered that during the next 150,000 years Britain was depopulated and became merely a haven for wild animals, as the earliest inhabitants had retreated south back into modern Europe. We know that between 127,000 and 117,000 BC the land bridge was being submerged by very high sea levels and the climate of this phase, known as the Ipswichian Interglacial, was considerably warmer than it is today. The growth of oak, elm, hazel, yew and water chestnut is attested by pollen samples. This phase was followed by another colder spell, the Devensian, and by 75,000 BC the land bridge was exposed again. Bison, reindeer and a mixture of carnivores, wolf, leopard, wolverine and large brown bear dominated the landscape with still no real indication of human activity in East Anglia. By 35,000 to 30,000 BC the first evidence of Homo Sapiens, modern man, is apparent in Europe, and towards the late Upper Palaeolithic phase we have some evidence of human occupation. Groups of hunters were arriving from Europe and the climate was steadily recovering towards the warmer conditions of the Flandrian phase, the most recent geological period in which we are still living today. By 11,940 to 11,370 BC hunters had re-occupied sites in Norfolk and Suffolk. It is from 8300 BC that we can see a real increase in population and observe the changes that occurred as the temperature rose.

We have now arrived at the Middle Stone Age or Mesolithic Period, when a microlithic technology was introduced. By this time the general topography of our landscape had reached its present form with its covering of Lowestoft Till and its pattern of river valleys. After a final very cold phase between 9000 and 8300 BC changes took place and human activity altered. Animal species which had previously been hunted, among them the woolly rhinoceros and mammoth, had become extinct, although there was still contact with Northern Europe across the land bridge. The landscape features that had been created by glacial activity changed and were marked by dense growth of birch in the river valleys while elsewhere birch, willow and pine covered the areas where deposits of Lowestoft till and the higher clay lands dominated the landscape. By 8300 BC a slow rise in temperature was occurring and reached an average 12 degrees Centigrade, only 2.5 degrees lower than our present July averages. Reindeer roamed the landscape but, as the tundra grasses and fern declined, new species of trees replaced them and threatened their lifestyle. Dense forests of hazel, elm, oak and lime heralded this next phase that we call the Middle Stone Age. Slowly, as this phase progressed, the large herds of reindeer, together with Arctic hare, fox and white grouse were replaced by aurochs, giant Irish elk, red deer, wild pig, wild cat and badger. Wolves still roamed wild as they had in previous phases, and they provided the first hunting dogs. Cubs were caught by hunters and their pack instincts led them to regard the hunters as pack leaders whose commands they obeyed, thus becoming the first hunting dogs.

Most of the southern area of the North Sea adjoining Norfolk and Suffolk was still fresh water fen and lagoons which provided rich hunting grounds for groups coming across the land bridge from Denmark and the Baltic area. Many hunter-fisher communities were situated near the land bridge. In 1931 the Lowestoft trawler *Colinda* set sail for the fishing grounds 25 miles off the Norfolk coast, north east of Cromer in the vicinity of the Leman and Ower banks. There at a depth of 35 metres they dredged from the sea bed a lump of peaty moor-log with a barbed bone point of red deer antler encased in the wood which has since been dated to between 9800 and 7000 BC. Other examples of this type of artefact have been discovered associated with the early phase of the Mesolithic Period. Finds of harpoons, bone fish hooks and nets with bark floats in the Gipping valley in Suffolk make it likely that sea and river fishing went on there. Fish traps were used to catch fresh water salmon and sturgeon. Sometimes dams were built across streams and the trap placed in an opening in the dam, the fish being caught as they tried to swim through the opening. There is evidence for the use of dug-out canoes and boats that could be used along the coast, up rivers and on inland lakes. They made distinctive flint tools including backed long blades, scrapers and burins which were used like a chisel[3]. Many production sites for such tools have been found in Norfolk and Suffolk, especially in the river valleys of the Waveney and the Dove, where flint workers used quartzite hammerstones, sandstone abraders, small antler hammers and antler punches to produce their implements. Spear launchers were used to extend the throw of a spear or javelin, which might be tipped with flint or antler bone, while others had their wooden point hardened by slow scorching in a fire which made the tip of the wood very hard. Many of these early sites will never be found as by 6500 BC the sea level had steadily increased to submerge totally the land bridge and thus make Britain an island. From this time onward the pattern of life must have changed considerably as the limit of hunting territory was now restricted to the boundaries imposed by an island. Weather patterns also changed as we find much of the heavier soils were now covered by dense mixed forests. This restricted the movement of larger animals and more wild species, including the reindeer, became extinct. We see a change in lifestyle and the introduction of new tools made from flint and other stone, the most important being the tranchet axe, which was probably the first type of axe to be fitted with a wooden haft, and the microliths. Significant evidence of activity in this period has been discovered along the course of the river Waveney at Flixton, and from the gravel terraces in the South Elmham parishes where there are also small flint scatters on the heavier clay land towards the valleys feeding the Blyth, where finds of this period have been recorded in Chediston by Gilbert Burroughes. Clay land areas have also produced flint work at Metfield and Weybread. This pattern of finds is also evident along the course of the river Dove and its tributaries at Thornham Magna and Gislingham.

Microliths are a feature of this phase and geometric forms were produced including trapezoids, crescents and triangles, many being minute with some as small as half an

Figure 2.2 *Mesolithic harpoon used for fishing, made from bone. Microliths and reconstructed arrows displayed at West Stow to show how the tiny flint blades were used.*

inch across, showing the great skill required for their production. In some cases their use is still a mystery, but certainly they were used for arrow tips that could be coated in a lethal poison. The choice of poison came from their knowledge of plants and roots acquired over many centuries of travel, and one person in the group must have had specific expertise in this subject learned from previous generations. Other uses of microliths reflect the production of composite tools in which fixing several of these flints into a holder of bone or wood created saws and reaping hooks, as well as barbed hunting spears.

Several areas have revealed indications of small settlements where groups lived together in summer or winter, with the presence of hearths and shelters being revealed by areas of burning and by postholes. Clearance of forest areas by fire increased and concentrations of waste flakes of flint suggest manufacturing areas. What these people looked like is becoming clearer and possible burial rites are indicated by finds of skeletons, including some from East Anglia such as a skull discovered on the banks of the river Yare at Strumpshaw in 1954. As new scientific procedures are applied to archaeology our understanding of ancient times becomes more definite. Already we can see that while the Mesolithic was a relatively short span of time compared to the preceding Palaeolithic, advances in knowledge, technology and social activity were immense. It is still regarded as a hunter-gatherer phase but as more evidence is collected we find indications of early settlements. As a result experts have revised the dates and time spans of different phases, so that in one significant example the change from Mesolithic to Neolithic has been moved back to about 5000 BC[4].

The Neolithic or New Stone Age period is a time of many changes, marked above all by the establishment of farming. While the beginning of this new age has been pushed back steadily so that it can be considered as starting about 5000 BC, it ended by 2500 BC, when metal was introduced. More woodland was now being cleared to make fields in which to grow crops of einkorn, emmer wheat[5] and vegetables. Evidence for woodland clearance comes from the flint axeheads and other stone tools found at Thornham and along the Waveney valley. The axeheads have sharp edges and were fixed into wooden handles so that they could be used to fell substantial trees, which also provided timber for building houses and other structures. Some of this land was probably cleared by applying slash and burn methods to remove more areas of natural woodland. During this time there was a noticeable decline in elm trees and one of the reasons for this might have been the chopping of branches for fodder to make up for the lack of open grassland pasture, but they may also have been subject to attack by disease caused by beetles similar to those responsible for the decimation of the elms in recent times. The climate was probably slightly warmer than now and also slightly wetter. Farm stock at this time included cattle, pigs, sheep and goats, while additional food came from hunting wild animals including roe and red deer. The antlers of these deer were used in making various tools similar to those found at the Neolithic flint mines of Grimes Graves. They also made high quality flint scrapers which were used to clean animal skins.

As part of the farming process they no doubt enclosed some fields, possibly two to five acres in size, to provide grazing for domesticated animals just as later inhabitants recognised the value of this land for dairy farming and livestock fattening. Remaining forest areas would provide grazing for pigs as we see with the later practice of pannage. This was the start of the farming activity that has been continuous in parts of this landscape ever since. It is worth emphasising that the number of finds in the Thornhams

Figure 2.3 *Neolithic axes found at South Elmham. The upper one has been polished to create a smooth surface, while the lower one was used in a rougher state but had an equally effective cutting edge.*

and Elmhams and to a lesser extent in Mendlesham suggest that there was significant activity, presumably by people setting up farms, this far into the heavy clay lands of 'High Suffolk' as early as the New Stone Age. We sometimes forget that our familiar landscape of fields and hedges, whether they survive or have been replanted, is the product of unceasing human activity since the work of the first farmers in the New Stone Age. Examples of this type of early landscape can still be seen, largely unaltered, on parts of Exmoor, Dartmoor and the Yorkshire Moors as well as in certain areas of Cornwall.

One of the most important advances in this period is the introduction of pottery to make containers for the storage of seed and for the preparation and cooking of food. People realised that clay can be shaped and decorated, then fired in a clamp kiln which produces a fairly porous type of pot. This provides a very important source of archaeological evidence as crucial dating can be determined from ceramics because, unlike so many other materials, they survive even in acidic soils. Because pots are fairly easily broken but the broken pieces survive in the ground, we can collect fragments left on the surface after ploughing. The evidence provided by these fragments of pottery can be lost for ever if they are left on the surface once they have been exposed by the plough as they sometimes break up quickly due to the friable nature of the clay. By careful plotting of these finds we can identify a number of areas on the Thornham estate where people were using pottery at this early date. So far nine sites have been identified with additional confirmation from the evidence of worked flint found nearby.

The sites are situated in low lying areas close to a water source with clay nearby. Evidence of clay extraction in this period could possibly survive as what nowadays look like ordinary field ponds, but we would need sophisticated scientific processes to prove this. Surviving evidence we do find from this period is represented by mounds of distinctive burnt flints, cracked in a different way from those broken by frost or by human activity. The flints tend to have a pink to orange hue on the surface. Those that show a particular pale blue/ grey colour which penetrates to the core of the flint have been heated to a very high temperature in a fire and then transferred by wooden tongs to a pot or other container full of water. The flints brought the water to boiling point without bringing the fabric of the container into direct contact with the flames. This enabled the settlement to enjoy cooked food even though the pottery fabric was not strong enough to be used in direct contact with the fire. Another reason for the large mounds of burned flint might be the use of communal washing areas. If the hot stones were drenched with water they would create steam and produce the effect of a Turkish bath and the whole area might have been covered by a large tent in a similar fashion to that used by North American Indians for their sweat lodges. This idea was discussed with the late Tony Gregory who was of the same opinion as us. One hundred and twenty one burnt flint areas were discovered in the Waveney valley and fourteen of these had associated flint work. So far in the Thornham area we have recorded six of these patches, of which five have associated flint work and pottery.

We find the products of intricate flintworking that produced, in addition to the axe heads, fine thumb nail scrapers for cleaning the animal skins and delicate but lethal arrowheads, some leaf shaped others oblique, which were used when hunting with bow and arrow. There are a variety of boring and cutting tools suitable for working leather and butchering meat. This supports the view that the farmers were rearing livestock as well as growing crops. It is notable that some of the axe heads, after being chipped to shape, had their blades polished with coarse sandstone, which worked like a natural sandpaper and produced fine cutting edges. A small but conspicuous group were polished all over which seems impractical for the part that needed to be fixed in the handle. This suggests that people were producing objects valued for their appearance, and leads some to think that they might have served some religious or ritual purpose, or indeed may have been regarded as a prestigious symbol that would be useful for barter. In the Waveney Valley area thirteen of the total recorded were polished and only two were left flaked. These came from fourteen parishes surveyed of which six produced no axes. At Thornham seven axes are recorded, four being polished and three flaked, one of these being made from greenstone. During the New Stone Age hides were used for clothing and for other purposes. Animal bones were also put to good use, including the production of darning needles and even making simple musical pipes. Bones were used to decorate pots by scoring lines and making stabbing marks. Many bones have been found ornamented with simple decorations, indicating early appreciation of art work. One of the major suppliers of axe heads to much of East Anglia was the extensive flint mining industry at Grimes Graves near Thetford, where some of the deep shafts have been examined closely. Access to the shafts was by simple wooden ladders and miners used antler picks to remove the layers of flint from the surrounding chalk.

The evidence from field walking at Thornham does not give us information about any structures built at this time. Many pits and post holes of this period have been excavated at Flixton and one Late Neolithic group of post holes suggests a timber circle about 18 metres in diameter[6]. Post holes are the visible evidence for the presence of timber structures, some of which were roofed buildings and others open air enclosures. The holes were created when digging a pit to hold a large upright post, as one does today when erecting a timber fence, and if the base of the post rotted in place this survives as a black mass which archaeologists call the post pipe. Careful excavation of these features provides vital information about early buildings. Across the River Waveney at Broome, Ditchingham there is a long barrow, a burial mound of this period which is an unusual survival in this region although it is likely that others have been destroyed by ploughing. They are lost more easily than those in regions with building stone, because the passage inside the grave was built with timber which rots away causing the mound to collapse making it more vulnerable to destruction. At Broome a bank and ditch encloses a C-shaped area of over a hectare with scattered potsherds and flints which may have been

Figure 2.4 *A fine barb and tang arrowhead found at South Elmham.*

24

the home of a community equivalent to a small village[7]. Excavation in 1972 revealed a palisade and wooden walkway built on top of the bank. Unfortunately no bones have survived in the acidic ground but study of pollen from excavations here by Cambridge University suggests that this land was cleared about 3500 BC for use as pasture, then ploughed for crops about 2600 BC but later reverted to pasture. Much of the pottery is of the Grimston-Lyles Hill tradition which is typical for a long period about 3000 BC. The C shaped enclosure was dated to 2217 BC. Two other burial sites are still evident on the heath, one disc barrow and one bell barrow, while others were mentioned in the past and a further nine possible barrows have been noted in this area which is situated on the sand and gravel terrace of the Waveney Valley. These few visible survivals clearly represent a much greater population of the area in the Neolithic times as indicated by the possibility of additional barrows at Burgate and Thornham Parva. In addition there is the evidence from our surface finds at Thornham and elsewhere in the region, particularly in Flixton. In the South Elmham parishes Neolithic axe heads were found at Mendham, Metfield, St. Cross and St. James[8] as well as scrapers, blades, a leaf shaped arrowhead and from St. Peter an oblique arrowhead. This area, which is situated at the junction of three streams in a low part of the field, also produced flakes of flint, three scrapers, a knife blade, a core made from a fragment of pecked flint quern and burnt flint. In Metfield a flint core had been discarded and then reused to heat the cooking water. On several sites throughout both the areas surveyed evidence of the re-working of flints is fairly common. Cores and large quantities of waste flakes show flints were being worked on the spot, and other materials including chert were also used. The majority of the burnt flint mounds in the Waveney Valley are of uncertain date (see Appendix 1).

A large clay mound in Thornham Parva, now concealed by woodland, looks like a Neolithic long barrow although so far we have no certain evidence about its origin, but it is similar to one found two miles away at Burgate by Basil Brown. However we do have examples of fine quality Neolithic flint tools from Thornham Parva, and in particular one field at the head of a rivulet near the church, about one and a half kilometres from the possible barrow, has produced large quantities of flint work. Here we have also found over 1400 sherds of prehistoric pottery ranging in date from Neolithic to Iron Age, including rims and bases and many pieces with various types of decoration. As our finds increase each season we find that sherds of decorated pottery of similar date have been discarded on the other primary sites raising the possibility that this might have been a production centre. Such an area was discovered by Basil Brown at Burgate, but only excavation can determine the answer here. In the Waveney Valley area a feature which, by its shape, might also be a long barrow was sufficiently conspicuous when parishes were created to be used as the mark for the junction of the three parishes of Weybread, Withersdale and Fressingfield. It was later used as the site for a gallows. Local legend would have us believe that it was the grave of a giant called Hulk. Although we have no datable evidence from this feature itself there are Neolithic flintworking sites nearby, and burnt flint patches. Although we have not found a henge in our area, this type of timber structure was introduced to the region in this period, as a fine example was excavated at Arminghall near Norwich. It could have been a major meeting place where the local Neolithic people assembled for religious worship and

Figure 2.5 *A selection from the many flints found during fieldwalking at Thornham including a core, scrapers and arrowheads.*

to trade in a market setting. The way of life was becoming more sophisticated for our local population and this was to experience another major change with the first use of a metal, bronze.

Bronze, the first metal to be used in this country for tools and weapons, is a mixture of several components. The basic ores used were those of copper and tin, with sometimes lead, manganese, iron, antimony and phosphorous added to the smelting process, and traces of these have been found in the bronze objects after scientific testing. Copper melts at 1083 degrees centigrade, which is why bronze was the first to be used as the production of good iron requires a temperature of 1350 degrees centigrade. Charcoal was used to create the heat required, assisted by the use of bellows placed at the mouth of the furnace to increase the flow of air. The molten metal was poured from crucibles into pre-shaped clay, stone or metal moulds to produce a varied range of objects. This was a significant advance in technology and, as neither copper nor tin occur naturally in East Anglia, the bronze must have been introduced to this region through some process of trade or exchange. Clues to this trading come from ingots, similar to one found at Thornham Magna. Ore from the rich sources available in Cornwall, Wales and Ireland must have been brought by some combination of overland transport and coastal trading boats. This would encourage the production here of a surplus of cereals, skins, wool and livestock that could be traded for metal through some kind of bartering. This trade would also be used to acquire the precious metals, silver and gold.

The early years of the Bronze Age also encompass an additional culture called Beaker after the style of pottery produced for drinking vessels, which are highly decorated. Some have a handle and are referred to as 'tigs'. This culture seems to have originated in modern Germany and also through the Low Countries, bringing a strong continental

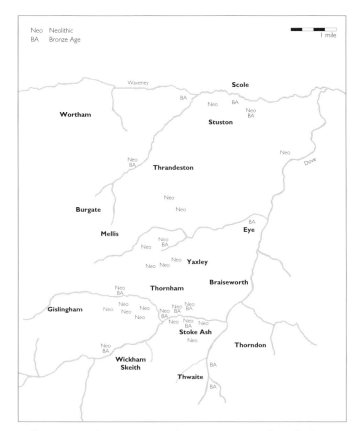

Figure 2.6 *Neolithic & Bronze Age activity at Thornham, based on finds made by field walking or reported as casual finds.*

influence to this country. This suggests trading links across the North Sea and there might have been some form of colonisation, which is believed to have started about 2700 BC, slightly earlier than the true Bronze Age which is currently said by Suffolk archaeologists to begin about 2350 BC and finish at the start of the Iron Age about 800 BC. Although metal was introduced, worked flint was still very important and many stone tools are discovered alongside metal ones with Bronze Age pottery. This is true on the Thornham estate and in the Waveney Valley. The production of bronze steadily increased and it became available more widely so that more efficient axes and other tools were made. During this period ash and birch trees showed a marked increase in numbers while weather patterns are marked by a decline in temperature, but an increase in rainfall. As conditions became colder and wetter, especially after 1200BC, there might have been a shift of emphasis from growing cereal crops to rearing livestock.

Significant finds of Bronze Age metalwork are recorded from Eye, Thorndon and Thornham Magna[9] in the valley of the River Dove. At Thornham fragments of two socketed axes and the solid type of axe head called a palstave by archaeologists, together with waste bronze, slag and furnace material marked by droplets of bronze indicate the presence of skilled smiths casting tools in moulds. People did not stop using flint, and it was during that earliest phase of the Bronze Age called the Beaker Period that some of the finest arrowheads were produced using the intricate barb & tang design. Three have been found in the Waveney Valley area and three in the Thornham area, as well as flint knives and neat scrapers for cleaning animal skins which could be converted into

Figure 2.7 *Neolithic & Bronze Age activity at South Elmham.*

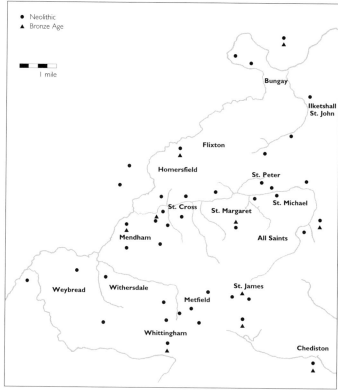

• Neolithic
▲ Bronze Age

I mile

Bungay

Ilketshall St. John

Flixton

Homersfield

St. Peter

St. Cross

St. Margaret

St. Michael

Mendham

All Saints

Weybread

Withersdale

St. James

Metfield

Whittingham

Chediston

clothing. Substantial pottery vessels were produced in which to store food and for use in cooking. A particular style of vessel takes its name, collared urn, from a distinctive band of decoration near the neck. Fragments of these have been recovered from the Thornham estate. Others were found in 1851 near the riverbank in Stoke Ash where they had apparently been used to hold cremated human remains. The Suffolk Institute of

Figure 2.8 *A long barrow on Broome Heath, Ditchingham. A rare survival of a Neolithic burial mound, protected by being on unploughed heath land.*

Archaeology, which is still the county society for archaeology and history, was founded in 1848 and in the second volume of its Proceedings there is a report of the meeting at which 'The Right Hon. Lord Henniker exhibited a British cinerary urn, found in 1851 at Stoke Ash, on the north side of the rivulet below the church ; and some fragments of other vessels, a celt, &c. The vase, shown in the annexed engraving, contained the bones of a young skeleton (human), probably those of a female. Four other vases, very much broken were found at the same time. The one exhibited was restored by C.R. Bree Esq., by whom the drawing for the above cut was kindly presented to the Institute.' The engraving appears to show a type of collared urn with simple decoration that was used for burials in the Bronze Age. Dimensions are given including a height of 15 inches, diameter of the top 10 inches and of the base 5 inches. His lordship did not obtain all the pieces as at the same meeting Henry Creed reported that 'five urns were taken out, but all of them were broken: the greater portion of two however have been preserved and are now on the table: the larger being sent by Lord Henniker on whose land they were found and the smaller of red earth beautifully ornamented is exhibited by the Rev. S.W. Bull, Rector of Stoke Ash.' This is our first certain evidence for systematic burials in the area. The finding of a fragment from the blade of a bronze rapier at Thornham Magna suggests more violent activity, as do a dagger with a bronze hilt from Homersfield and a sword, knife and spearhead found at Thorndon. It has been suggested that weapons for fighting were first produced at this time because the pressure of a growing population competing for land led to conflict. Presumably the demand for land was not based only on the need to produce enough grain and other agricultural products for people to feed themselves, but also on the desire to create a surplus that could be traded with those living in places with natural supplies of the much needed metal ores.

Along the main Waveney valley aerial photographs have revealed the crop marks of a significant number of ring ditches on the primary terraces above the flood plain of the river, particularly at Mendham and Flixton[10] and at Shotford Heath. Only some of these have been tested by excavation but they are likely to indicate the burial mounds known as round barrows which are typical of the Beaker or Early Bronze Age period. The primary terrace is the location of the best known areas of Neolithic and Bronze Age activity at Flixton where the first ring ditch was excavated in 1990, at Broome Heath, Ditchingham, which was excavated in 1972, and at Brockdish/Needham which has not been excavated. Unfortunately there are fewer air photographs for the Thornham area and those we do have only reveal former field boundaries, but the finds of metalwork and pottery show we did have an active population throughout this period. Beaker pottery has also been found in the Waveney Valley at Homersfield, close to the excavated Roman kiln[11], and by Basil Brown at Stuston and also on the parish boundary of Oakley by Mike Hardy. Beaker material and Bronze Age finds, including pottery, have been discovered by Gilbert Burroughes in Chediston, while in South Elmham St. James and St Margaret bronze axe heads have been found, all on the high clay lands. The axe heads are of the type known as palstaves which represent an intermediate stage in the design of axes from the simple flat blade of the early years to the more sophisticated socketed version used at the end of the Bronze Age. Examples are also recorded from Ilketshall St. Lawrence, again on the high clay land, and at Homersfield. Here a small hoard was discovered which included among its contents two socketed axes, a dagger and hilt, a

Figure 2.9 *Bronze Age pots: many fragments of similar pots have been found at Thornham, some of them showing the distinctive decoration used during this period.*

fragment of a spearhead and an arrowhead. This hoard was found on the edge of the clay land overlooking a minor river and worked flint was recovered close by. A late Bronze Age spearhead of the Conyger Hill type was found on the west boundary of Metfield and Fressingfield. People were certainly active in this period along the Waveney Valley and, given the density of finds, we can assume that much of the land was being farmed. While some people were making bronze implements in Thornham we might speculate whether others had started the pottery making that became a major industry in this area during later periods. This impact on the local landscape was to increase further when people started using iron.

Some 2800 years ago the introduction of iron for tools and weapons brought significant advances in technology, as the period we call the Iron Age began. It is important to recognise that the transition from what archaeologists call the Late Bronze Age to the Early Iron Age was a gradual process in which it is impossible to draw hard and fast lines of demarcation. Throughout Britain from about 800 BC more land was cultivated and this might have been the time when groups of people became established. Sometimes referred to as tribes, states or kingdoms their names

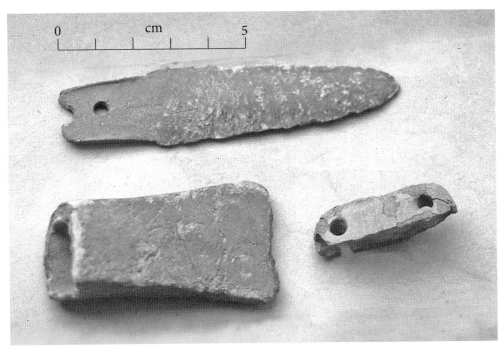

Figure 2.10 *Bronze Age tools: part of a small hoard of bronzes discovered at Homersfield. At the top is the blade of a small dagger showing the hole where a rivet attached it to a wooden or bone handle. Below are a socketed axehead and the hilt of a weapon.*

are first given to us by the Romans in the last century before the time of Christ. In our area these were the Iceni and the Trinovantes. At Thornham the population seems to have increased and extensive areas of farming are indicated by scattered finds of their pottery which was hand made and fired in clamp kilns. A more substantial Iron Age kiln recorded by Basil Brown at Burgate might have been the source of the unusually well fired pottery that we find in the Thornham area, but this has yet to be proved. The discovery of small fragments of pottery over a wide area shows that people had been manuring the fields by spreading domestic waste, in which broken pots were combined with human and animal dung and discarded vegetable matter. These tiny pieces of pot are heavily abraded, that is they show signs of wear and their edges are rounded by exposure to disturbance by the plough and the effects of the weather over a long time. Plotting the finds of this rubbish shows how much land was being farmed at this time. Areas that produce large numbers of fragments suggest places where people were living in the equivalents of modern farmsteads. These pieces of pottery generally tend to be larger with sharper edges as they have suffered less disturbance over the years. After being buried in pits or covered by the collapsed remains of buildings, they generally remained undisturbed until the recent introduction of deeper ploughing which brings them to the surface. A large fragment of puddingstone[12] quern of typical 'saddle back' shape was part of a hand operated mill to grind the cereals to make a coarse flour from crops grown on the farms. Much work must have been needed to create the flat grinding surface of this quern before it could be used in the time consuming task of producing flour. The quern was discovered in an area close to the river where many of their round houses would have been situated, with their fields spreading out from

Figure 2.11 *Part of a Pudding-stone quern found at Thornham.*

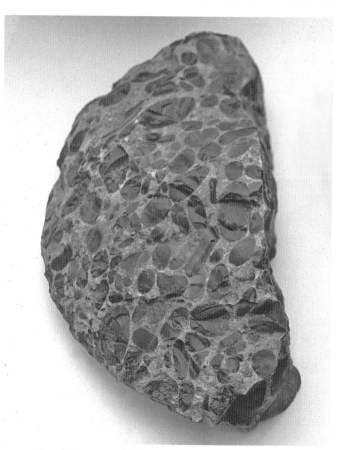

shape was part of a hand operated mill to grind the cereals to make a coarse flour from crops grown on the farms. Much work must have been needed to create the flat grinding surface of this quern before it could be used in the time consuming task of producing flour. The quern was discovered in an area close to the river where many of their round houses would have been situated, with their fields spreading out from the living area. Evidence of typical Iron Age timber round houses was found during excavations on the edge of the Roman settlement at Scole and Basil Brown noted signs of others nearby at Stuston. Perhaps one day excavation will reveal evidence of similar structures at Thornham, but meanwhile we have to rely on comparative examples from other parts of the region which do seem to be remarkably consistent.

More recently work on the Scole/Stuston bypass made it possible for Patricia Wiltshire to examine pollen deposits in the valley of the Waveney at Oakley[13]. She concluded that the landscape here had been cleared of most of its woodland by the Early Iron Age and certainly by the Middle Iron Age. Dense woodlands of oak and lime recorded here in the Bronze Age had gone, leaving mostly alder and hazel with some ash and beech trees. There was evidence of more grassland, probably used as pasture for livestock, and evidence for the cultivation of cereal crops. Heather and bracken was growing on open heath land. There appears to have been an interruption in the middle of the Iron Age when lime and elm trees increased at the expense of some farm land, which might have been caused by a decline in population or just by a change in the use these findings do support the impression from the field walking evidence set out below. The area was cleared of its primeval woodland and mixed farming was well established in a landscape that offered plenty of useful plants growing in a variety of soils.

The mapping of finds of Iron Age pottery, indicating the probable locations of farms and ploughed fields, shows that much of the land was being worked in a landscape that seems to have been totally managed. We can assume that pasture for grazing livestock and woodland for fuel and timber were also exploited as a contribution to the agricultural economy. Certain dense concentrations of pottery and coins suggest the presence of larger settlements. The most conspicuous is in fields west and north of Thornham Parva church where the amount of material recovered makes a strong case for seeing this as a market centre established before the Roman conquest. This area produces a significant amount of material representing all periods from the New Stone Age to the Middle Saxon so it might have been a focus of activity for a very long time. It is adjacent to the feature known as 'Grim's Ditch' which might be an ancient boundary (see Chapter 3) and it can be seen as the focal point for a number of long lanes which appear to be older than the Roman road. These lanes provided routes for travellers to cover long distances and for drovers moving livestock between grazing areas and driving them to and from markets. Another substantial Iron Age settlement might lie beneath the later Roman settlement south of Stoke Ash White Horse and may represent the nucleus out of which grew the large settlement in the Roman period. A few individual pottery sherds abraded by ploughing in a field immediately to the east of this settlement, and similar finds beyond the edge of a probable settlement near Stoke Ash church, look like manuring scatter spread on arable fields beyond the houses. These larger settlements might have been market centres, the early predecessors of market towns.

There are regional variations marked by particular styles of pottery in pre-Roman Britain and the designs of coins indicate different kingdoms or tribal units within the island, which became the Iceni and Trinovantes of our region. However all the inhabitants of Britain seem to have adopted the culture known as Celtic on the continent and they may all have been ethnically related to the peoples known to the Greeks and Romans as Celts, Gauls or Galatians. However it may be that they simply shared similar possessions and perhaps a common language as we should remember that it would not take them long to travel down the river and then across the sea to the continent, so communication with mainland Europe would not be a problem. We have to remember that what we know of these people historically comes from writings of Greeks and Romans, as no native Celtic writing survives. Most of our information reflects the attitudes of the Romans who saw their own culture and language as the only real civilisation. In particular they were uncomfortable with the rural culture of the continental Gauls and the Britons, who never seem to have been really converted to the urban aspirations of Rome. Romans used the general term 'barbarian' to describe all those foreigners who did not speak Greek or Latin and tended to dismiss their culture as inferior, except when seeking images of the 'noble savage'. The quality of their artistic style which we call 'Celtic' or 'La Tene', the sophistication of their coinage and the evidence of their agricultural efficiency, suggest this view is far from being an accurate impression.

Figure 2.12 *Iron Age evidence at Thornham, showing places where concentrations of finds indicate the presence of farmsteads.*

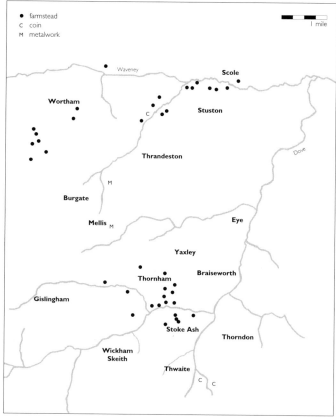

It seems from the archaeological evidence that about 100 BC new cultural influences were brought over from Europe and features that we label as Belgic spread through southern and eastern England. We should not be surprised if these ideas, and perhaps even some Belgic people themselves, reached our region by sea at an early stage and spread up the river valleys. They brought the first pottery in this region to be made on the wheel, which was to become a major industry in the Waveney valley after the Roman conquest. In fact some of these immigrants might have been skilled artisans, who became the first people in the region to use the wheel in making pottery here. Perhaps we should see them as early entrepreneurs. We cannot tell how the people of our valleys related to the largest urban settlement in East Anglia at Colchester, which was growing in size and in the decades before the Roman conquest became the capital of King Cunobelinus (Shakespeare's Cymbeline and possibly the Old King Cole of popular song). He dominated much of southern Britain but our people might have been far enough north to maintain independence or to have joined the kingdom in northern East Anglia that was known to the Romans as the Iceni. Either way it is likely that they were familiar with the Roman world long before they became part of it. We cannot tell how early traders from the Mediterranean reached our rivers but the Iceni were probably the Great Ceni who exchanged embassies with Julius Caesar himself in 55 and 54 BC. Afterwards we can assume they maintained some direct contact with Rome, as we know that the Trinovantes certainly did. There is a remarkable possibility[14] that as early as 216 BC the Romans had recruited the Iceni, and the Cantii (if 'Cantini'

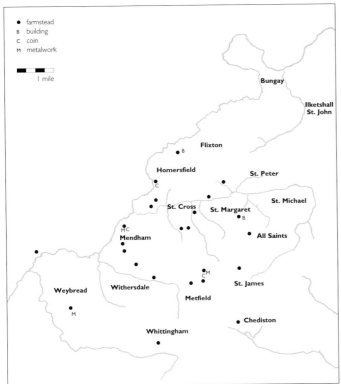

Figure 2.13 *Iron Age evidence at South Elmham.*

were the Cantii of Kent) from Britain to join Gauls from modern France in helping them to defeat Hannibal's Cathaginian army in Italy according to Polybius. However we should be cautious as there are several examples of Celtic peoples in Gaul (France and northern Italy) using the same names as contemporary groups in Britain.

The Waveney valley was no doubt a busy area with its accessible waterway and further down the river a number of parishes in the Elmhams and the Mendham area have produced evidence[15] of settlement in the pre-Roman Iron Age including two sites in St. James which continued into the Roman period. Of four sites in Mendham one was on the 35 metre contour of the gravel terrace on the high ridge overlooking the Waveney at a multi-period site with evidence of occupation as early as the New Stone Age: one of the sherds of Iron Age pottery came from the neck of a small decorated vessel and was apparently associated with crudely worked flints which are typical of the Iron Age when rough tools were produced without the careful workmanship typical of Stone Age flintwork: another Mendham site on the ridge produced sherds of the sophisticated 'Belgic' type of pottery typical of the immediately pre-Roman period: also on the boulder clay ridge overlooking the Waveney a multi-period site had Iron Age buff-orange pottery with white grit filler and a bronze brooch of type La Tene III, made sometime within the century before or after the birth of Christ. Such brooches are a kind of safety pin used to fasten clothing so a very practical part of ancient clothing. There were three sites in St. Cross which all continued into the Roman period. One of these on land that was formerly part of Greshaw Green close to a water course produced the rim of a clay crucible similar to one found at Burgh[16] that was used in the manufacture of small decorative items in bronze, silver or gold. This process created

Figure 2.14 *'Belgic type' pottery used in the first century AD. Several large fragments found at South Elmham enable us to see the shape of the complete vessel.*

an area of scorched clay and sand noticed in this location. Of two sites in St. Margarets one continued into the Roman period and the other contained an Iron Age building revealed by excavation of a farm lagoon. This exposed two postholes and possibly two more enclosed by a shallow ditch and nearby was a pit containing Iron Age pottery of buff-orange colour in a flint gritted fabric, which were excavated by Mike Hardy. This is the one site that has produced clear evidence of an actual timber building of the Iron Age. In Homersfield there were seven distinct sites and fragments of pottery typical of manuring scatter confirmed agricultural activity with domestic refuse, presumably after composting, being spread on the fields. Two sites have been identified in All Saints, three in Metfield and two in St. James. People continued living on several of these sites into the Roman period, as they did on the edge of a watercourse in Chediston where they left much broken pottery. If all of these were farms it suggests most of the land was being used at this time. We are looking at an intensively managed agricultural landscape which must have made a significant contribution to the productivity of this region. At Flixton excavations by Stuart Boulter in advance of quarry workings have produced evidence that on part of the site a new rectilinear ditched field system was created in the first century BC. He describes this being laid out at the base of the north facing slope at a point that marks the boundary between the clay soils of the Lowestoft Till to the south, rising up the side of the Waveney valley, and the Bytham Sands and Gravels on the valley floor to the north. This occupation continued through the Roman period into at least the third century AD. Features surviving from the Iron Age, in addition to the boundary ditches and some pits, were four-post and six-post structures that might well have been granaries and the top stone from a rotary quern which would have been used as a handmill to grind grain. We cannot say whether these granaries, if that is what they were, represent purely domestic supplies or the storage of a surplus to be transported on the nearby river. However if a larger building supported on posts and attributed to the early Roman phase was a granary, then this does suggest a commercial scale of operation here. Finds of triangular clay loom weights speak of the weaving of cloth on the site, but there is no reason to suppose this was any more than a domestic operation, producing clothing for local residents. However in the Roman period heavy woollen cloaks from Britain were highly valued, so spinning and weaving must have become commercial operations.

Oliver Rackham[17] suggested that the 'semi-regular geometry' of small fields in the Elmhams and Ilketshalls which are shown on the Ordnance Survey map of 1882–3 preserve a prehistoric field system related to parallel sinuous lanes forming the main axis of a pattern with irregular cross-hedges. He suggests the pattern, which we are unable to date with any precision, is similar to the Bronze Age 'reaves' of Dartmoor and sees the medieval greens as inserted into this ancient pattern, as are the parish boundaries. We can detect the vestiges of a similar pattern in the Thornham and Yaxley area where Tom Williamson has mapped some of the evidence[18]. He has shown how the Roman 'Pye Road', the modern A140, appears to cut across an existing pattern of fields. This suggests that the field system must be earlier than the Roman road and relates to a series of long tracks or droveways, which we discuss in more detail in the next chapter where we consider their relationship to the main Roman road. It seems that some elements of a planned landscape, which was divided into fields before the Roman conquest, survive into the modern countryside. It is clear that some field divisions have been altered over the generations but the orientation survives and dictates the general direction of the boundaries. Confirming that some field boundaries can survive, John Fulcher has found in his excavation of a Roman farm at Coddenham that at least one boundary marked by a ditch dug before the Roman period is still marked by a hedge today. Williamson has refined his study of these ancient landscapes in an article on the 'Scole-Dickleburgh Field System'[19], where he concentrates on the area immediately north of the River Waveney at Scole. He sees the field pattern laid out in relation to the Waveney but ignoring tributary valleys and other topographical features. He sees this system as extending north from the Waveney onto the higher ground as far as the watershed between the valleys of the Waveney and the Tas where it coincides in part with the medieval hundred boundaries. Having found similar evidence in Hertfordshire, he suggests these planned systems originate from schemes based on large territorial units, much larger than medieval manors or parishes, where people sought a balance between arable land and areas suitable for woodland and pasture. Both the 'Scole-Dickleburgh' system and that in Yaxley and Thornham are cut through by the Roman road, so we are justified in suggesting the general pattern of tracks and land divisions were laid out before the Roman period, although it remains impossible to say how long before. They create a pattern for the economic use of the natural resources of the valley on both sides of the Waveney. They might support the idea that the large 'Estate of Faustinus', which we see as a major feature of the Roman landscape, could have originated from part of a large pre-Roman territory over which some powerful individual was able to impose a scheme for the use of the land. The ancient tracks that run through this system show that long distance communication was possible by land as well as along the rivers and coast before the introduction of Roman roads. As the local population was already organised to make maximum use of the natural resources of our area, and had acceptable communication links, we can see them contributing to the economic activity described by the geographer Strabo, who was writing in the years between the visit of Julius Caesar and the conquest by the emperor Claudius. He recorded that the Britons were exporting to the Roman Empire grain, cattle, hunting dogs and slaves. This required the production of surpluses well above the immediate needs for the subsistence of the local population and must have depended on intelligent planning of the use of all the available land.

There is evidence that in the later part of the Iron Age before the Roman conquest better equipment was being developed for the spinning and weaving of woollen textiles, and improved strains of cereal crops were being introduced. Presumably farmers in this region took full advantage of such innovations because their prosperity must have depended on producing a surplus that could be traded for items not available in East Anglia, particularly metals, as iron is the only metal that occurs naturally in the region. However it seems that some of the land which is highly productive under modern agricultural methods was still not being exploited in the pre Roman Iron Age as the intensive field walking of Mendlesham has produced no evidence of Iron Age activity. Fifteen Roman sites have been identified and all of them are in the part of the parish that lies north of the watershed, where the relatively level high land slopes towards the Waveney catchment area as opposed to the south of the watershed which feeds the headwaters of the River Gipping (pers. comm. Roy Colchester). This did not prevent the land having economic value as woodland providing timber and fuel as well as offering feeding areas for pigs. This is supported by the fact that over a thousand years later Domesday Book recorded a high proportion of such use of land in Mendlesham with reference to woodland for 1000 pigs on the main manor (Domesday Book for Suffolk 1; 76).

Gold and silver coins were introduced for the first time in the later Iron Age from about 100 BC and these carry designs stamped onto blanks produced in moulds. The earliest issues were gold coins of a type derived ultimately from Greek staters of Philip of Macedon. We can see the differences between designs produced by the people we know from Roman authors as Trinovantes centred on Colchester and the Iceni centred somewhere in Norfolk. The earliest gold coins produced in Norfolk show an animal described as a 'wolf'[20], but it has been suggested that early Trinovantian gold coins were also used throughout Norfolk for some time[21]. The Iceni were certainly producing their own silver coins by about 35 BC. Examples of the clay moulds used to produce the metal blanks for Icenian silver coins have been found in the Waveney valley at Needham[22]. Here a Roman road later crossed the river and the site produced Belgic pottery of the type used in the immediately pre-Roman period as well as local wares of the Iron Age. Close to the same road in Weybread a bronze terret ring was found. It showed a curvilinear design enriched with red enamel decoration and was an ornate rein guide from a horse drawn chariot made in the first half of the first century AD[23] by skilled artisans. The number of such decorated rings that have been found in East Anglia, along with finely manufactured swords and high value gold torcs, suggests the presence of expert metalworkers and wealthy patrons prepared to pay for their skills or able to command their services. There was more to the local economy than agriculture, important as that clearly was. This was the countryside that produced chariot driving warriors and their supporters to fight under the leadership of their queen Boudica (Boadicea) against the Romans in the great rebellion of AD 60.

Numbers of Icenian coins have been found along the Waveney valley between Scole and Homersfield. At Scole 153 silver Icenian coins were found in a pot and twenty silver Icenian coins are recorded from Homersfield, including four of the 'ECEN' type and three of 'ANTED', as well as a Trinovantian gold quarter stater of Cunobelinus. It is generally thought that Anted is most likely to be the name of a ruler but Ecen could be a version of Iceni, although some think it too is a personal name and it would certainly be unique in Britain if the name of the kingdom appeared on coins. Further down the river Ditchingham is one of eight sites in Norfolk from which more than twenty Iron Age coins have been recovered[24]. Others include the major settlements at Thetford, Saham Toney and Caistor St Edmund so this suggests it was a place of importance and John Davies points out that non-Icenian coins have also been found at Ditchingham which might imply a major trading centre on the river. A number of silver Icenian coins have been found at Thornham, including small silver coins sometimes referred to as minims. The Thornham coins are of the type described as 'pattern-horse' because they have the ubiquitous Iron Age horse on one side and a pattern including two back to back crescents on the other: it is unclear whether the designs indicate different groups within the Iceni or different periods of issue. These coins were made from silver of sufficient value to be worth taking care of and the metal could easily be melted down and used to produce new coins or valuable objects, so it is reasonable to suppose that only a very small proportion of the coins in circulation will have survived until the present day. Most precious metal is recycled and the material of much modern jewellery must have been used many times over. Based on the number of coins that are found the economy of the region was clearly sufficiently advanced to make considerable use of coins which indicate trade involving high values. The use of standardised coins with recognised values, and produced to an accuracy measurable in fractions of a gram[25], only makes sense in trading activities on an organised basis. This was far from being a simple subsistence economy. However as the coins were of gold and silver, no bronze issues being known, they would be of relatively high value, so suitable only for expensive purchases or exchanges between wealthy individuals. For everyday shopping a system of bartering might have been more acceptable.

Figure 2.15 *Iron Age coins of the Iceni found at Homersfield, showing the distinctive pattern used on many of their issues: similar examples have been found at Thornham.*

The presence of a mint, producing coins, at Needham, which is on the River Waveney and was later linked to the Roman road system, suggests an early phase of the industrial activity along this river valley which is more clearly revealed by evidence from the Roman period. We begin to see a busy community that was farming, working metals, trading with others, driving livestock on long cross country routes and sailing down the rivers to the open sea. This was already a productive landscape with a substantial population.

Notes

1 Wymer, J, 1983 The Lower Palaeolithic Site at Hoxne, *PSIAH* **35**, 169.
2 Named after Saint Acheul, near Amiens, northern France.
3 Wymer, J, 1999 Late Glacial & Mesolithic Hunters, in Dymond, D, and Martin, E (eds), *An Historical Atlas of Suffolk*, Ipswich.
4 Jacobi, R, 1984, in Barringer, C (ed), *Aspects of East Anglian Prehistory: twenty years after Rainbird Clark*, Norwich.
5 Einkorn is *Triticum monococcum*, Emmer wheat *Triticum dicoccum* and modern Bread wheat is *Triticum aestivum*; see Reynolds, P, 1979, *Iron-Age Farm: the Butser experiment*, London.
6 Martin, E, 1999 The Neolithic, in Dymond, D, and Martin, E (eds), *An Historical Atlas of Suffolk*, Ipswich and recent annual reports of Archaeology in Suffolk, in *PSIAH*, particularly *PSIAH* **39** (1997), 96.
7 Wymer, J, 1994 The Neolithic Period, in Wade-Martins, P (ed), *An Historical Atlas of Norfolk*, Norwich.
8 Mike Hardy – records of field walking in the Waveney valley. In addition Neolithic material from Fressingfield, Linstead Parva and Wissett is recorded in VCH Suffolk and has been found in Chediston by Gilbert Burroughes.
9 Details of finds in Pendleton, C, 1999 *Bronze Age Metalwork in Northern East Anglia*, BAR **279**, (note particularly 208–9).
10 Lawson, A, 1981 *The Barrows of East Anglia*, EAA **12**.
11 *PSIAH* 1968.
12 Puddingstone is a natural conglomerate stone formed from large numbers of pebbles bound in silica which hardened to form a very solid rock. It occurs in natural deposits of which one is known in East Suffolk on a farm at Leiston Abbey.
13 See Wiltshire, P, and Murphy, P, in Davies, J, and Williamson, T (eds), 1999 *The land of the Iceni: the Iron Age in northern East Anglia*, UEA, 141ff.
14 Durschmied, E, 2002 *From Armageddon to the Fall of Rome: how the myth makers changed the world*, London.
15 Most of this evidence comes from regular systematic field walking by Mike Hardy.
16 Martin, E, 1988 *Burgh: Iron Age and Roman Enclosure*, EAA **40**, 25.
17 Rackham, O, 1986 *The History of the Countryside*, London, 158.
18 Dymond, D, and Martin, E (eds), 1999 *An Historical Atlas of Suffolk*, Ipswich, Map 19, 'Ancient Landscapes'.
19 *The Annual Bulletin of the Norfolk Archaeological & Historical Research Group*, **12**, 2003, 13ff.
20 Mack, R, 1964 *The Coinage of Ancient Britain*, London, type 49.
21 Cunliffe, B, 1991 *Iron Age Communities in Britain: an account of England, Scotland and Wales from the seventh century BC until the Roman conquest*, New York, 124–5.
22 Frere, S, 1941, in *Antiq. J.*, **21**, p.41–55.
23 Found in 1976, it was of Spratling's sub group VIIIA.
24 Davies, J, 1999, in Davies, J, and Williamson, T (eds), *The land of the Iceni: the Iron Age in northern East Anglia*, UEA, 36. His table on page 37 shows a total of 48 coins..
25 Chadburn, A, 1999, Tasking the Iron Age, in Davies, J, and Williamson, T (eds), *The land of the Iceni: the Iron Age in northern East Anglia*, UEA, 168.

Chapter 3

The Iceni and the Romans

Initial surveys of the arable fields at Thornham have produced a much greater density of pre-Roman Iron Age material than would be expected on these higher clay lands according to the traditional view that such land was unsuited to agricultural use before the Roman period. It is becoming clear from other work in and around the Waveney valley and in other parts of East Anglia that most of the land in this region was being farmed long before the Roman invasion. However the quantity of pottery, the scatter of metalwork and the complex series of apparently early tracks that focus on one location suggest that it was not just a farm but was a focal point, perhaps a marketing and administrative centre at or near the southern boundary of the Icenian territory on the fringe of Trinovantian lands. It may be significant that when the Romans built their main road, now the A140, from the south into Icenian territory it ran directly from the crossing of the Gipping at Combretovium (modern Baylham House in Coddenham parish) to Thornham and Stoke Ash. This may have been built soon after the conquest in AD 43 when the Trinovantes were incorporated in the Empire but the Iceni remained independent allies. From Stoke Ash the road was extended, probably after the Boudican rebellion had been suppressed in AD 60 and the Iceni themselves became subject to Rome, but on a slightly different alignment directed to Caistor by Norwich. This makes sense if there was already a significant settlement, equivalent to a small market town, here at Thornham close to the border between the Trinovantes and Iceni.

The evidence from the distribution of coin finds mentioned in the last chapter shows that the vast majority of Iron Age coins found in the Waveney valley were minted by the Iceni so it is reasonable to suggest that the people living here, and as far south as Thornham, were part of the Great Ceni named by Julius Caesar in the account of his campaigns in Britain with a Roman army in 55 and 54 BC. He said they sent an embassy to make their submission to him and this would bring them into closer contact with the political and commercial world of the Romans, as it was transformed from Republic to Empire. They followed Roman practice by stamping the names of their leaders on their coins. Examples of these have been found at Thornham suggesting the local population were being drawn into the trading relationships which the geographer Strabo records before the actual conquest of Britain as including exports to the Roman Empire of grain, cattle, hunting dogs and slaves: as well as gold and silver in which trade the Iceni may also have been involved even though they had no natural deposits of these in their own territory. An enigmatic clue is offered by the group of five lead ingots stamped ICENES or similar out of 271 ingots from a shipwreck from Sept Iles off the

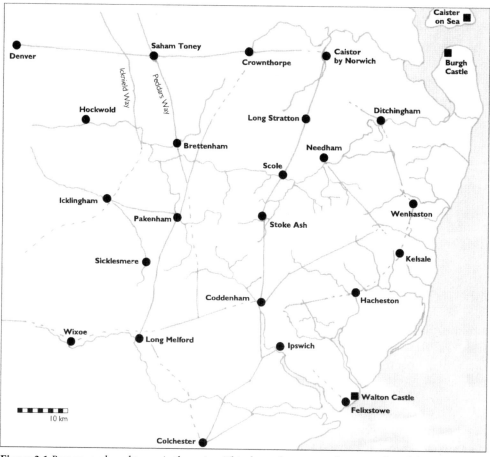

Figure 3.1 *Roman roads and towns in the region. This shows the pattern of main roads and the main market centres based on our current knowledge.*

coast of Armorica, France dated as Gallo-Roman from the presence of tegulae roof tiles made from Armorican clay; other ingots being stamped Brigantes suggesting a cargo from varied sources[1]. Were the Iceni actually processing lead, perhaps to extract the more valuable silver? The Iceni are best known for their last queen Boudica (Boadicea) who led a rebellion against the Romans in AD 60. We have yet to find here any of the ornamental bronze fittings from horse harness and chariots that are a feature of their products, although a terret ring was found at Weybread as mentioned in the last chapter. However large quantities of fragments of their pottery have been found, particularly near Thornham Parva church and in the same area as the Roman settlement at Stoke Ash. A number of their silver coins have also been found suggesting it was a prosperous place. There is evidence that this was already a planned landscape of fields with a complex of trackways, some of which survive as roads and footpaths. Some of these tracks appear to extend over long distances with one leading to the crossing between the head of the Rivers Waveney and Little Ouse, while others may have served to link local fields to facilitate the movement of grazing livestock. The waterways also played an important role in the settlement pattern and presumably played a significant part in the communication system over both long and short distances.

One piece of evidence from the reign of Henry III may be a clue to the boundary between the Iceni and the Trinovantes. A thirteenth century document (B.L. Harleian MS 52 A.49) refers to a Grim's Ditch in Thornham Parva 'in campo qui vocatur Grimisdich' and this field name of 'Grimsditch' still appeared on nineteenth century maps to the south of Howe Lane which comes from the direction of Mellis and may follow the line of a sunken lane south of Thornham Parva churchyard and continue east across the A140 towards the swampy margins of the River Dove at Eye. In Anglo-Saxon times earthworks of unknown origin were often attributed to Grim (an alternative name for the god Woden), just as later people called such things 'the Devil's work', so this may record the line of an ancient ditch perhaps constructed in Iron Age days being marked out by the powerful king Cunobelinus to define his enlarged kingdom after taking over the Trinovantes in addition to the Catuvellauni and moving his capital to Colchester. This would define his boundary with the Iceni in the same way that an interesting theory suggests Aves Ditch and Grim's Ditches in Oxfordshire marked the western boundary of the Catuvellauni[2]. We might note that one of the defensive ditches at Colchester itself is called Gryme's Dyke and this has been dated by Philip Crummy as being constructed in the Roman period, probably soon after the Boudican revolt[3]. Unfortunately we do not as yet have any evidence for the date of construction of the Thornham Grim's Ditch. It may be relevant that about 3 miles further up the A140 a location, now marked by a petrol station on the junction with the road to Diss, is called 'The Devil's Handbasin' which suggests that here as well an unexplained feature in the landscape was being attributed to the devil.

The distribution of Iron Age coins in the Waveney valley area might also provide a clue to the territorial boundary as a significant number of Trinovantian gold coins have been found here as well as many Icenian silver and potin coins. These coins and coin moulds for the production of Icenian coins found at Needham, which was presumably the site of a mint[4], suggest we are within, but perhaps near the southern edge of, Icenian territory where high value Trinovantian coins were also in circulation. It is possible that the area between the River Waveney and the River Dove at Thornham was home to a distinct group of people who owed allegiance to neither the Iceni nor the Trinovantes. Similar independent groups have been suggested for the occupants of the valley of the River Blyth, the later Hundred of Blything and for the area of the Wicklaw Hundreds which might have centred on the earthwork enclosure at Burgh by Grundisburgh[5]. If so the eight Roman silver coins found at Needham might have been the pay of a Roman soldier stationed on the edge of Icenian territory in the last years of its independence: they include three Republican coins issued before 62 BC and five from Julius Caesar, Augustus, Tiberius and Nero, the latest being minted in AD 60 just before the Boudican revolt which could have prompted the soldier to conceal his savings[6].

By examining nineteenth century and earlier maps Tom Williamson[7] has demonstrated that the landscape north of Grim's Ditch towards Yaxley appears to be a pre-Roman field system cut by the Roman road. He argues that this may be part of an ancient co-axial field system in which fields are defined by parallel but slightly sinuous lanes and boundaries, and have few prominent continuous features running in a transverse direction[8]. This type of system is described as Bronze Age on Dartmoor where the boundaries are called Reaves. The evidence in East Anglia is not so clear and merits further research because some field boundaries certainly do appear to be earlier than the Roman road, which would mean that some elements of the Iron Age field system survived into modern times. There are some changes south of the apparent line of Grim's Ditch where the boundaries that can be identified seem to be aligned on the Roman road so may result from later changes. The possible pre-Roman alignment is followed by a major route through the estate known for part of its length as Cowpasture Lane (Plate 5); from Stoke Ash this crosses the River Dove at Waterhouses and follows the alignment of the present village street of Thornham Magna, then continues as a private drive to the Hall where it becomes Cowpasture Lane leading to Mellis Green; then extends by Stonebridge Lane and Bugg's Lane in Burgate to the market at Botesdale and arrives at the watershed between the rivers Waveney and Little Ouse. Debenham History Society (pers. comm. David Aldred) have suggested that this is part of a much longer route starting from the large Iron Age ditched enclosure at Burgh by Grundisburgh, near Woodbridge, and running on the line of the present B1079 to Helmingham, then along a lane past Bocking Hall and a footpath to Winston Green, then past Poplar Hall (in 1361 Cattenhaugh) to the springs at the head of the Deben (TM 158636) above Debenham, then by a way north described in 1621 as a processional way to Old Hall after which the precise route is lost through Wetheringsett, but picked up as 'Deadmans Way' through Stoke Ash. They suggest the route continued north west to Swaffham in which case it would form a fairly direct route from the east coast at Felixstowe via Woodbridge to the Fen edge and the Icknield Way. Although impossible to prove it may be that this was a major alternative way providing a cross country alternative to sailing round the coast of Norfolk. This route would cross the major Iron Age site at Saham Toney which John Davies points out has produced a notable number of non-Icenian coins[9].

After the Romans invaded Britain in AD 43 they soon built a system of main roads. That road which became the modern A140 through Stoke Ash was part of the highway which ran from the major Roman town at Colchester to the Icenian centre at Caistor by Norwich. Colchester, the Roman Camulodunum, had the high status of a colony originally founded to house retired legionary soldiers with full citizen status and was the only really Roman town in East Anglia. Caistor by Norwich, as Venta Icenorum, became the official administrative centre for the Iceni and later received massive defensive walls but remained relatively small as if the Icenian culture was predominantly rural and never absorbed the urban attitudes of Roman society. Evidence so far available suggests that the Iceni continued farming the productive lands of East Anglia much as they had before the Roman conquest. They used Roman style pottery, both imported and locally made, converted their wealth into the coins that were current throughout the empire and collected silver plate and gold jewellery to the latest designs but lived on farms and in small towns that had few distinctively Roman features. East Anglia was probably of particular value to the Roman administration as a source of food for its armies. One clue which may be significant is that in the fourth century[10] the emperor Julian took steps to restore the protection for the transport of grain from Britain to the Rhine, as we are told that in AD 359 while campaigning in Germany he built granaries in place of those which had been burnt, to store the corn regularly brought from Britain. The Roman sources also tell us that, where the Rhine flows into the Atlantic Ocean at a point on the coast 900 stadia, about 103 miles from Britain, Julian had timber gathered from the forests around the river and 800 boats larger than galleys built which he sent to Britain to convey grain. We are told that before Julian's time corn was shipped from Britain over the sea and up the Rhine, but the barbarians had blocked transport up the Rhine so ships unloaded in coastal ports and transport from there by wagon instead of river was very expensive. Julian provided more ships and re-opened the Rhine navigation which was seen as an important achievement. We are not told about transport of the corn in Britain but presumably every effort would be used to achieve river transport for East Anglian corn to the sea. This traffic might have been controlled by officers based in the so called 'Saxon Shore Forts' on the coast at Caister on Sea and Burgh Castle near Great Yarmouth which dominated the Great Estuary through which the Waveney as well as the Yare entered the sea. It must also be very likely that some of the grain required for the garrison troops on Hadrian's Wall was transported by sea from the East Anglian ports to the supply base at South Shields on the River Tyne.

The site of the White Horse public house on the crossroads at Stoke Ash could well be the very one where a Roman mansio or guest house complex stood. The purpose of this was to provide facilities for weary travellers, and in particular officials using the Imperial Post, for provision of the link between the military and administrative bodies controlling the outlying areas of the Empire. Tired horses were changed for fresh mounts at the mansio and the traveller might have enjoyed a visit to the existing local market centre. They had many similarities to the present day system of Travel Lodges that are linked with modern motorways as they made it possible to wine, dine and relax in the bathhouse. Here the latest gossip from Rome could be discussed, and after an overnight stay the refreshed travellers could continue their journey. However in the absence of specific archaeological evidence so far this can only be a matter of speculation. Initial construction of roads was carried out by the army and the military entrenching tool found here may have been lost by a soldier engaged in this work, although no Roman fort has yet been identified in the area. A few other metal objects

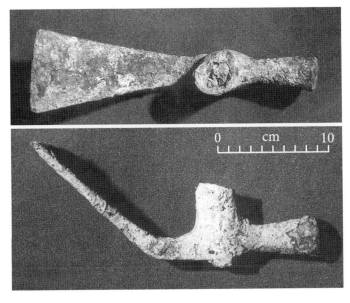

Figure 3.2 *Roman entrenching tool found at Stoke Ash. This seems to have been an item of standard army issue.*

that might have military origins, including a broken lance head, could also have been lost by troops who were involved in the building of the road or who were marching along it. Those items that might have belonged to Roman soldiers that have been recorded in our area have all turned up close to the main road near Stoke Ash or near Scole, where a few military items have been found. The modern crossroads may also have served the Roman west to east route from Ixworth, where an early Roman fort has been partially excavated, to Wenhaston near Halesworth. If so it would have been a busy junction. It is an appropriate point to mention that the highways we know as 'Roman roads' were built for use by the army and the accompanying administration, but many lesser routes had been developed generations before to meet local needs. These either continued as they were or would have been improved to carry heavier Roman traffic. Such ordinary roads were by far the greater in number and while they are impossible to date, it is safe to assume that many that are in use today are much older than those we recognise as Roman. Where the two systems of roads do meet it often appears that the local lanes ignore the Roman roads, and this suggests that they were already there when the Roman engineers cut through them. We feel that the local lanes that led to the focal point at Thornham would have linked to the new Roman highway much as our minor village roads today are linked to the new motorways.

This stretch of the A140 from Coddenham to Norwich is often referred to by its medieval name 'The Pye Road' and is numbered 3d by Margary. In Coddenham parish where the road crossed the River Gipping about six miles upstream from Ipswich at the settlement called Combretovium by the Romans the road was sectioned by Stanley West north of the Roman forts revealed by air photographs but never excavated[11]. The road was 32 feet wide with a raised carriageway, the agger, 1 foot 6 inches high made of rammed sand and gravel. It was reported that 'Near Baylham House … a section cut to the north of Mill Lane showed the road well preserved, of gravel 18 inches thick, apparently 23 feet wide at first, but later widened on the west side to 32 feet above a pit containing Claudian pottery dated to about AD 50. From the absence of silting it was obvious that the pit cannot have been long closed before the road was constructed.' Another description said that 'work of Ipswich School … assisted by Mr. S.E. West of Ipswich Museum … found road width of 22–26 feet rammed sand and gravel 1 foot 6 inches thick. Samian ware of Claudian date was found in a pit below the road and a coin of AD 77–8 was stratified in the road make-up.' The authors of 'The Archaeology of Roman Suffolk' in 1988 suggested the construction date of the Pye Road as about AD 70. Why? Even at that date the coin recorded by West has to be a later intrusion which either worked down into the road or was lost during repair work. It seems more likely that this military highway was constructed towards the Iceni soon after the initial conquest and extended to Venta once the Iceni were fully incorporated in the province.

It is only possible to study the structure of the road where the modern route deviates from it, thus in 1936 Rainbird Clarke tried to trace the road from the point where the A140 leaves it at Swainsthorpe to Caistor and suggested it was laid out about AD 70. He says the road was examined in 1936 by Thrower & Long west of Scole Bridge across the river Waveney a few yards beyond the county boundary. It was 21 feet wide and made of packed flints with a ditch on its west side containing fragments of Roman pottery and was making for a ford across the Waveney of which traces still existed[12]. Roadside ditches recorded on the Suffolk side of the river show that the Roman road ran on or close to the same line as the modern A140. Portions of three other roads, probably Roman, may connect with the main road at Scole Bridge. The first runs north and south on Stuston Common, with a surface of compact gravel with good camber 18 feet wide. The second is south east from the bridge, having a gravel surface 11 feet wide, and the third at Waterloo in Scole parish was 12 feet wide, also made from gravel, running south east towards Scole Bridge and immediately south of it were piles and timbering regarded by Gale as a wharf with wooden and flint buildings but this is uncertain although we should expect to find that small barges were travelling this far up the river. Scole was certainly the site of a small commercial settlement with industrial premises located near the point where the main road crossed the river[13]. An artificial water channel leading to timber structures, which included re-used roof timbers from an earlier Roman building, appears to be part of a malting and brewing complex. There was also an area of iron working and smithing and evidence of furniture manufacture: large quantities of worked leather were found in a well, where it was in good state of preservation as completely waterlogged, and these included parts of shoes of different sizes and the soles of some were heavily studded, showing the standard Roman practice of protecting the leather soles of outdoor footwear by inserting rows of metal studs.

For the main road across our area we do have one important written document. The Antonine Itinerary is a collection of routes across the Roman Empire, possibly compiled from records prepared for imperial journeys. One route (Iter V) includes the stretch of road between Colchester and Caistor by Norwich and features a location called 'Villa Faustini' meaning the Estate of Faustinus. It is worth remarking that although archaeologists use the term 'villa' for a Roman style house its use in Latin, the language of the Romans in which the Itinerary was written, usually refers to a country estate and not just the house of the estate's owner. Arguments have been put forward at various times suggesting that either Scole or Stoke Ash is the 'Villa Faustini'. The suggestion that Villa Faustini might be the large villa site at Stanton Chair north of Ixworth[14] seems much less likely. The use of a villa name in the Itinerary is not unique since one is listed in Italy and no less than seven in Africa. The central building of the villa estate was not necessarily beside the road and the record could well refer simply to a road-station dependent on it which might have been developed by the estate owners to take advantage of the passing traffic. The Roman author Varro, writing in the first century BC, had suggested that for a villa estate near a road it was a profitable side line to own an inn[15]. There is a problem about the actual distances listed in the Itinerary. The total mileage for the whole of Iter V from London to Carlisle is an accurate sum of the individual stages but the distance allowed between Colchester and Caistor is inadequate and this affects Villa Faustini. A detailed study of this problem was made by Leo Rivet[16] who concluded that there are two acceptable textual emendations which are easy errors for a later copyist to make, either changing the figure of xxxv (for 35 Roman miles) from Colonia (Colchester) to Villa Faustini to xxxx (40 miles) so that it falls at Scole, or changing the xviii (18 miles) from Villa Faustini to Icinos (Caistor St Edmund) to xxiii (23 miles) it becomes Stoke Ash. We propose a possible alternative based on the suggestion[17] that the routes were compiled from the milestone survey prepared when each road was built, and that these were measured from a fort or the capital of a civitas, that is the local administrative unit generally based on the pre-Roman people. In Iter V Caistor by Norwich is named as Icinos, presumably using the name of the people of the civitas, as is often found on the continent, rather than the individual name of their main town which is given as Venta Icinorum ('Market of the Iceni') in Iter IX. If the road was measured north from the colonia at Colchester to the northern limit of the territory of the Trinovantes directly governed as part of the new Roman province this would give the figure of xxxv miles to Stoke Ash. We think that after the Boudican revolt this became the northern limit of the territorium of the colonia of Colchester as the whole of the northern part of the territory of the Trinovantes was attributed to the colonia, and the southern part to Londinium so that the Trinovantes lost their independent existence. When the Iceni were incorporated into the province the section in Icenian territory was measured north from the River Waveney at Scole to Caistor by Norwich, giving the correct distance of xviii miles. Thus the two distances of xxxv and xviii are correct, but the property of the estate (villa) of Faustinus is excluded. This omission may have arisen because this was a large estate extending for some five Roman miles along the road, and of unknown extent to either side although it could have included Eye & Hoxne, which was not included in either the territory of the colonia of Colchester or the civitas of the Iceni, so that it was missed from the milestone survey. Perhaps the owner of the estate maintained the main road through his land, but it is more likely that this was part of the land in this region that was made into an imperial estate in the personal ownership of the emperor. It may then have been sold or leased to Faustinus. Rivet & Smith may not find the inclusion of Villa Faustini in the itinerary surprising, but it is unique in the British routes suggesting a large and important estate that might have been established in the border territory between the Trinovantes and Iceni. This is particularly interesting if Grim's Ditch in Thornham Parva can be suggested as the northern boundary of Trinovantian territory. It is notable that Stoke Ash marks the only major change of alignment in this road which runs fairly directly from Combretovium to this point then makes a significant change towards Caistor by Norwich. It is worth recalling a nineteenth century comment by J. Raven in his 'History of Suffolk' 1895 (p.41) that 'From Stoke Ash a gravel road goes northward by Scole, Dickleburgh and Long Stratton to the great camp Ad Taum at Caistor, near Norwich. Those who work at the pick and shovel on this road say that there is a great difference in its character north and south of Stoke White Horse.' Until the end of the nineteenth century the main road made a curious deviation north of the crossroads along the curving route now marked by Chapel Lane, and it is possible that this resulted from some post-Roman obstruction of the direct route, but it is possible that here, as is found elsewhere, the Roman road was diverted to avoid a large burial mound (a tumulus) perhaps of Bronze Age origin, as a number of apparent Bronze Age burials are recorded below in the Dove valley. If so this mound would have been a conspicuous feature of the landscape marking the last resting place of some hero from the past. The modern crossroads at the White Horse might well echo one from the Roman system as there was probably a route from the market town at Wenhaston in the valley of the river Blyth near the east coast to the towns at Pakenham/ Ixworth and Icklingham to the west. From the White Horse crossroads it is possible to suggest a line that diverges slightly north of the modern road to Thornham so that it passes through Street Farm in Thornham Magna and on by a bridleway in a straight alignment to join Clay Street towards Finningham and then perhaps by a change of alignment through Westhorpe on the modern road, then by a line of footpaths and boundaries between Badwell Ash and Walsham le Willows.

J. Raven ('History of Suffolk' 1895, p.25) records an early find of Roman material near the cross roads:

> 'My friend and correspondent, Mr. H. Watling, of Ipswich, thus writes to me about Stoke Ash, after treating of Baylham, Coddenham, Crowfield, and Stonham, all abounding in fictile and other remains: "Stoke Ash is decidedly the most important place, and the finest description of pottery is found here … just below the White Horse Inn on the same side. … It is a curious fact that the opposite side was devoted to burial purposes. Some vessels containing calcined bones were inverted on a square tile" (April 4, 1892). About this time the Master of Pembroke College, Cambridge, wrote an account of the find here. The position had attracted attention early in the century, when Lapie, probably from measurements only, placed Villa Faustini at Little Thornham, close by Stoke Ash. I visited the place on May 30, 1892, in company with one of my sons. The spots where the fictile fragments were discovered, as related by Dr. Searle and Mr. Watling, were indicated to us, and the landlord of the White Horse brought out several coins found thereabouts, of which one bears the head of Crispus, the eldest son of Constantine the Great, with a reverse referring to Vota Vicennalia of that unhappy prince.'

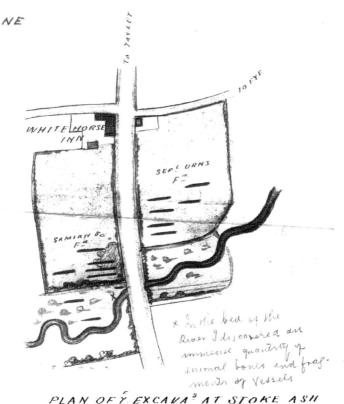

PLAN OF Y̆. EXCAVAˢ AT STOKE ASH

Figure 3.3 *Hamlet Watling's plan of Stoke Ash, showing where he found Roman material. This is taken from his complete map of 'the Ninth Iter' made in 1871 and now in Ipswich Museum.*

Hamlet Watling became schoolmaster at Earl Stonham in 1855. In 1867 he was finding much Roman material in the valley between Little Stonham Hall and Earl Stonham Rectory. This led to his interest in the Roman road and other likely sites on it[18]. Rev C E Searle had been curate of Earl Stonham from 1864 to 1870, before becoming Master of Pembroke.

Searle's account of the circumstances in which the Stoke Ash finds were made is worth quoting as it appears in a letter to the editor of the 'Quarterly Journal of the Suffolk Institute of Archaeology' for June 1869, p.43

'Dear Sir, – As in the first number of the 'Journal of the Suffolk Archaeological Institute' you invite communications of antiquarian interest, I venture to send you notice of a small 'find' of Roman remains at Stoke Ash, in this county, which I acquired in October last. The Stonham postman observing some labourers digging gravel in a field by the side of the high road leading from Ipswich to Norwich, saw them toss out several fragments of strange-looking pottery, which he brought to me. They consisted of the ordinary kinds of pottery usually found in Roman sites – brown, blue and grey: the most interesting were the Samian, of which there were portions of several vessels – one, a hunting scene, with potter's mark (Albuci), is very spirited. The rim of the light brown vessel, too, is singularly elegant, and the handle of the amphora is interesting for the name Ennius Julianus (abbreviated). I went myself to identify the spot, but unfortunately the pit was filled; but, from numerous fragments scattered over the surface, I judged that the men were right when they said that they had buried a considerable quantity. From them I obtained five 'old halfpennies', which were found with the pottery; these were second brass coins of Domitian, Hadrian, Antoninus in bad preservation, and third brass coins of Tetricus the Younger and Salonina – very good and legible. I picked up a flint arrow head, and have another curious chipping from the same place, which was probably a knife. The whole field looked very inviting for excavation, and I heard that old pots were frequently turned up in an adjacent field. If you think this humble discovery worthy of a corner in the journal, you will probably encourage me to intrude again upon your pages. Yours faithfully, C.E. SEARLE. Earl Stonham, March 1869.'

More recently at Stoke Ash fine pottery, metalwork and coins have been found in the area of the settlement. Systematic field walking reveals a concentration of evidence suggesting that this was a small town extending for about a mile north to south along the road from north of the White Horse crossroads to south of Stoke Ash church, where finds in the 1960s led to the naming of a road as 'Roman Way'. More surprisingly it stretches at least three quarters of a mile east to west, in the area between the Dove and the road west from the White Horse crossroads. This area is large enough to suggest that in the Roman period this town was a major market centre for the surrounding farms. Finds include two brooches of a distinctive type based on a coin of Hadrian showing cavalry soldiers and three infantrymen above an eagle. Sometimes called the 'adlocutio' type, seven found at Hockwold have been claimed as evidence for a religious site so perhaps there was a temple near the river. A small excavation near the point where the main road crossed the river in Stoke Ash has revealed two distinct periods of activity separated by a level surface of clay that might be the floor of a building. The first period belongs to the early phase of Roman activity as it contains large pieces of pots that were made before the middle of the second century, early brooches and first century coins including one of the emperor Vespasian. There was also a fine blue glass bead, the silvered bowl of a spoon, a pair of bronze tweezers, and a small scoop with a long handle that might have belonged to a toilet set held by a bronze ring. The level above the clay floor showed continuing activity late into the Roman period, which is confirmed by the presence of a fifth-century coin. Among other items a fine jet toggle was found. There was evidence of meat preparation as there were many animal bones, including cow, pig, horse and sheep as well as dog and a small bird. A significant number of bones showed cut marks typical of butchering and some had been split open to extract the marrow. A study of the pollen[19] in these deposits showed that in the Roman period local trees included birch, oak, pine, beech and alder with hazel and holly bushes. There was plenty of grass pollen but also wheat (*triticum*), mugwort, chicory, campion, cruciform weeds, plantain, nettles and at this site close to the river a fern.

Field walking has also revealed additional groups of pottery, indicating that a number of other places on the estate were being farmed. This confirms the picture we

Figure 3.4 *Early Roman stamped pottery found at Thornham. This unusually fine plate or shallow dish was apparently copied from imported 'terra nigra' (black earthenware) types. Continental examples have the potter's name in the central panel which survives in the bottom corner of this fragment.*

are building up from fieldwork throughout the region that in the pre-Roman Iron Age and right through the Roman period East Anglia was intensively farmed to produce grain and meat that were exported and made an important contribution to feeding the Roman army. Indications of dairy farming come from the number of cheese presses recovered during the survey. Some of the produce may have been transported by small boats on the River Dove and we are sure that the River Waveney through Scole was used for transporting bulk goods as carriage by water was so much cheaper than using road vehicles. Excavation at Waterloo in Scole in the 1930s revealed evidence of the timber structures that probably belonged to a wharf on a short channel linked to the River Waveney[20]. The Waveney offered direct access via the Great Estuary past the fort at Burgh Castle near Great Yarmouth to the North Sea. This rich farming area with direct access to the river may well have been the source of wealth for the estate of Faustinus. So far we are not finding very much Roman building material on the estate but it is likely that most houses, even large ones, were timber framed, as are so many of their seventeenth-century successors, with substantial walls of wattle and daub roofed with thatch, all of which rot down completely over the years becoming unidentifiable components of the farm land under the plough. It seems that in East Anglia very few people chose to invest in expensive country houses of the type recognised by archaeologists as Roman villas, numerous examples of which have been identified in some parts of the country including the Cotswolds, which was a comparably rich agricultural area. The only examples of the largest type so far recognised in Suffolk are at Castle Hill, Whitton, Ipswich and Stanton Chair near Ixworth. Although some large buildings may have gone undetected it seems unlikely that many had the large mosaic floors, under-floor heating systems and tiled roofs of the great villas. However it is worth noting that a fine group of roof timbers, from at least two buildings, were found reused in a brewing complex at Scole. This may be the first time such parts of a Roman roof structure have been found in Britain and are a reminder that in this region the building of large timber frames has always been highly developed, although we only find evidence when the timbers are preserved in waterlogged conditions. These are rare examples of the survival of components of large timber framed houses and commercial buildings that were common features of the Roman countryside in East Anglia, and it is worth emphasising that we only need to look at examples in Suffolk that survive from the sixteenth century and earlier to see that such houses could be large and comfortable; also that as long as the footings are kept dry and the roof is watertight these buildings can last for hundreds of years. There is other evidence of 'villa type' houses in our area because a mosaic floor was reportedly found in the mid twentieth century on a site parallel to the Halesworth to Bungay road ('Stone Street') but then buried, and crude red tesserae from a simple 'tessellated' floor were found at South Elmham St Peters.

The production of pottery in the Waveney valley during the Roman period should be seen as a major industrial enterprise, with a series of factories producing pottery on a large scale. This was not some rustic craft centre, but a considerable manufacturing operation of the kind that one would expect to find sited in an urban location in today's environment. Perhaps we should compare it with the sequence of industrial sites along the Severn valley in the Ironbridge Gorge at the start of the Industrial Revolution. The largest complex of pottery making in Suffolk during the Roman period has been found in the Wattisfield area[21] above the head of the Waveney only about six miles from Thornham. It made use of a good local source of clay for pot making which was still used through the Middle Ages and in more recent times. The clay contains a high proportion of mica, a mineral that gives the fabric of the pots a distinctive glint or sparkle. They were sold over a wide area and represent about forty percent of the finds at Thornham and Stoke Ash. It is possible that the Roman industry grew from Iron Age production using pit-clamp firings suggested at a poorly recorded site at Pear Tree Farm, Wattisfield[22]. This pottery industry, which spread into what are now the neighbouring parishes of Botesdale, Rickinghall and Hinderclay, must have consumed much wood for fuel and local woodlands were no doubt coppiced to produce a regular supply. It is important to note that firewood is a totally renewable resource. It is well established that in the Middle Ages local woodlands were carefully managed to produce a steady supply of 'underwood' which provided material for such uses as fencing poles and tool handles as well as logs and bundles of brushwood for fuel: cropping areas of coppiced woods at intervals of twelve to fifteen years allowed the trees to grow back naturally from the 'stools', while a limited number of larger trees, including oaks, were left to grow for many years to provide structural timber. By Roman times such a system would have been embraced, as without woodland management timber would have been in short supply, so the woods were managed as much as fields were. It has been suggested[23] that the owner of the large villa at Stanton Chair which is not far from these potteries might have derived his wealth from this industry. This is one example of pottery production on a commercial scale by specialist potters which is found at a number of locations in Roman Britain, many, like this one, in rural locations. To operate on this scale they must have depended on the ordered society and reliable communication system under the auspices of the Roman empire, so the collapse of imperial government may have been the most significant factor in the loss of these industries and of the highly developed potting skills on which they relied, because the whole tradition of fine pottery production that had developed in Britain during the Iron Age and Roman period disappeared at the start of the fifth century.

There was a plentiful supply of the right type of clay at Homersfield and Mendham that was used to produce jugs with face masks made in special moulds[24], as well as a wide variety of household wares. The clay here also contained some mica but not in as high a quantity as that found in the Wattisfield area where the pots have a definite 'twinkle'. The Mendham site was producing pottery during the whole Roman period from the first to fourth centuries AD, with evidence of a very active pottery manufacturing industry during the second and third centuries. This is attested by the many thousands of pottery sherds recovered from the site, with many appearing to be pottery wasters, that is pots that went wrong when fired in the kiln. A pottery sherd, an Iron Age brooch and an Icenian coin indicate earlier activity here, as do finds from the Homersfield kilns, both being close to the River Waveney. Fragments of cheese presses indicate that dairy farming existed, and the large number of loom weights suggest that weaving was carried out, perhaps producing the everyday clothing for the settlement. The large number of Roman brooches and coins suggest a centre of commercial activity and would point to the growing importance of pottery production as opposed to farming. Some of the pots produced at Homersfield in the second and third centuries AD were decorated with

Figure 3.5 *Fragments of Roman pottery from the kiln site at Mendham. The top row are from cheese presses and the middle row from colanders. At the bottom is half a circular loom weight.*

distinctive stamped designs and fragments of these have been found nearby at Flixton as well as at Stoke Ash. At Homersfield pre-Roman Iron Age coins of both the Iceni and Trinovantes have been found; 25 Iceni coins including some of early 'boar' type, 4 potins and one gold coin of Cunobelin. There were also Roman coins starting from Republican issues of Mark Anthony, which although minted in the first century BC could still be in use throughout the first century AD, with additional coins discovered on site extending through the fourth into the early fifth century AD. Nearby at Flixton they were producing tiles, including both tegula and imbrex types for roofing, from kilns spread over at least ten acres, as well as the box flue tiles for hypocaust heating systems and thick tiles suitable for flooring or for use in the tile courses of buildings. Some fragments preserve the delicate fingerprints of women or children employed in the manufacture and the distinctive signatures of the tilers were discovered on many of the samples found indicating continuous production over a long period of time. The tile works were located on higher ground up the valley side above a pottery production area and additional activities, including weaving, are indicated by the loom weights, while farming would have been necessary to support the large community that had developed around the industrial centre. The tiles were being made in an area with a good supply of clay, marked by the naming of 'Heavy Land Wood', where there was extensive woodland for fuel and a beck providing plenty of water: this would have helped in preparing the clay but is not of sufficient size for the tiles to be transported

Figure 3.6 *Roman tiles with makers' marks and fingerprints found at Flixton. These are perhaps as close as we can get to the many labourers who produced our earliest structural ceramics. (See also plate 4.)*

by water so they were presumably carried about two miles by pack animals or wagons downhill to the River Waveney where they could be loaded into barges. It is notable that very few pieces of Roman tile have been found on the Thornham sites although they have been found on two sites in Wickham Skeith, and there is an unconfirmed report of tesserae with roof and box tiles in Thrandeston. Quantities of fragments of both tegulae and imbrices used to tile roofs have been found on the sites along the Waveney valley. One site in St. Peter, which has produced much Roman material suggesting the home of a wealthy farmer, did better than just a beaten earth floor as it has produced some tesserae cut from plain red tile. Tesserae were also found at a site in Oakley on the edge of the Scole settlement, although this might have been a temple rather than a large house. Tesserae, in the form of small cubes, were used to make the decorative floors known as mosaics, the earliest type being monochrome and later in a variety of colours, depicting scenes of mythological characters and rural life. The only other find of tesserae in our area is an unconfirmed report from a site in Brandeston which certainly had much Roman pottery. The very small number of mosaic floors found in Suffolk, with none in the north east, remains remarkable. Pottery evidence suggests a substantial population in Flixton, and in the neighbouring parish of St. Margaret's, continuing from the first century, with much 'Belgic type' material, into the fifth with quantities of Samian, Nene Valley and Oxford wares. There were other substantial structures supporting the case for significant commercial activity in Flixton where one early Roman building appears to be a large granary about 12 metres by 14 metres, supported on timber posts[25] in a location that produced evidence of a number of Iron Age four-post structures which were probably granaries. Three Roman pottery kilns have been found at Needham[26], where the settlement on the north bank of the River Waveney apparently had an Iron Age mint on the basis of a find of coin moulds and this was probably the destination of the road from Peasenhall (Margary Road 35) as there is no evidence of a northward continuation to Pulham, although this must remain a possibility.

One pottery at Ellingham specialised in the production of mortaria, the strong mixing bowls with a heavily gritted inner surface: no Roman kitchen was complete without one of these bowls that could be used in pounding herbs and fining down any mixture before cooking, and we might equate a slave using a mortarium and a pestle with the modern electric food mixer. At the Ellingham site[27] the mortarium kiln included stamped mortarium fragments in its structure showing at least two and possibly four makers using the kiln, of whom one was called Regalis. He is also known to have worked at Colchester and some of his mortaria have been found at South Shields so presumably he was supplying military units in the north by sea in the period between the campaigns of the emperors Hadrian and Severus, as he was probably working at Ellingham about AD 170–190. A total of 837 sherds of mortaria were recovered during the excavation, of which some represented between 37 and 49 individual types, stamped by Regalis. These kilns were also producing flagons. Regalis' mortaria have also been found at Scole. Altogether the Waveney valley was a busy manufacturing area, no doubt taking advantage of water transport along the river and through the Great Estuary to northern East Anglia and thus to the sea. Other production centres were manufacturing mortaria and examples of Nene Valley types, local grey wares, imported samian (Plate 6) and later Oxford ware were distributed throughout the Waveney Valley and Thornham areas.

The Roman pottery, of which we find broken pieces in many parts of the estate, includes fine decorated red tableware of the type we know as Samian which was made in Gaul (modern France) as well as large jars (amphorae) in which wine, olive oil and fish sauce was brought from the continent and quantities of ordinary storage and cooking pots, and mortaria, some of which were made locally in the Waveney valley. Bronze and silver coins turn up from all the Roman periods: including ones struck before the invasion of Britain and even one, only one so far, gold coin[28] of the emperor Honorius who was on the throne when the Roman army and administration were finally withdrawn from Britain in AD 410. Much of the Samian pottery came from the factories in East and South Gaul which suggests it probably came on ships trading from the Rhine estuary, perhaps forming a return cargo for ships that carried East Anglian grain to the Roman garrisons on the Rhine frontier. The continental site at Domburg near Walcheren on the southwest side of the Rhine estuary by the Scheldt was a trading centre with links to England in both the Roman and Anglo-Saxon periods. Mark Hassall[29] reports the finding of over 150 altars at Domburg and Colijnsplaat, 25km from

Figure 3.7 *Roman coins: a first century silver denarius of Vespasian found at Stoke Ash and a fifth century gold solidus of Honorius found at Thornham. In their time these were high value coins.*

Domburg itself, from shrines to the goddess Nehalennia, some dedicated by merchants including four declaring themselves as trading with Britain (*negotiator Britannicianus*) of whom two are in the pottery trade (*cretarius*).

Millstones may also have been included in return cargoes as from Roman times until the later Middle Ages the hard volcanic lava from quarries in the Rhine valley at Niedermendig was valued for grinding grain in mills turned by hand or driven by slave, donkey or waterpower. This stone is coloured from grey to black and with distinctive honeycomb appearance is easily recognised when fragments turn up on fields or are seen incorporated in church walls. We also find fragments of fine glass bowls and dishes near the Stoke Ash White Horse, and these also appear on a number of sites down the Waveney valley so the houses were certainly well equipped. (Plate 7.)

The estate of Faustinus which as we have seen was identified in the official Roman guide, the Antonine Itinerary, may have extended from here to the crossing of the River Waveney four miles up the road at Scole. Certainly somebody wealthy lived near here as a magnificent treasure of gold and silver from late in Roman times was found in 1992 about five miles down the River Dove at Hoxne[30]. It is now in the British Museum and included some 14,865 coins of which 569 were gold and most of the rest silver which were of very high purity but many of them have been clipped which is unlikely to have been done before the final collapse of the rule of Roman law in Britain. There were about 200 other gold and silver objects including 29 items of high quality gold jewellery, the solid silver tigress handle from a large vase, four elaborate gilded silver statuette pepper pots, 78 spoons and 20 ladles mostly in matching sets as well as four silver wine strainers. One silver spoon does carry the name Faustinus, although a whole set of ten are inscribed Ursicinus, both common Roman names. A collection of 600 gold coins of similar date that had been buried at Clint Farm, Eye, was found about 1780, but the records tell us little about them. However in the second volume of the Proceedings of the Suffolk Institute of Archaeology it is reported that at a meeting held at Eye in 1854 'The Rev. C.R. Manning exhibited ten gold Roman coins found at Eye, Suffolk, in May 1781. Several hundred coins were found at the time, chiefly of the Emperors Honorius and Arcadius, in a leaden box; and near them were found some human bones.' In the same volume Henry Creed recorded that 'in 1781 a leaden coffer was turned up near the river on the Clint Farm by some labourers. It contained several hundred aurei [presumably gold solidi] of the Roman emperors Valens & Valentinianus, Gratian, Theodosius, Arcadius & Honorius. I have seen several of these in the possession of a lady lately deceased and ten of them, in the finest preservation, are now on the table being exhibited by Rev. C R Manning.' However we note that although within Eye, Clint Farm is actually just across the river from Braiseworth at a point where burials, which may be early Anglo-Saxon are said to have been found[31].

A site on high ground beside Clay Street, on the north side of the presumed Roman road, has produced evidence of significant Roman occupation including, unusually for Thornham sites, ceramic building materials likely to be part of an underfloor heating system (hypocaust), several coins (fourth century), enamelled bronzes and pottery with first century greyware and later mortaria manufactured in the Nene valley, and others from Ditchingham in the Waveney valley. An unusual item from this site is a piece of Roman pottery with a fabric incorporating crushed shell which was made in the Lakenheath and Mildenhall area, suggesting it was the container for some commodity transported from the edge of the Fens. It is likely this was the site of a substantial building occupied throughout the Roman period. Less than a mile south west of this area, slightly south of the projected continuation of Clay Street, but just inside the parish of Wickham Skeith surface finds suggest the presence of a really substantial Roman building that might be described as a villa with a bath house. Quantities of roof and flue tile have been found high on a south facing slope which is likely to be the site of a villa with a hypocaust heating system while at the bottom of the slope more tile is found, and in the sides of a stream which feeds into the River Dove there are substantial concrete footings with Roman floor tile embedded in the top: perhaps this is the base of the latrine for the bathhouse, flushed directly by the stream. As well as substantial quantities of pottery, including samian, several brooches and a cosmetic grinder have been found[32]. This site overlooking a tributary of the Dove may have had a long history as it has produced Bronze Age and Early Saxon material. Not far away a hoard of 130 Roman coins was found with brooches. There are also reports of square section ceramic pipes, presumably to carry a water supply, being found in an area with Roman pottery on the other side of the stream at Wickham Skeith, nearer to the church. These could well have been prosperous farms upstream from the settlement on the main road at Stoke Ash. The substantial amount of roof tile, easily recovered when walking across the site of the Wickham Skeith villa, contrasts with the experience of walking the sites in Thornham and Stoke Ash which produce much Roman pottery, brooches and coins but hardly any tile and no substantial pieces of roof tile: this is true even of the site on Clay Street. We must conclude that the buildings of the extensive settlement in Thornham and Stoke Ash, presumably a trading town centred on the main Roman road, all had thatched roofs and it was only a few large houses in the countryside that had the tiled roofs of tegula and imbrex type that we associate with really Romanised structures. Apart from the incomplete reports about a site in Thrandeston which appears to have been a substantial building with a tiled roof and heating system, the only other site producing significant amounts of tile near our Thornham area is some four miles north of Stoke Ash at Oakley where finds include some tile and coarse red tesserae, indicating a plain tiled floor rather than a coloured mosaic, but Judith Plouviez *pers. comm.*suggests this might be a temple on the edge of the small town at Scole. It seems that in the Thornham area the local residents continued a local tradition of building timber framed houses, the size and design of which we cannot so far determine, and giving them thatched roofs. These could be large comfortable residences that would last for several centuries as long as the roof was kept watertight and the walls were maintained. The Romanised buildings we refer to as 'villas' were clearly the exceptions to the norm, presumably the equivalent to the 'stately homes' of more recent centuries. It is possible that all the inhabitants of the Thornham area were tenants of the estate of Faustinus but we have yet to discover the total size or administrative centre of this estate. It might have belonged to a wealthy Briton or to some absentee landlord with estates in several provinces of the empire.

The population during the Roman period seems to have been significantly higher than during the preceding Iron Age or the following Saxon periods because, after looking at some 29,000 acres of land, we have evidence of 116 sites of Roman activity on farmsteads and larger settlements. There are 85 in the Waveney valley area of study and 31 on the Thornham Estate, all surrounded by land on which a thin scatter of abraded pottery indicates manuring of the fields with the rotted remains of household waste in addition to animal dung. They suggest that each farmstead was working about 200 to 250 acres of land which is reasonable if they are tenanted farms on large estates. People probably enjoyed a longer life expectancy as a result of a better standard of living with improved sanitation and medical care, as well as a better diet marked by the introduction of new vegetables, fruits, nuts and herbs. The farms are generally sited to include a mixture of soil types with the buildings on rising ground above a reliable source of water. Finds from these sites suggest a prosperous economy, doubtless producing significant quantities of grain and meat, with evidence of efficient butchery, but also dairy products and wool processing. Some sites involved industrial activity including pottery and tile manufacture, leatherworking, metal work, furniture production and brewing. The presence of coins on the larger settlements and on most farmsteads in the Thornham area (although on few of the Waveney farms) implies the production of surpluses for sale either on the open market or to contractors supplying the army. This prosperity seems to extend throughout the Roman period in most of the parishes studied with the exception of Metfield where there is a marked decline in the fourth century. As many of the Metfield sites were on low lying sites in marshy ground near the river it is possible that they became too wet towards the end of the period or had been exploited to their limit and became unproductive through exhaustion of their natural resources.

Only one extensive stretch of land on the Thornham Estate has failed to produce any evidence of Roman or other early activity: the fields on high and wet ground behind the Swatsfield moated site have revealed no pottery or other finds despite repeated field walking, so we suggest it was woodland, no doubt managed to produce both timber and fuel. It is notable that in the Roman period we find evidence of activity right up to the edges of watercourses while in the Iron Age people seem to have avoided occupying these areas close to the water so liable to flooding. Indeed there are signs that in the Roman period watercourses were being actively managed.

The distribution of sites in the region where Roman pottery is found suggest that the majority are individual farms or small farming communities situated about half a mile apart. Where they can be related to known or likely main Roman roads they are set back from the line of the road as we might expect farm buildings to be. However in a limited number of places occupation is immediately beside the road as is the case at Stoke Ash where the market town seems to extend along, and border directly upon, both the main Roman road from Colchester to Caistor by Norwich (the modern A140) and the most likely line of the road from Ixworth/Pakenham to Hacheston which crosses at right angles at the White Horse. This extensive area of intensive occupation suggests a commercial centre of some size which is supported by the presence of significant numbers of coins, as these tend to be much less common on farm sites or even in villas except where groups of coins appear to have been deliberately concealed for safe keeping. Bronze pins, brooches for fastening clothing, a bronze spoon and rings have been found. We were excited and delighted to find from this area a complete enamelled seal box (shown on the cover). The reason for our excitement was that complete boxes are quite a rarity, and could mean that our area had been one of importance, which

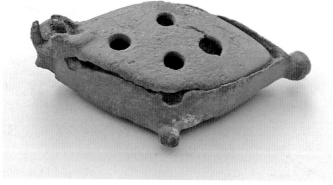

Figure 3.8 *The back of the seal box, showing holes for the ties that secured the wooden writing tablet. The knot inside the box was protected with a wax seal. Found at Stoke Ash. The front of this box is shown on the cover.*

supports the theory of it belonging to the Villa Faustini, and that official documents were being handled in this area. Seal boxes were used to protect the wax seal bearing the impression of the seal ring worn by the sender of a message, which covered the knot fastening together the two leaves of a writing tablet in which the message was written in wax panels inside the wooden frame. They were used to preserve the privacy of commercial or official messages while in transit and remind us of the importance and ubiquity of written documents throughout the Roman world. Finds from Hadrian's Wall have revealed that ordinary messages were often written in ink on thin wooden tablets which might contain routine daily ration returns for soldiers or a communication between mother and son about new socks and undergarments, but these have usually disappeared as completely as the average modern memo or personal letter. It is worth noting that a seal box lid has been found at South Elmham St. Margarets, suggesting that here too there may have been more than just a farm. The neighbouring parish of South Elmham St. Cross has revealed evidence of iron working in the form of an acre of residue a deep orange colour and of conical pottery crucibles on ground which was later covered by Greshaw Green. Edward Martin suggests this may be from the making of iron brooches and compares his finds at Burgh by Grundisburgh. Apart from the Thornham area, thorough field walking studies have produced evidence for the distribution of farms and ceramic manufacturing centres near the Waveney in and around Weybread, Mendham, and the South Elmham parishes. There were also farms

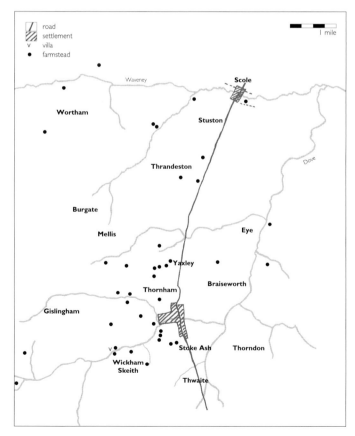

Figure 3.9 *Roman sites at Thornham, showing the extent of the Roman market town and the distribution of farms identified by field walking.*

Figure 3.10 *Roman sites at South Elmham. The distribution of known farms between the two main roads at the east and west of our area of study.*

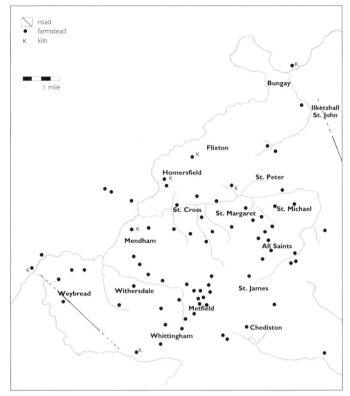

on the high plateau in Mendlesham where Roy Colchester has identified fifteen Roman sites. Similar patterns are indicated by the results of less thorough studies in a number of other parishes across the region. At Scole, where there has been much actual excavation of sites, the evidence suggests commercial and industrial occupation directly beside the roads, close to the river crossing, but over a smaller area than at Stoke Ash. In fact the settlement close to the main road at Stoke Ash is at least twice the size of that at Scole and extends significantly further along the edge of the river. This is based on the minimum extent so far mapped by field walking and metal detector finds at Stoke Ash/ Thornham. Both modern and nineteenth century finds of large pieces of Roman pottery with no signs of later abrasion in the area near the River Dove crossing at Stoke Ash reinforce the view that this was the site of a substantial settlement that we can call a market town. The fact that we have here a considerable amount of Iron Age material suggests the commercial centre may have had a predecessor before the Roman conquest.

Worked flints have been recovered from many of the Iron Age and Roman period sites, but these are not products of the early prehistoric styles. They are poor quality flakes roughly struck and crudely worked to produce scraping and cutting tools suitable for simple tasks on Iron Age and Romano-British farms. Even today farm workers will often use a freshly struck flint to cut binder twine rather than looking for a knife. They remind us that the basic technology of using stone tools has never entirely disappeared.

Finds from field walking reveal a difference, so far unexplained, between sites in the Thornham area and those along the valley of the Waveney as in the Thornham area the pottery we find for the later Roman period includes significant amounts of Hadham type wares for which production sites are known in Hertfordshire and Essex but not much Oxfordshire ware, while the Waveney valley sites have much Oxfordshire ware and little Hadham type ware. This may reflect some feature of the supply routes, but there may be some other factor which also led to the apparent scarcity of roofing and heating tiles in the Thornham area. For the post-Roman period it is notable that despite extensive field walking in the parishes along the Waveney valley only South Elmham St. Margaret has produced any concentration of Middle Saxon Ipswich type pottery and only it and its neighbours of Flixton and Bungay have produced Early Anglo-Saxon wares, but all three parishes of Thornham Parva, Thornham Magna and Stoke Ash have produced significant amounts of Ipswich type wares (so has one site at Mendlesham[33]) and both Thornhams have produced Early Anglo-Saxon wares. It may be that we are seeing evidence for significant foci of activity in these areas continuing into the post Roman period. Scole has produced some late Roman material but no Middle Saxon Ipswich Type ware has been found there.

The Hadham type wares are sometimes called Romano-Saxon pottery because some of them are decorated with designs also found on early Anglo-Saxon pottery, particularly bosses or dimples. Some people have argued that they were being made for an immigrant Saxon population, but this is not now generally accepted, and it is not clear whether these designs did originate outside the Roman empire or were copied by Anglo-Saxon potters from the Romano-British designs after they became fashionable in the Roman empire. Apparently Hadham wares were in circulation in the third century and reached the height of their popularity in the fourth century[34]. The typical Hadham pots are coated with a red slip: they were produced at Little and Much Hadham in Hertfordshire near Bishop's Stortford from about AD 250 to 400 and appear along the east coast mainly during the later fourth century. It is possible that these wares were also produced at Essex potteries, including Inworth near Tiptree, which would be better suited to heavy loads of pottery being transported by water to markets in our part of eastern England.

Government from Rome came to an end about AD 410 but the survival of the main road and some elements of the field system show that people did not stop farming here. There was probably a decline in population and some Anglo-Saxon immigrants arrived from Germanic lands beyond the North Sea, nobody made pottery to the standard achieved by previous generations or brought in new coins. People adopted Germanic designs and different burial customs. It is very likely that even before AD 410 there was a considerable Germanic presence in East Anglia, as many regular troops in the Roman army were of Germanic origin and there were doubtless extensive trade contacts with the Rhine valley, which would lead to social contact and probably some intermarriage. These people might have come from either side of the Rhine, that is from either inside or outside the empire. It is worth remembering that the Roman empire was cosmopolitan and non-racist. There is no evidence of racial prejudice as such. People were probably expected to be capable of using Latin in everyday life but the educated were literate in Greek as well as Latin, and other languages were tolerated: a number of Greek inscriptions have been found in Romano-British contexts, and some in eastern languages including Palmyrene on a memorial at South Shields[35]. If people lived inside the Roman Empire they were required to accept Roman law and frequently chose to adopt Roman names which concealed their ethnic origin (from another part of the empire we might note the typically Egyptian mummy head in the Ipswich Museum collection which has the full tripartite Roman name of the person, Titus Flavius Demetrius, inscribed in perfect Greek lettering, a fusion of three great cultures). The attitude seems to have been truly multicultural and there is no way of telling the ethnic origin of a person by the country of origin of their possessions (owning a Japanese video recorder and car does not make a modern Englishman Japanese). However the combination of archaeological evidence and the limited historical record do support the possibility that the population of Romano-British eastern Britain contained a significant number of people of German origin. It is sometimes suggested that the Roman army in our region only contained what are described as 'Germanic mercenaries' towards the end of the Roman period, but there are specific references to troops of Germanic origin who surprised the British by swimming across wide rivers during the initial conquest of Britain and Batavians from the Rhine valley formed an important part of the regular army from the campaigns of Agricola in the first century to the late garrisons on Hadrian's Wall. As the wooden writing tablets from Vindolanda have revealed, troops from different units were regularly posted to forts other than the headquarters of their units and we might expect troops from the coastal territories of Batavia and Frisia to be serving with the fleet along our coast, so we should consider that regular Roman soldiers who were ethnic Germans were probably a common sight in Suffolk and may have felt sufficiently at home to settle here when they retired. It would be easy for them to keep in touch with their ancestral homelands across the sea.

Gildas, writing his book 'De Excidio Britonum' (The Ruin of Britain) in western Britain about AD 540, refers to events immediately after the departure of the Romans, about a century earlier. He tells us that Scots and Picts attacked northern Britain but after a famine they went home but later at a time of plague these enemies returned so the ruling council and the proud tyrant (?Vortigern) invited Saxons to help. The Saxons arrived in three keels which Gildas says was their name for war ships, they gripped the eastern side of the island, and these were followed by more Saxons in ships. The Saxons, as fighting soldiers, claimed from the British annonae, that is provisions from annual produce as a tax payment, so they were settling as soldiers but clearly not as farmers. Later they complained their monthly allowance (*epimenia*) was not sufficient so broke their treaty (*foedere rupto*) and plundered the whole island. The reference to them receiving payment suggests we should see them as setting up, initially at least, military communities where they and their families got their food from the British and did not farm the land themselves: their task was to fight, just like the Roman army but not the British civilian population who had been forbidden to carry weapons under Roman law. When the British refused to provide as much as the Saxons demanded the latter turned aggressive and raided all the way across Britain before returning to the eastern side of the island, which matches our experience of finding early evidence of an Anglo-Saxon presence in Suffolk.

One local place name might provide evidence that later landowners took notice of the previous Roman settlement and its sports centre when naming their villages.

The Wickham in Wickham Skeith is a name which it seems was invariably used for a settlement next to a Roman site as recognised by Margaret Gelling[36], confirming the recognised status of the Roman presence at Stoke Ash; but Skeith is an uncommon Scandinavian word for a racecourse while Thwaite is Danish for a clearing so these names show a Danish or Viking influence in naming places presumably during the time when this was part of the Danelaw from AD 870 to 917. The use of the Scandinavian Skeith for a racecourse may be comparable to a number of instances of Camp as another place name close to a Roman site, including Bulcamp close to the Roman settlement at Wenhaston and Campsey Ash close to Hacheston. The derivation of camp could be from the Roman campus as in Campus Martius, which was the large open area beside the River Tiber close to the city of Rome used originally for public assemblies, exercise and games. Did the Roman towns in Suffolk each have an open campus, which in some cases retained its Roman name in use by the local population even after they became subject to Anglo-Saxon rule? Perhaps the death of King Anna of East Anglia and his son Jerminus in AD 654 at the hands of King Penda of Mercia at Bulcamp, on the River Blyth opposite Blythburgh, was the result of a violent conflict staged on the ancient campus. It may be that use of the campus was the origin of the game of camping which could be played on these open spaces. Camping as a local ball game is referred to by Thomas Tusser in his 'Five Hundred Points of Good Husbandry' published in its final form in 1580. For December he instructs his readers 'Get campers a ball, to campe therewithall' and expands this by saying 'In medow or pasture (to growe the more fine)/ let campers be camping in any of thine:/ whiche if ye doe suffer when lowe is the spring,/ you gaine to yourselfe a commodious thing.' (Spring here refers to shoots or young growth). However it seems that generally a special place was designated for camping and Norman Smedley[37] identifies an earlier reference to a 'camping pightel' in a deed of 1486. Camping was a violent and potentially dangerous team game involving keeping possession of a ball and passing it within the team[38]. It may be that this game developed in the middle ages to be played on the open campus outside Roman settlements and later other open areas were designated as Camping Closes or Camping Lands[39]. Its origin is unknown and it must be just possible that it was directly descended from one of the ball games enjoyed by Roman players on the original campus. It is possible that the feature recognised by the Scandinavian settlers as a skeith some time before the Domesday Book was compiled in 1086 could have originated as a Roman campus which remained an open space. The location of this campus at Wickham Skeith might still be marked by a number of landscape features as the church stands immediately at the east end of an enclosure marked by a substantial ditch curving away from the north west corner of the churchyard. The north side of this large enclosure is marked by a track, in places a solid causeway that reaches the north side of the church directly from the south end of the Roman town at Stoke Ash, passing south of Wood Hall. Finds suggest that there was activity in the Roman period along this route between Stoke Ash church and Wood Hall. The track continues eastward directly to the site of the Roman villa noted above. The south east corner of the campus has been destroyed by the landscaped grounds of Wickham Hall but its southern side is marked by a pronounced bank and ditch along the minor road west from the Hall gates. Its south west corner is marked by a rounded ninety degree bend in this road at Daisy Green where the west side is a field boundary that appears to be the original line of a diverted footpath. There is a substantial moat outside this south west corner. It seems most likely that the northern side of the campus is the south side of the present Green with its pond which lie between the campus and the most likely line of the track to the villa site. The modern road running north from the Green (and from the north west corner of the campus) leads straight to the river crossing at Wickham Street, which might take its name from this Roman road if such it is, and the track beyond the crossing leads straight up hill to join Clay Street which we argue to be a significant Roman route. The enclosure lies on an extensive fairly level plateau.

It is impossible to say how long the pottery and coins typical of the Roman period remained in use but we might note the large number of silver coins in the Hoxne hoard which had been clipped, a misuse of stamped coin unlikely to take place, and certainly subject to severe penalty, before the end of Roman government, so they were almost certainly in use for some time after AD 410. Further down the Waveney at South Elmham St. Margaret a high proportion of Roman sites remained in existence throughout the fourth-century and also produce metalwork and pottery of the early Saxon period and Middle Saxon Ipswich type wares as well as Thetford type wares which take us right up to the Norman Conquest and so strongly suggest continuity of occupation. At Flixton two fourth-century Roman bronze coins were found, both of which had been drilled so that they could be strung and worn round the neck. These were found close to an Anglo-Saxon burial with sixth-century brooches and an unusual glass claw-beaker[40]. The beaker of green glass marks this as a high status burial and we have noticed that Flixton was a busy place in the Roman period. A single fourth-century coin, similarly drilled, was found at Thornham Magna close to the river, where evidence of fifth century occupation has also been discovered. In the sixth century Roman coins were still being valued although we cannot say whether they were worn as ornamental pendants or strung together as a safe way of carrying money. In either case it is likely that they were respected because they carried the portrait of the Roman emperor when the Wuffing royal family of East Anglia were proclaiming their descent from the deified Roman Caesar. The new rulers did not break all links with the past.

Notes

1   Chadburn, A, 1999 Tasking the Iron Age, in Davies, J, and Williamson, T (eds), *The land of the Iceni: the Iron Age in northern East Anglia*, UEA, 165.

2   See Sauer E, 'Aves Ditch: an Iron Age Tribal Boundary?' *Current Archaeology* **163**, 268–269. Edward Martin discusses the evidence regarding the boundary between Trinovantes and Iceni in Davies, J, and Williamson, T (eds), 1999 *The land of the Iceni: the Iron Age in northern East Anglia*, UEA, 83. He suggests, page 90, that Black Ditches, Cavenham might mark part of an Iron Age boundary.

3   Crummy, P, 1997 *City of Victory*, Colchester, 90.

4   Chadburn, A, 1999, Tasking the Iron Age, in Davies, J, and Williamson, T (eds), *The land of the Iceni: the Iron Age in northern East Anglia*, UEA, 168.

5   Martin, E, 1988, *Burgh: Iron Age and Roman Enclosure*, EAA **40**, 72.

6   Diss, *Mercury* 15 January 1993.

7   Dymond, D, and Martin, E (eds), 1999 *An Historical Atlas of Suffolk,* Ipswich, 48.

8   For further discussion of this field system see Edward Martin in Davies, J, and Williamson, T (eds), *The land of the Iceni: the Iron Age in northern East Anglia*, UEA, 52 ff.

9   Davies, J, and Williamson, T (eds), *The land of the Iceni: the Iron Age in northern East Anglia*, UEA, 35.

10 Zosimus, III, 5, 2 and Eunapius, Fr.12, and Ammianus Marcellinus, XVIII, 2, 3 cf. Libanius, Oration 18, 82.

11 West, S, 1956 A Roman Road at Baylham, Coddenham, in *Antiq.s J.*, **35**, 73 and *PSIAH*, **27** (1954), 42.

12 Clarke, R, 1952 Roman Norfolk since Haverfield, in *Norfolk Archaeol.*, **30**, 142; *Norfolk Archaeol.*, **26** (1937) 120–1 and 161–2; Gale, C, in *PSIAH* **22** (1936) 267 and *Journal of Roman Studies*, **27** (1937), 239.

13 Rogerson, A, 1977 Excavations at Scole, in Wade-Martins, P (ed), *East Anglian Archaeology*, EAA **5**.

14 Proposed by Rodwell in 1975 (*Britannia* **6**, 76).

15 Varro, Rerum Rusticarum I.ii.23.

16 Rivet, A, and Smith, C, 1979 *The Place-names of Roman Britain,* London.

17 Rivet, A, and Smith, C, 1979 *The Place-names of Roman Britan,* London.

18 For more information see Plunkett, S, 1997 Hamlet Watling, Artist & Schoolmaster 1818–1908, in *PSIAH*, **39**, 48.

19 Gurney, D, 1986 *Norfolk: Settlement, religion and industry on the Fen-edge*, EAA **31**, 64 ff.

20 By John Fulcher who kindly supplied the information.

21 *PSIAH* **22** (1936), 263–286.

22 Spread over parishes of Wattisfield, Botesdale, Hepworth, Hinderclay, Market Weston, Rickinghall Inferior and Superior (Swan, V, 1984 *The Pottery Kilns of Roman Britain*' RCHM, 115).

23 Swan, V, 1984 *The Pottery Kilns of Roman Britain,* RCHM, 54.

24 Moore, I, with Plouviez, J, and West, S, 1988 *The Archaeology of Roman Suffolk*, Ipswich, 62.

25 Smedley, N, and Owles, E, 1965 A face-mould from the R-B kiln site at Homersfield, in *PSIAH* **30**, 211.

26 *PSIAH* **40** (2001), 95-6.

27 *PSIAH* **23** (1939), 236.

28 Hartley, K, and Gurney, D, 1997 *A mortarium Kiln at Ellingham, Norfolk*, EAA Occasional Papers **2**.

29 Gold coin found *c*.1980. Present location not known.

30 Britain and the Rhine Provinces: epigraphic evidence for Roman Trade, in du Plat Taylor, J, and Cleere, H, 1978 *Roman shipping and trade: Britain and the Rhine Provinces*, CBA Research Report **24**.

31 Bland, R, and Johns, C, 1993 *The Hoxne Treasure*, London.

32 West, S, 1998 *A Corpus of Anglo-Saxon Material from Suffolk*, EAA **84**, 264.

33 Found by a group field walking with Stanley West (Saxon finds include brooch, buckle, sleeve clasp).

34 West, S, 1998 *A Corpus of Anglo-Saxon Material from Suffolk*, EAA **84**, fig.158.

35 Roberts, W, 1982 *Romano-Saxon Pottery*, BAR **106**.

36 Collingwood, R, and Wright, R, 1995 *The Roman Inscriptions of Britain*, Oxford (RIB)1065.

37 Gelling, M, 1978 *Signposts to the Past*, London, 72.

38 Smedley, N, 1976 *Life and Tradition in Suffolk and North East Essex*, London, 141.

39 Detailed description in Moor, E, 1823 *Suffolk Words and Phrases; or an attempt to collect the lingual localisms of that county,* Woodbridge, and in Claxton, A, 1954 *The Suffolk Dialect of the Twentieth Century*, Ipswich.

40 Dymond, D, and Martin, E (eds), 1999 *An Historical Atlas of Suffolk,* Ipswich, map 70 and the accompanying article by David Dymond.

41 Archaeology in Suffolk 1990, *PSIAH* **37** (1991), 268.

Chapter 4

Anglo-Saxons, Danes and Normans

Did the Roman lifestyle continue long in our region after the withdrawal of imperial government and how did the later changes come about? Patient study of tiny pieces of evidence, carefully interpreted, can lead to some answers. Many of these answers remain tentative as we search for more clues, but we will try to show how some of the problems can be solved. We face a real challenge in this chapter: to give an account of some 650 years in which important events took place and people in our area faced difficult times, but left very little evidence. Yet this is the period when the great ship full of treasures was buried at Sutton Hoo, so we know there was considerable wealth in our region. Who created that wealth, and how did they do it? Clearly people were farming the land and living in communities that are now represented by little more than elusive stains in the ground, where wooden objects and buildings have rotted away. Hence the excitement when the first stains in the soil that represented decayed buildings were revealed in Dr Stanley West's excavation of the houses at West Stow. But why do we get excited about finding tiny pieces of pottery? One reason is that we have so little tangible evidence, because many everyday objects were made from wood or bone that do not survive well in the ground. We value our few scraps of pottery because they do start to shine a little light into what many call the Dark Ages. Broken fragments of metalwork tell us of the people who pumped the bellows for the furnaces and forges where they made brooches and decorated pins. Poor scraps of pottery give us clues to how people responded to the end of the Roman imperial economy's direct impact on Britain. They help us to see how far new people were moving in across the North Sea, the people we refer to as Anglo-Saxons who converted our region into the eastern lands of the Angles, East Anglia. But they leave us unsure how many of the existing British families survived and perhaps married new immigrants, adopted their fashions and became indistinguishable from them.

During the last years of Roman government in Britain the Empire was suffering severe disruption under pressure from those outside its boundaries. Its economy was breaking down and Britain felt the effects of being remote from the centre and vulnerable to attack from the sea. Whether the Britons lost confidence in the competence of imperial administrators or the central government tired of running a distant and difficult land is unclear, but the result was the same. When it lost the guidance of Roman administrators and the funds that the empire sent to pay the army guarding the province, Britain gradually lost its Roman character. The Britons had been used to accepting the rule of Roman law and a Roman lifestyle. They paid taxes and sold much produce to feed the Roman army as well as supplying it with manufactured goods. They did not carry weapons or fight unless they joined the Roman army, when they might be posted to anywhere in the empire. Some Roman soldiers, even complete military units, might have remained in Britain after AD 410, but we know the main field army had accompanied Constantine III to the continent and never returned. Presumably British leaders had to find ways to pay soldiers to protect their people against pirates and raiders, and to keep the peace. It is no surprise that, at least in Eastern England, they turned more and more to warriors from free Germany north of the Rhine, who were like themselves outside the Roman Empire. Thus Angles, Saxons, Jutes and other Germans, collectively referred to as 'Anglo-Saxons', probably came as replacements for the Roman soldiers, paid to protect the freedom of the Britons. It was only gradually that they took advantage of the indecision of British leaders to take control and claim ownership of land and the right to govern. Gildas suggests this started with a dispute about the rates of pay, and when this was unresolved the Germanic peoples took land and brought more of their families as immigrants. No doubt they found it easy to bring increasing numbers across the North Sea and into East Anglia, sailing through the estuaries of the Orwell and the Yare which gave ready access to the Gipping and Waveney valleys, their tributaries enabling them to travel far inland. Others might have used the Wash and its rivers. Having already paid the early immigrants to serve as soldiers, it seems that many Britons found themselves paying rent to the newcomers or even working as their slaves. No doubt some married them and the racial distinctions became blurred as later generations became increasingly mixed. As time went by natives and immigrants combined to become the English.

We have noted evidence for a continuity of settlement and farming after the end of Roman government about AD 410, but we do see changes that are marked in our area by different types of pottery and metalwork. The pottery used in burials at this time is quite different from that of the Roman period as the vessels were hand made, without use of a potter's wheel, and many have distinctive decoration. Archaeologists mark a change from 'Early Saxon' to 'Middle Saxon' about AD 650[1] when these pottery vessels that were hand-made and fired in bonfires were replaced by wheel-made pots fired in kilns. These new pots are mainly small globular cooking pots with a sagging base, which is sensible if pots are not to be placed on a flat surface, storage jars and spouted pitchers. So far kilns for making this pottery have only been found in Ipswich although the pots have been found as far afield as York and London. It is generally referred to as 'Ipswich Ware' or, as some may have been produced elsewhere, 'Ipswich type Ware'. This Ipswich Ware pottery is named after the kilns discovered in the Carr Street area of Ipswich in the 1920s. The pots were studied in the 1950s by John Hurst and Stanley West[2] and the latter excavated evidence of the industry in Cox Lane behind Carr Street. The excavations revealed that many vessels, including the distinctive round bottomed cooking pots, were being made here using a slow wheel[3]. Finds of this pottery indicate a major industry with distribution throughout East Anglia but extending further afield, reaching Yorkshire and London. From about AD 850 the kilns in Ipswich were producing a different type of vessel with a flat bottom and made on a fast wheel. Additional production centres were established and this later style is called Thetford Ware, as the first examples were identified by Group Captain G M

Knocker at Thetford. A series of kilns were discovered there during excavations carried out along the Brandon Road between 1964 and 1970[4]. They manufactured a variety of vessels including storage jars, cooking pots, pitchers, spouted bowls and costrels, all with relatively flat bases and many of them highly decorated. The fabric of the pottery was stronger and finer than the preceding Ipswich Ware. Many fragments of both these types of pottery have been found on the Thornham Estate and in the Waveney Valley. In addition we have found on the estate pottery imported from production centres in Cambridgeshire, Huntingdonshire, Bedfordshire, Northamptonshire and Lincolnshire. The dense shell inclusions visible in the fabric of this pottery make it easily recognisable. It is referred to as 'Saxo-Norman' St Neots Ware and was produced from the 900s to the early 1200s. As on a number of sites we have recovered a greater proportion of this

Figure 4.2 *Thetford ware and St Neots ware pottery provide the best evidence for Late Saxon activity. The stirrup mount is an example of the fittings that were required by warriors riding across country.*

Figure 4.3 *Pole lathes reconstructed at West Stow. Powered by a springy pole operated by a foot treadle, this left the turner free to use both hands to create rounded shapes from a block of wood with his chisel.*

ware along with Thetford type wares it would seem these date from the earlier end of the production period. Those found in association with sherds of thirteenth century and later pottery can be attributed to the period closer to 1200.

For the Early Saxon period a major problem generally is the comparative lack of pottery. We can be confident that some domestic vessels simply do not survive because they were made from wood and bone. Use of these materials is confirmed by evidence from West Stow and Sutton Hoo, so we should not under rate the technical skills of wood turners, carvers and bone workers at this time. For example bone combs were widely used and many examples have been recovered from excavations in Ipswich and Thetford. The pottery that was produced, being hand made and fired in clamp kilns, was not as strong as that made during the Roman period and does not survive well in plough soil. More and more evidence is suggesting that significant numbers of the better pottery vessels produced in very large quantities during the Roman period continued in use long after the end of the Roman administration. Even samian pottery, which had gone out of production long before, might have been kept in circulation as its antique value is confirmed by the many pieces found that had been repaired with metal staples. It is notable at sites in Withersdale and South Elmham St Margaret we find Early Saxon metalwork associated with Roman pottery but no trace of Saxon pottery. It may be that the presence of so much old, but still usable, pottery was one factor in the complete collapse of the industry producing new high quality pots. A single Roman coin which had been drilled for use as a pendant was an isolated find on the south side of Water Lane in Thornham Magna, but it was close to the large spread of material discovered on

Figure 4.4 *Anglo-Saxon stamped pottery found at Thornham. These fragments show the typical style of decoration used on early pots.*

the other side of the river. Drilling coins seems to have been common practice during Anglo Saxon times and many have been discovered throughout the county. There is no way of knowing whether these were chosen purely as decorative items or if this was seen as a secure way to carry coins that could still be used for trade purposes in the absence of newly minted coinage.

The earliest Anglo-Saxon evidence from the heart of the Thornham estate comes from three areas close to Parva church, one close to Magna church and the most prolific site which is close to the river. This particular area, which lay at the western edge of the Roman market town, has shown evidence of activity in the Neolithic period and has apparently been used continuously until modern times. For the Early Saxon period we have found on the surface of this field stamped pottery, black burnished ware, a spindle whorl and various metal objects including a wrist clasp. The site expanded during the Middle Saxon period as Ipswich Ware pottery was recovered from this field and from a second area close by, while Late Saxon material was also found here. It is often assumed that finds of Early Saxon metalwork denote a burial site, but with so many finds of early metalwork from the surrounding parishes, many of them certainly from burials, we seem to have an imbalance between cemeteries and settlements (Plate 8). Where there is evidence of continuous occupation over a longer period we believe there is a stronger case for thinking these are more likely to be settlements where people lived than cemeteries where they buried their dead. This applies to the key site in Magna described above and to a site in Wickham Skeith further up the same valley. This site is marked by a large amount of Roman material which suggests a villa, but the Early Saxon period is represented by three brooches, a buckle and a wrist clasp with a mid period key and a bronze ingot. To the south of this site a hoard of silver coins was found ranging from Harold I to Edward the Confessor, which brings us to the end of the Late Saxon period.

Finding spindle whorls and loom weights, pieces of which have also turned up on the same field at Thornham, show the domestic activities of spinning and weaving which do not seem to be represented in burials. Wrist clasps might be lost from a dress worn about the house or survive from the costume in which somebody was buried, but there is no sign that tools of the trade such as spindles or looms were placed in graves. We do see that warriors were buried with their weapons and shields but these are marks of high status in communities whose original aim was defence of the land and keeping order, just as jewellery no doubt represented the wealth of successful civilians. Loom weights were rings of dried, but generally not fired, clay that kept the vertical threads hanging straight on the loom. They survive where the wooden frame does not so are usually the only evidence for weaving as is shown by the many sets found in houses at West Stow. The spindle whorls of stone or fired clay are smaller discs which gave weight and momentum to the drop spindle used when spinning woollen thread by hand. They were clearly more personal items than the loom weights and many carry simple decorations, but they still do not seem to appear in graves. Would you want to be reminded after death of one of life's more mundane tasks? For us however these weights and whorls are reminders of the woven fabrics that were the setting for the colourful jewellery. It is often assumed that the vegetable dyes used in antiquity gave only earthy colours but much of the woollen and linen fabric, in clothing, bed covers and wall hangings was probably very bright. Madder mordanted with clubmoss gives a strong red, weld with clubmoss a good yellow, but with iron a distinctive green, and the famous woad, when mordanted with urine an essential ingredient for dyers, gives a clear blue. These are only some of the possibilities to brighten up the Anglo-Saxon village.

An isolated find of an Early Saxon wrist clasp is recorded from the edge of the Park near Thornham Magna church and another has been found to the east of Thornham Parva church. The finding of wrist clasps, sometimes called sleeve clasps or cuff fasteners, is interesting as they are seen as distinctive of the area associated specifically with the Angles. They show a regional style of costume in the sixth century which is not apparent earlier or later but is confined to northern East Anglia, the east midlands, Lincolnshire and Yorkshire[5]. It seems that at least some local people adopted a style of costume associated with the Angles at a time when regional identity may have been more important than a national one. People were probably more conscious of being East Anglians than English, if the latter concept even existed as distinct from some concept of being British because they were living in the land that had been known to the Romans as Britain. These wrist clasps are seen as evidence of at least some people here in the fifth century being Anglians, connected with North Germany and Scandinavia (that is possibly with Norway & Sweden as well as Denmark and North Germany) as distinct from Saxons in Essex where there are no wrist clasps. North east Suffolk was part of the Anglo-Saxon kingdom of East Anglia with the presumed royal palace of the Wuffing kings at Rendlesham and their burial ground at Sutton Hoo linked to King Rædwald who died about AD 625. There was also a royal presence in the north east at Blythburgh which was associated particularly with the Christian king and saint Anna who ruled from AD 636 to 654. We know that kings and nobles of this period appreciated music, which is confirmed by the presence of a lyre in the Sutton Hoo ship. Remarkably the bronze bridge from such a lyre has been found at Oakley where our River Dove joins the main stream of the Waveney. It incorporates two backward facing animals with open beaks and has notches for the six strings[6] and was found with a bronze tuning peg. A number of these lyres are known from sites, mainly burials, including Snape, Taplow and Prittlewell in England and Hedeby, Dorestadt and Cologne on the continent that might be seen as belonging to the North Sea zone. This location has also revealed a number of decorated bronze items including a small long brooch, an open work swastika, wrist clasps, tweezers and a zoomorphic bucket fitting. Three gold coins of sixth to seventh century dates, included one of Theodobard II, minted by the moneyer Aribordus of Clermont-Ferrard about AD 605. Here we see signs of an individual who was cultured and wealthy. Perhaps an early version of the Beowulf story was sung in his hall, which stood near the outskirts of the Roman market town at the Scole river crossing.

Close to Thornham early Anglo-Saxon cemeteries have been found at Eye[7] where about 150 cremation urns were found by men digging a pit for sand on Abbey Farm at Waterloo Plantation in 1818. At Thorndon finds of 'weapons, brooches, beads, etc.' reported about 1870[8] suggest an inhumation cemetery with grave goods. Also further up the river valley beyond Thornham at Finningham[9] the digging of a cutting for the railway in 1849 revealed a mixed cemetery of cremations and inhumations with spearheads, 'ornaments of brass' and urns. There is also a record that human remains and urns, which might have been Saxon, were found in 1810 at Braiseworth[10] just across the river from the large hoard of late Roman coins at Clint Farm, Eye. There are also records of some early Saxon finds at Wetheringsett[11] and Gislingham. Tom Plunkett has drawn attention to recent finds in Yaxley of Anglo-Saxon brooches distorted by fire, showing an unusual variation where the dead were presumably burnt on a pyre in full costume including bronze jewellery. This includes large decorated brooches, one with empanelled groups of S-motifs. Individuals or groups seem to have been buried in distinctive ways, rather than all conforming to a single fashion. We should allow for personal taste in such matters but some general trends can be identified.

The area east of Thornham Parva church where the wrist clasp was found has also produced a fairly large collection of Ipswich Ware pottery. This site is beside the line of Grims Ditch and evidence of continuing occupation comes from Thetford Ware pottery which extends into the field adjoining the church. A late stirrup terminal was found with the pottery. During this time the settlement expanded as new areas were developed along the line of the road leading to Thornham Magna, and in many of the areas we consider to have been part of the later holdings of the Hermitage based at the Chapel of St Eadburga. Ipswich Ware has been found close to the parish boundary between Thornham Magna and Gislingham, on a site which has shown evidence of activity from Neolithic times to the Roman period, and on two sites relatively nearby. An early cruciform brooch was recovered south of these sites. These finds, those from Wickham Skeith and the Early Saxon material on the Thornham estate show a considerable presence in the valley of the River Dove and its tributaries. It is impossible to say at our present state of knowledge whether these finds belonged to immigrant Anglo-Saxons or members of established local British families who adopted Anglo-Saxon fashions. It is also unclear whether we are seeing the influence of new settlers in the last years of Roman government in the late fourth to early fifth centuries or in the 'Dark Age' fifth to seventh centuries. However they support the argument for continuity of occupation, in which people carried on farming this productive land. A further seven Middle Saxon sites have been discovered by Roy Colchester in Mendlesham parish.

We can build up a picture of steadily increasing settlement around the Thornham Estate, particularly notable in the Late Saxon period for which additional sites have been identified following the line of Clay Street which is situated on a high clay ridge overlooking the river valley. This growth of settlement culminates in our first documentary record for the area, the Domesday survey of 1086. It is difficult to convert the Domesday evidence into figures for the total population as it was only intended to record taxable assets. However whatever basis is used for the calculation it seems that the population of our region was significantly lower in 1086 than it had been during the Roman period. This discrepancy needs to be explained. Did some disaster reduce the numbers living in East Anglia, causing the loss of large numbers of the farmsteads that filled the Waveney Valley during the Roman period and of the extensive settlements in and around the Thornham Estate? During the 650 year span of the Anglo-Saxon period how important were changes of climate which must have had a great impact on farming? These remain unsolved mysteries but our best written source for the early years of the period is Gildas. He was a British historian writing about the state of the church and of the government of western Britain. His main work 'The Ruin of Britain', written about AD 540, opens with an account of the earlier history of the whole of Britain including a virulent plague which killed so many in a short time that the living could not bury all the dead. This seems to have happened about AD 450 and another plague, probably the Bubonic version which was to cause the Black Death in the fourteenth century, struck Britain about a hundred years later. This was preceded in the first half of the sixth century by major climatic changes which led to the failure of crops and this would have made the population more susceptible to illness. Our evidence is not sufficient to say with certainty what happened, but it does suggest that in the sixth century farming was carried on with the land managed in larger estates. These were worked by a reduced population from fewer centres, which formed the basis for renewed expansion from the seventh century onwards.

In the Thornham area by the Middle Saxon period after about AD 650 greater quantities of pottery, fragments of the simple grey cooking pots of Ipswich type ware, turn up near Thornham Parva church which may once again mark a focus of settlement. It may then have been the site of a Christian church although no structure survives from this early date when it was probably a timber building. A significant amount of Ipswich type pottery has also been found near Stoke Ash church suggesting that there was activity here too in middle Saxon times although we cannot say at present whether this occupation was in fact continuous from Roman to modern times. There are also records of Ipswich Ware finds not far away at Mendlesham[12] and at Gislingham. Occupation sites with pottery of this period are relatively uncommon in the interior of East Anglia so these finds are significant and suggest our area was of some importance.

At some stage Thornham and Stoke Ash received their names from the presence of thorn bushes and one or more distinctive ash trees, or could it have been a mass of ash from cremations? Many of the parishes in our area certainly do have names derived from trees: Thorndon, Occold (oak copse[13]), Oakley, Brome (broom), Palgrave (grove for poles), Walsham le Willows, Badwell Ash, the Ashfields, Hinderclay (land with elder), Wattisfield (place for growing wattle for building material and perhaps to fuel the kilns). Perhaps the different varieties of useful trees were used as a way of distinguishing individual settlements within the original single Roman estate that we have suggested for the area. We also have the Scandinavian names Thwaite (clearing) and Skeith (racecourse) in Wickham Skeith, referred to in the last chapter and presumably marking immigrant landowners who perhaps arrived during Danish domination of this area when it was part of the Danelaw. We may suppose that the new owners translated the names of these settlements into their own language, rather than necessarily thinking of them as creating new villages on unoccupied land. This Scandinavian element is marked most prominently in our region by the group of names ending '-by' in the Flegg area on the original estuary of the Waveney and Yare river systems.

The emphasis on tree names is not surprising when used by people who were certainly skilled in working wood. We know that they were shaping and joining large timbers for the frames, walls and plank floors of their houses. They were also making cups, bowls and even bottles from wood. These were presumably turned on a pole lathe that will, in skilled hands, produce a perfectly rounded shape. They must have been able to achieve a high quality result as wooden bottles, decorated with gilded silver mounts, were considered good enough to include in the royal burial at Sutton Hoo. On a more mundane level we can imagine them turning legs for furniture, as a pottery lid from the Early Saxon cemetery at Spong Hill in Norfolk is a perfect representation of a figure sitting on a wooden chair. It is not clear whether any features of it are turned as they might all be of square section and we have no idea how common chairs and similar items of furniture were, but the possibilities are apparent. We do have evidence for skilled carpenters, woodturners, joiners and coopers all dependent on the management of woodland to provide suitable timber. Apart from specialist tools all of these skilled artisans were using various types of axe, the most fundamental tool for working with wood. There must also have been many charcoal burners producing fuel that served the furnaces of blacksmiths and others working metal and provided a less smoky, more efficient fuel than simple logs for domestic hearths.

We have yet to find early horseshoes in our area, but they were used in Saxon times, at least from the ninth century as examples have been recognised at Thetford. We do have strap mounts of ninth- or tenth-century type at both Thornham and Homersfield. These and many other metal fittings from horse harness of the Anglo-Saxon period in this area show the importance of horses to local people. They remind us of the record in the Anglo-Saxon Chronicle that in 866 the Danish invaders, called Vikings when making violent raids, took horses from this area after they landed and before they moved inland to attack Northumbria and Mercia. We do not know how the East Anglians viewed their position when this Danish army to whom, according to the Chronicle, they had peacefully provided horses returned in AD 869 and killed King Edmund the last king of East Anglia, soon to be recognised as a protective saint. Throughout the history of this region we need to bear in mind that it was part of a North Sea zone which gave it links to peoples across the sea in lands that were more readily accessible by ship than was western England by slow and expensive travel over land. Our people had easy access to the homelands of the Danes and no doubt maintained commercial

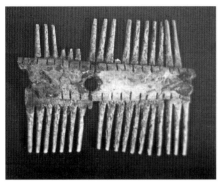

Figure 4.5 *A closer view of the stirrup mount found at Thornham Parva and a typical Saxon comb from West Stow.*

contacts with them. Of course they were also exposed to attack when more violent elements from Denmark and other Scandinavian countries came by ship either to seize valuable spoils or to take permanent possession of lands. Certainly some of these new immigrants gave settlements names in their own language, sometimes apparently translating existing names.

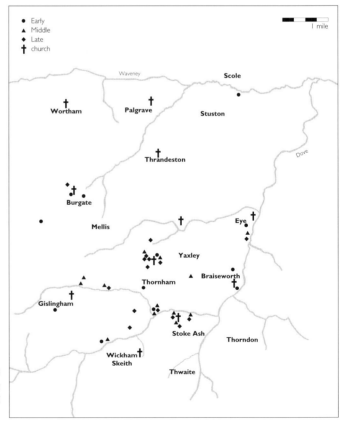

Figure 4.6 *Anglo-Saxon evidence at Thornham, including churches thought to have been founded before the Norman Conquest.*

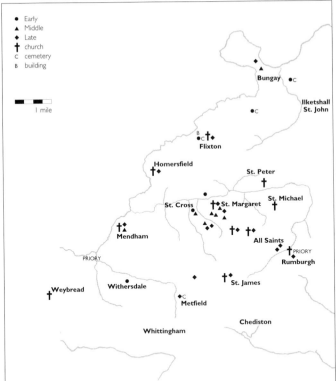

Figure 4.7 *Anglo-Saxon evidence at South Elmham, including churches thought to have been founded before the Norman Conquest. Apart from Flixton where both cemetery and houses have been excavated, it is difficult to tell whether finds originated from burials or from houses.*

We have noticed evidence of activity through the Early Saxon period and a significant quantity of Middle Saxon pottery. As far as we can tell from this Thornham was still a significant centre of activity, as it had been in prehistoric and Roman times. The distribution of Saxon materials suggests a focus of activity within the Thornhams running from the River Dove at the up-river edge of the main Roman settlement along the line of Water Lane and the Street of modern Thornham Magna village, itself the valley of a small stream. It seems to continue up the original, almost straight, road to the field west of Thornham Parva church. It is possible that this reflects the continued use of a direct route that had been in use before the Roman conquest. The main focus of activity in the area of significant Saxon activity further down the Waveney valley follows a similarly straight line from the river valley in Flixton up to higher ground in St. Margaret. The rivers must have been an important focus of activity. The new influx of people to the region, whether as traders or immigrants, came from the continent by sea. We would expect many to take their boats on up the navigable rivers until they reached a point where they needed to use smaller craft for the upper reaches of our streams, or could take advantage of the substantial Roman roads which were still useful communication routes. We can be sure that our riverside communities included experienced boatmen, boat builders and fishermen. We tend to think of Ipswich, Norwich and Thetford as inland towns, but all were important ports with significant sea-going trade as a vital part of their economies. Smaller towns much further up our rivers had harbours or simple staithes to take advantage of the considerable economic value of transporting goods, and people, by water.

We have seen evidence that there was continuous occupation at South Elmham St. Margaret in the Waveney valley from the last years of the Roman period through Saxon times. It has been suggested that the boundary of the group of Elmham parishes might mark the edge of a large Saxon estate. If so this estate would have included the seven South Elmham parishes and Flixton, an area about three miles by four, and might have originated in Roman times. Certainly St. Margaret, situated in the centre of this South Elmham group of parishes, proved from the field walking survey to be the most important centre of this early Saxon estate with hand made Early Saxon pottery recovered from a ten acre field bordered on two sides by streams. The area also revealed later Saxon pottery of the Ipswich Ware and Thetford Ware types. In a separate area on the northern boundary of the parish, on a predominantly Roman site, fifth-century cruciform brooches were discovered. The Roman sites in St. Margaret gave the clearest evidence of later occupation, which possibly resulted from the creation of the estate and this is also indicated by the unusual zigzag line of the southern boundary of the parish which looks as if it followed the edges of existing fields. Each corner was marked by a small collection of Ipswich Ware pottery, possibly rubbish dumps placed at the edge of strip fields. Two other areas, of which one was just inside the parish of St. Nicholas, had Ipswich and Thetford ware sherds in larger quantities. A major site discovered in a field known as Elden Hall spread into the adjoining field. This too has an unusual position in the parish, suggesting it might have been taken originally from the adjoining parish of St. Nicholas and added to St. Margaret. Pottery from this site spans the Ipswich, Thetford and pre-Conquest wares and then stops. Among the

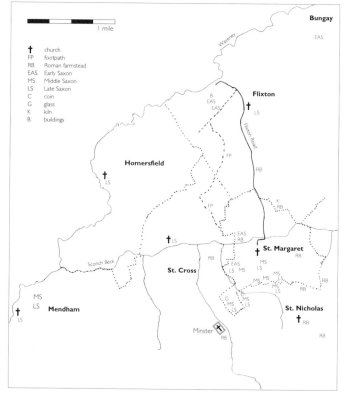

Figure 4.8 *South Elmham St Margaret showing its remarkably complex parish boundary.*

Saxon pottery were small fragments of samian and colour coated wares produced in the Roman period but perhaps introduced to this site during the Saxon period. Included in the finds were fragments of glass, one of which had a grozed edge and showed stains from its wooden frame, showing that it had been used to glaze a window. Similar glass has been recovered from religious sites in the area of Staunch Meadow, Brandon, during excavations by the Suffolk Archaeological Unit. Certainly this area of the Elmhams was the property of the Bishops of Norwich (Bishops of Thetford until 1094) straight after the Norman Conquest and they might have changed the boundary with St. Nicholas to incorporate an important religious site. Additional material of the late Saxon period was recovered from an area close by in St. Nicholas, including a bronze stirrup mount and the small copper alloy pommel of a sword or a seax, which could have been a small single edged sword or a large hunting knife. The system of tracks and roads in this area leads directly to the Flixton burial site where, in 1990, the fifth-century claw beaker was discovered. This showed that the ditch of an Early Bronze Age burial mound, a round barrow, had been used for the burial of a woman in the Early Saxon period, a practice that seems to have been common at that time.

Excavations at Flixton[14] have revealed that after the Roman period a large Saxon burial

Figure 4.9 *Anglo-Saxon glass claw beaker found at Flixton. This has been reconstructed completely because all the fragments of glass from the broken vessel were recovered by excavation.*

81

Figure 4.10 *An Anglo-Saxon house reconstructed at West Stow. The latest version of a series of buildings based on careful study of the evidence from excavation.*

ground was created here serving a substantial settlement on the gravel ridge, where at least twenty one buildings have been identified. These included large rectangular hall buildings and smaller houses with hollows beneath the floors, which are sometimes called 'sunken featured buildings' (SFB's) or *grubenhauser*. Both these types were recognised and reconstructed by Stanley West at West Stow near Bury St. Edmunds and were typical of early Anglo-Saxon building design in our region. The reconstruction of the early settlement at West Stow, under the guidance of Stanley West, has taught us much about the tools and methods of building used and how people might have lived in the houses. He has shown that some at least of the SFBs had plank floors covering

Figure 4.11 *Inside one of the Anglo-Saxon houses at West Stow. Furniture and fittings are based on information from excavations of the remains and from early writings.*

the sunken feature, which would form a storage cellar with access through a trap door. While West Stow appears to have been a hamlet just outside the small Roman market town of Icklingham, other developments which presumably replaced the small market towns of the Roman period occupied places that were already significant settlements in Iron Age and Roman times. As at Flixton a similar succession of occupation has been found at Bloodmoor Hill, Carlton Colville, further down the Waveney valley. There at least 33 SFBs and 8 'halls' of early Saxon date were built within a Roman field system marked by a considerable amount of pottery suggesting more than just agricultural activity[15] so presumably there had been a Roman settlement nearby. Similar evidence has emerged at RAF Lakenheath/ Eriswell in West Suffolk, and recent excavations at Ipswich have revealed early Saxon buildings constructed on a site that had been occupied throughout the Roman period[16]. It is difficult, and might be impossible, to determine whether this evidence shows unbroken continuity of occupation but it seems that any break was relatively short.

Perhaps we have signs of those Anglo-Saxon warriors of the fifth and sixth centuries whom Gildas describes as being paid regular sums to replace the Roman army as guardians of the civilian communities, who presumably went on farming the land and providing sufficient surplus to feed the warriors they employed. At Bungay, during development of housing at Stow Park, the graves of two Saxon warriors were found. They had been buried with their spears, shields and knives. Later excavations close to Bungay castle revealed Ipswich Ware pottery and by the time of Domesday it was a thriving town, destined to become a major seat of the powerful Bigod family. Norman Scarfe suggests[17] that nearby Ilketshall took its name from Ulfketel or Ulfkill Snilling who led an army in 1004 that stopped the invading Danes under their King Swein, although he was himself killed during another Danish invasion in 1016. However if he owned an estate here it might well have kept the name of a man so famous that East Anglia was then known throughout the north of Europe as Ulfkell's Land[18]. As Scarfe points out if it received its name as late as the eleventh century there is no reason to doubt that it had been occupied for long before that under another name since totally lost. It is clear that in our region changes of ownership often led to the giving of new names and this seems particularly true in the Danish period.

To date no Saxon material has been recovered from the other South Elmham parishes, but their churches are all recorded in Domesday Book, as is evidence of the monastery at Rumburgh. Close to the church at Flixton a collection of Thetford Ware sherds was recovered, and in land adjoining Homersfield church a tenth or eleventh century stirrup terminal was found. The tower of Flixton church is an architectural challenge because it was rebuilt by Anthony Salvin in the nineteenth century. However he claimed that his work was faithful to the original Saxon work, including the roof which is of the Saxon type known as a Rhenish Helm because it is common along the banks of the Rhine but only found in England at Sompting in Sussex. The original tower at Flixton had collapsed in 1835. Experts still argue about Salvin's claim that he was faithful to the original, as he frequently created his own versions of medieval architecture. Further along the River Waveney at Mendham is the site of a priory that was documented in the will of Bishop Theodred in AD 951, which also mentions a church here. Late Saxon material was discovered in the ditch surrounding this

Figure 4.12 *A closer view of the dress tag found at Mendham and window glass from South Elmham. It shows the elaborate decoration on the head of the tag which might have fastened garters or a purse. The edge of the glass is shaped to fit into a window frame.*

churchyard and two Middle Saxon dress tags were found on a site overlooking the church in an area that has revealed predominantly Iron Age and Roman material. Close to Thorpe Hall in the adjoining parish of Withersdale five Early Saxon brooches were recovered. Two of them were cruciform, two square headed and one was a small long brooch; there was also a girdle hanger. Inside the parish church the font appears to have early Norman decoration but to have been cut from a stone worked in the Saxon period, which might have been removed from Mendham church when it was rebuilt and deposited at Withersdale. At Metfield two areas have shown evidence of Late Saxon pottery and at the one in the south western part of the parish somebody lost a coin minted in Thetford by a moneyer called Eadric some time between 1035 and 1044, during the reign of Harthacnut or that of Edward the Confessor. As yet we have no archaeological evidence of the Saxon presence in the Domesday parish of Whittingham which adjoined Metfield, but the Domesday survey tells us that a thane called Wulfric held a manor of one and a half carucates (180 acres) in this parish before 1066. He also held manors at Mendham and Weybread/ Instead.

One of the sites in the Elmham parishes where Ipswich type ware pottery has been found has also produced Middle Saxon window glass[19]. It is very near to South Elmham

Figure 4.13 *The early font in Withersdale church, showing the Norman decoration including the tree of life and rosettes.*

Hall and is on higher ground overlooking the area known as 'The Minster'. We would only expect to find this glass in a building of importance, so the tradition associating this Elmham with the Anglo-Saxon bishops of East Anglia may have some basis in the archaeological record. However the argument about whether it was the seat of one of the two early bishoprics that preceded the see of Norwich is confused because the early bishops had property at both South Elmham in Suffolk and North Elmham in Norfolk. They never distinguished them as 'North' or 'South'. The single diocese of the East Angles was established by the first Bishop, St. Felix, in AD 630 with his seat at a place called Dommoc which was almost certainly Felixstowe[20]. Theodore, a Greek monk who had been appointed by the pope to be Archbishop of Canterbury, improved the administration of the church and created more dioceses. In this process some time between AD 673 and 680 he used the illness of Bisi, whom he had himself consecrated as Bishop of East Anglia, to divide the diocese. He left one see to continue at Dommoc, and apparently located the second at one of the Elmhams as at the Council of Cloveshoe in AD 803 Bishop Alhheard signed as 'Elmhamis ecclesiae episcopus' (Bishop of the church community of Elmham). When the see was restored in AD 955, after the Danish intervention following the death of King St. Edmund in AD 869, the single bishop was named as 'Bishop of the East Angles' without any reference to his seat. Stuart Rigold[21] suggests he had two seats which were then Elmham and Hoxne[22]. It was only Bishop Herfast[23] who called himself 'Bishop of Elmham or Thetford' after he had actually moved his seat from Elmham to Thetford about 1071[24]. At no stage are we told whether the references are to North or South Elmham. The archaeological evidence is inconclusive as none of the surviving structures at either site can be shown to be that old. The enigmatic ruin in the parish of South Elmham St. Cross known as 'the Minster' stands inside a rectangular earthwork and both structure and earthwork have so far resisted efforts to assign a date[25]. Finds of pottery suggest the earthwork might have been dug in the Roman period, although it is more likely that it was dug later through the remains of a Roman settlement which field walking suggests extended outside the enclosure. The present stone remains are believed to date from the eleventh century and appear never to have been completed, but may have replaced an earlier timber building. We can say that the minster might be the site of an early church which was presumably intended to be the centre for a community of priests, a monasterium, serving the Elmham parishes, including Flixton and Homersfield. Occupation of the site with the Saxon window glass seems to have ended in the eleventh century so it might have been Bishop Herbert de Losinga who moved the bishop's residence to the nearby moated site of South Elmham Hall. Perhaps he then started building the stone church for a proposed new monastic foundation, a 'minster', down in the valley. It was probably the site with the glass that became known as 'oldhallestede' in medieval account rolls and its early importance might explain the strange deviation of the parish boundary to include it in St. Margarets. Herbert's interest here is confirmed by his gift to his new Cathedral Priory of the property at Elmham in Suffolk which he bought from William de Neveris. Perhaps he was recovering more property that had once belonged to the bishopric.

Thus the early Christian bishops held property and had serious interests in the Flixton/ Elmham area where occupation may have continued without a break from

Roman to Saxon times. The will of Theodred, Bishop of London, in AD 951[26] certainly refers to minsters nearby at Mendham and Hoxne, with a specific bishop's holding at the latter. This was the time when church properties were being restored after the period of Danish (Viking) control during which all religious institutions seem to have lost their endowments. Presumably at this difficult time Theodred, as well as being Bishop of London, was responsible for the diocese of East Anglia with a seat at Hoxne, although it is not clear whether we really should call this a cathedral. When Theodred made his will in AD951 he requested that all the men on the Hoxne estate be made free but by 1066 the people of Hoxne were apparently all villeins (40) or bordars (15) with four slaves. Presumably the free men took the opportunity to move to other parishes, many of which had significant numbers of free men by 1066. It seems the later bishops preferred to keep a village of tenants subject to the manorial court rather than have free independent farmers on the home estate. Fifty-five tenants owing service to the manor would provide a valuable work force. In his will of 1035 the second Bishop Aelfric of East Anglia[27] left fenland worth a thousand pence to the priests at Hoxne, but did not forget the great abbey of Bury St. Edmunds as he left it Worlingworth 'as he had received it from King Cnut'. Norman Scarfe has pointed out that both this Flixton and Flixton in Lothingland had episcopal estates and probably took their name from the first bishop, St. Felix in the seventh century. Homersfield was the other major episcopal holding with its churches, and Norman Scarfe derives its name from Hunberht the last bishop of Elmham before the Danes in AD 869 killed King Edmund, who was later canonised as Saint Edmund. When the Bishop of Norwich was granted a market and fair here in 1218 and received a charter for the fair in 1226/7, these might have been confirmations of ancient rights.

These continued as the main holdings of the bishops in Suffolk after the great Norman bishop Herbert de Losinga moved the seat of the see in 1095 to his new cathedral at Norwich. Tom Plunkett suggests that when Folcard in his Life of Botolph reports that this seventh-century saint[29] visited a remote estate granted to him in a valley fed by a stream, far from the sea, in a vast solitude where he built two churches dedicated to SS Peter and Paul the reference might be to Hoxne and Eye where the churches do have this dedication. Folcard recorded that Botolph reached this valley through dense thorny spinneys and Tom Plunkett sees this mention of 'spinosa loca' as a possible reference to Thorndon and the Thornhams. This would link the religious connection at Hoxne to one of our earliest saints who is recorded as giving instruction to Ceolfrith who was sent by Bishop Wilfrid to study at Iken. Ceolfrith went on to become founding abbot of the monastery at Jarrow where Bede was his pupil. It may be that Botolph also travelled through Thornham to visit Botesdale which was named after him and had a chapel dedicated to his memory, so perhaps remembered as part of his estate. We have already referred (Chapter 3) to the long distance route to Botesdale from Debenham via Thorndon and Thornham which would be the obvious route for anybody coming from Iken.

We should set this in the context of the history of Christianity in East Anglia. We know little about the situation in the later years of Roman rule, but Christianity was the official religion of the Empire from the time of Constantine early in the fourth century. In East Anglia we have evidence of Christian structures of the fourth century at Icklingham, with several lead tanks on which the chi-rho monogram might indicate fonts, and at Colchester. In addition we see Christian symbols on a pewter plate from Icklingham, on items in the silver treasure from Mildenhall and, close to Thornham, on silver spoons, ladles and a necklace in the Hoxne treasure. However many items of the time, including the great dish from Mildenhall with its central head of Oceanus and circling figures from the story of Dionysus (Bacchus, god of wine), suggest that the new religion had not completely displaced the worship of previous deities. We cannot tell how far Christianity survived the transfer of power to non-Christian Anglo-Saxon rulers because our best record of the time comes from Bede who has been described by Sam Newton as 'wielding the weapon of withering silence' on matters that do not fit his views. Bede was adamant that Christianity was introduced to England by St. Augustine when his mission was sent from Rome by Pope Gregory in AD 597. We need not doubt this did mark the conversion of some of the ruling families of English kingdoms, but there may have been many Christians among their subjects descended from the original inhabitants. Bede does tell us that sometime before AD 616 King Raedwald of East Anglia, whose body probably lay in the ship under mound one at Sutton Hoo, was converted at the court of King Aethelbert of Kent to the extent that he set up an altar to the Christian god beside pagan altars to pre-Christian gods in a temple which probably stood at Rendlesham beside the River Deben. It may be that Raedwald welcomed the opportunity to encourage the loyalty of the Christians in East Anglia as well as those believing in other gods, although Bede is strangely silent about any priest who accompanied him from Kent. It is difficult to believe that he was not supported by a senior priest from Augustine's mission. His son Earpwald was baptised but soon killed and it was left to another son Sigebert to establish a strong Christian presence in AD 630 or 631 by seeking the help of Archbishop Honorius to bring Felix from Burgundy where he may have followed the Irish tradition of St. Columbanus. He established a see, and probably a religious community, certainly Bede speaks of a school, at Dommoc which was almost certainly the Roman fort of Walton Castle at Felixstowe. Sigebert also gave another Roman site to an Irish missionary, St. Fursa, who reached East Anglia from Ireland even before St. Aidan established his base on Lindisfarne off the Northumbrian coast. Despite the dispute about the date of Easter and other matters about which Aidan and other 'Celtic' Christians disagreed with Rome, Bede specifically states[30] that Aidan was highly respected by both Honorius of Canterbury and Felix of East Anglia, so there is no reason to suppose hostility between Felix and Fursa. St. Fursa set up his monastery of Cnobheresburg within the Roman walls of either Burgh Castle or Caister on Sea, overlooking the Great Estuary of the Rivers Waveney and Yare where he claimed to have a powerful vision of the life after death. This monastery was later supported by King Anna but destroyed by King Penda of Mercia some time before he killed Anna at Bulcamp near Blythburgh in AD 654. Earlier Sigebert had retired to another monastery he founded, probably at Betrichesworde which became Bury St. Edmunds. We are told in the Anglo-Saxon Chronicle that in the year of Anna's death St. Botulph began to build his monastery at Icanhoe, almost certainly Iken on the River Alde. It was Anna's daughter St. Etheldreda who gave rights over much of south east Suffolk to the monastery she founded at Ely. As a precedent we might note that when Etheldreda was married to Ecgfrith king of Northumbria they gave much land, including Carlisle, to Lindisfarne monastery and were said to be obedient to Bishop Wilfrid.

We know of only one early monastery north of the Waveney and that is St. Benet's beside the River Bure, which was said to have been founded about AD 800[31]. However Felix has been claimed as founder of a number of northern churches, including Loddon and Reedham on the Great Estuary and Babingley near Kings Lynn. The entry in the Liber Albus of Bury St Edmunds[32] reads in full 'In the wall of Loddon church a certain inscription was found. Felix bishop and Werned Abbot and Luthing Aetheling. He maden the kirke at Lodne (Loddon) and the Kirke at Redeham (Reedham) and the halige kirke at Babingeley. At Mendham a bishop was found in a wooden coffin and in a leaden tablet was contained – Hier lieth biscop Eadmund Kinges thean. He sette Lodne and he sette Redham and he sette Mendham and there hise bones restan.' It is not clear who was buried at Mendham with this inscription as there is no record of a bishop Edmund of East Anglia, so could this be a royal thegn called Biscop Eadmund (Edmund Bishop) who funded the establishment of these three significant churches? Certainly this record emphasises the importance of the minster church of Mendham at an early date, as well as confirming the association of Felix himself with the Waveney valley. A powerful Christian presence seems to have been established in East Anglia and we can imagine them converting the holy trees and sacred springs (holy wells) honoured by pagan worshippers and seeking out families who retained the native Christian tradition from the days of Roman rule. We can note in this context the dedication of a chapel at Thornham to St. Eadburga[33] an eighth-century royal abbess from Kent and successor to St. Mildred who was herself honoured by a chapel at Ipswich. These confirm links by sea down the coast to Kent as well as across the sea to the Rhineland[34] and Denmark, not forgetting the Irish who may have travelled through the Great Glen to Inverness before sailing down the east coast. The dedication to Mildred at Ipswich has been seen as linked to the Wuffinga royal family[35] and we might see Eadburga as marking a similar royal connection at Thornham.

Two early Anglo Saxon gold coins of the type known as 'thrymsas' have been found in the Elmhams. These coins might be regarded as shillings and are thought to have been valued at three or four silver pennies, 'sceattas', to the gold shilling (Plate 9). They were modelled on the Merovingian tremisses of the kind found in the Sutton Hoo ship burial, which were each worth a third of a gold solidus. These two shillings show two emperors below a victory in a design copied from fourth-century Roman gold solidi issued by joint emperors and are said to have been issued about AD 660–675[36]. Such coins are rare and suggest the presence of wealthy individuals. The coins date from the period when the East Anglian diocese was first divided between Dommoc and Elmham by Theodore the Archbishop of Canterbury in line with his policy of increasing the number of bishops (a topic on which he was in dispute with Bishop Wilfrid of York). As Fletcher points out[37] bishoprics had to be endowed with adequate landed estates and this might be related to the substantial area of the Elmhams in the Waveney valley which can be seen as a busy and wealthy area that was in the hands of the bishops. Could the estate have been a royal gift to the new bishop?

More frequently found than the early gold coins are the silver 'sceattas' which presumably mark an increase in trade. Had people been using the old Roman coins until the shortage made it necessary to create new ones? Were late Roman coins found in Anglo-Saxon contexts actually being used until they were finally lost or converted into jewellery or even new 'Saxon' coins? In the tenth century more new coins were in circulation. We have seen that the pottery, while still fairly basic and almost invariably grey, was finer and made to a higher standard, being known to archaeologists as Thetford ware. As these vessels were now made with flat bases, were people becoming accustomed to the use of flat table tops and shelves in their timber framed houses? This pottery, although first recognised by archaeologists at Thetford, was made at several places in East Anglia including Ipswich. A number of the fragments of Thetford Ware pottery found near Stoke Ash church appear to be from wasters, pots that went wrong when fired, suggesting there was a kiln here making this type of pottery. Thetford Ware continued in use into the twelfth century so does not help us distinguish activity before or after the Norman conquest in 1066. It is equally uncertain whether the earliest features of the existing stone church at Thornham Parva were built before or after the conquest. Domesday Book does refer to a church here saying that three parts, presumably three quarters, of a church with ten acres were held by Robert Malet[38]. Experts have drawn particular attention to the round window at the west end of the nave which is regarded by many as typical of pre-Conquest work.

In 1086, when the Norman conquerors recorded their survey of property throughout the country in the Domesday Book, Thornham was in the Hundred of Hartismere. Hundreds had existed as administrative divisions of the county for judicial and taxation purposes as early as the tenth century and may have been based on much earlier land units[39]. Norman Scarfe[40] remarks on the impressive ditch that marks the southern boundary of Hartismere against Bosmere, suggesting that this was an ancient and important division. Thornham is central to the hundred and we are left wondering about the location of the hundred's original meeting place which was presumably a pool associated with deer, called the hart's mere. Some locate it on the north of the Waveney at Diss, part of which was then counted in Suffolk even though it gave its name to a Norfolk hundred. There is still a substantial mere in the centre of Diss today. It is true that the jurisdiction of the Hundred of Hartismere in Suffolk together with that of the Half Hundred of Diss in Norfolk was attached to the king's manor of 'Diss in Hartismere' which included four carucates and a church with 24 acres. Domesday Book (Suffolk 1.8) confirms that this was held by Edward the Confessor before the Norman Conquest. Apparently the jurisdiction of Hartismere was kept by the king but he had divided the half hundred of Diss evenly with the abbey of Bury St. Edmunds[41]. Presumably these arrangements were the result of some compromise when the separate counties of the North Folk and South Folk were created with the division based on the River Waveney, but not always following it. It is not known when the eastern part of the single kingdom of East Anglia, which might have included originally more than just modern Norfolk and Suffolk, was divided into Norfolk and Suffolk. Dr. Steven (Tom) Plunkett has suggested it might have been as early as the time when King Sigeberht, who ruled from AD 629 to 636, shared power with his cousin Ethelric (Ecgric)[42]. Ethelric might have had stronger links towards Northumbria, as he married Hereswith, sister of Hild of Whitby, so he might have ruled Norfolk. If the hart's mere was not the Diss Mere we do have a number of wet places where it might have been, including perhaps the mysterious Devil's hand basin. Norman Scarfe has pointed out[43] that the great green of Mellis, which extended over almost 180 acres immediately north of the Thornhams, was apparently administered by the Hundred presumably as an asset common to all its constituent parishes. We might compare the record in Domesday Book that there was a pasture in Colneis common to all the men of the Hundred. The many lanes that led towards the green would provide routes by which men could move their livestock to and from the common pasture. This might have been a very ancient tradition that provided pasture for animals without having to open the arable fields for grazing after the harvest.

Cattle and sheep were pastured on the commons or in the fields, but some pigs were fed in woodland. Domesday Book records the amount of woodland used for pigs. The entries from Thornham support the evidence from field walking that most of the woodland had been cleared to accommodate a large number of farms, using most of the land as fields, whether for cereal crops or livestock. Woodland is recorded for only 34 pigs of which 30 were held by Isaac under the abbey of Bury St. Edmunds. The area behind Swatsfield is the only land we have found without any evidence of early occupation, so we can suggest this formed part of Isaac's manor. Robert Malet's holding did include 25 pigs but without reference to woodland. Did he have a more domesticated breed kept in the medieval equivalent of modern fields of 'pig arks'? Oliver Rackham considers that depending on 'pannage', driving pigs into woodland in the autumn to fatten by grazing on acorns and beechmast, was not a reliable proposition in England and that this measurement of woodland had become more of a notional exercise. Perhaps it was just being used as another way of extracting additional taxes. In Eye Robert had reduced his woodland from 120 pigs to 60 pigs, perhaps reflecting its poor economic return.

In Burgate a freeman's substantial manor of 5 carucates, taken over by Aubrey de Vere, had woodland reduced from 100 to 40 pigs but his other pigs increased from 23 to 80. He was presumably converting woodland to pasture fields, as his number of ploughs was unchanged but he had increased his sheep from 63 to 176, his goats from 40 to 57 and his cattle from 7 to 12. In the process he increased the value of his manor from the already high £16 to over £19, at a time when most manors were only valued in shillings, and Eye itself was worth £15 rising to £21. This wealth presumably explains the presence of an early castle at Burgate of which only a ring ditch survives[44]. Aubrey de Vere was lord of the manor of Lavenham, which his family kept for many generations after becoming Earls of Oxford. Having taken over these holdings from Wulfwin, who was described as King Edward's thane at Lavenham and simply as a free man at Burgate, de Vere seems to have kept Lavenham for himself but leased the substantial five carucate manor of Burgate, and its dependent holdings including that of a freeman called Wulfmer in Thornham, to a man called Adelelm[45]. Presumably the descendants of this Adelelm prospered so that they were able to build the earthwork castle at Burgate and adopted the parish name as their own. Certainly Sir William Burgate who died in 1409 was able to afford a magnificent memorial for himself and his wife. They are shown as two fine brass figures, described by Pevsner as 'the best brasses of their date in Suffolk', on a great tomb chest standing in the church where the font carries what are thought to be his arms and its stepped base has an inscription including his name. The church itself, its churchyard surrounded by high banks, stands in a prominent position on the highest land in the area. Perhaps the plain but substantial stone coffin lid standing upright against the outside of the west wall of its great tower had covered an earlier member of this family. The de Vere Earls of Oxford rose to national prominence and it was John de Vere, 13th Earl of Oxford who survived the Battle of Bosworth Field in 1485 and as a supporter of the new King Henry VII officiated as Lord Great Chamberlain, being rewarded by the king 'with many lucrative offices'.

At Thorndon a large wood for 200 pigs was reduced to 120 pigs. Wetheringsett was the only manor in Hartismere that belonged to the abbey of Ely and it retained in 1086 woodland for 400 pigs, but reduced from a massive 500 pigs in 1066. Much of the land in these two parishes lies on the high ground between the valleys of the River Waveney's tributaries and the headwaters of the River Deben. Mendlesham lies in a similar position between the Waveney and Gipping valleys. Here the manor of seven carucates held by the king, after confiscation from Earl Ralph, was valued at £25 and had woodland for 1,000 pigs reduced to 800. Here we have clear evidence for the retention of extensive woods on this higher ground which has now been cleared and converted into huge arable 'prairie' fields. However the manor had enough arable in 1086 to require 17 ploughs, so as field walking confirms even then much of this land was being farmed as it had been in Roman times. Looking elsewhere we find in the Elmhams a total of woodland for 72 pigs but this is divided between several holdings spread over a wide area, so accords with our earlier conclusion that these parishes were heavily farmed, as was Flixton with woodland for 32 pigs divided between four holdings. In Homersfield the bishop, on his manor of five carucates, had extensive woodland for 600 pigs, reduced by 1086 to 200 pigs. Although this parish includes fields beside the river, it also stretches up the slope of the valley and this woodland was no doubt on the higher heavy clay land, which retained much woodland into modern times being incorporated in a park. The bishop had woodland for a further 250 pigs in Hoxne, on his large manor of nine carucates, which might be land that later formed the bishop's park.

Down the Waveney valley, below the 'Bishop's Hundred' of Hoxne, Wangford Hundred, probably taking its name from Wainford – 'the wagon crossing' over the Waveney, contained two particular units that were perhaps formal subdivisions or Ferthings and may have been ancient estates. One is the group of parishes known as 'The Elmhams' or 'The Saints' which are all the South Elmhams plus Flixton and Homersfield, sometimes known as South Elmham St. Mary. South Elmham St. Cross was variously called Sancroft, later giving its name to a significant family, and South Elmham St. George. Domesday Book records that the bishop, that is Bishop William of Thetford, had jurisdiction (sac and soke) over the whole ferding of Elmham included in his manor of Homersfield. It may be that all this land, in an area closely associated with the bishops, was originally served by a group of priests who formed a college at the bishop's minster community of Elmham, wherever it was based. Perhaps here on his own estate the bishop set an example of official practice in the ninth century by dividing the minster's territory into a series of separate parishes. Each would have its own ordained priest, drawn from the minster's college of priests, and a church to which the residents could be required to pay their church taxes. Much of the land in the Elmhams was still held by the bishop at Domesday and it remained an important episcopal estate. John Ridgard[46] has suggested on the basis of a later reference to the boundary between Elmham and Bungay as the 'hundryd mere' that South Elmham might once have been a separate hundred or part of the Bishop's Hoxne Hundred rather than Wainford Hundred. The other group of parishes was the Ilketshalls adjoining Bungay itself. The Elmhams were associated with the bishops of East Anglia, while the Ilketshalls may derive their name from belonging to Ulfketill, an ealdorman of East Anglia and later became part of the Bigod holdings centred on Bungay Castle.

Domesday Book records that Robert Malet's church of St. Peter at Eye had an unusually large landholding of two carucates (240 acres). This suggests that it may have been the senior church of the area, a minster with a religious community from which priests were sent to serve the smaller churches round about including the Thornhams. If so this arrangement presumably came to an end soon afterwards when Robert included Eye church with others nearby in the endowment of his new Priory of Eye. However under the new arrangement Eye Priory did receive the right to appoint the priest to a number of churches, so the role of the religious community in meeting the needs of local parishes was continued.

According to Domesday Book much of the land in both Thornham Magna and Parva, as well as Stoke Ash and some land in Gislingham, was held by Robert Malet the Norman lord of Eye[47]. The abbot of Bury St. Edmunds had 15 free men in Thornham[48] and Isaac had a manor here under the jurisdiction of the abbot of Bury[49]. Before the Norman conquest the evidence from finds suggests that Thornham might have been a centre of commercial activity, although there is no sign of this in the Domesday record, as the holdings are relatively small and show no significant change between 1066 and 1086. It seems that the land was being worked by a number of free individuals with small farms. If we rely on the pottery evidence the only significant date of change is that from Middle Saxon (Ipswich type ware) to Late Saxon (Thetford type ware) which is generally dated to about AD 850 so the change in significance may have happened some considerable time before the Norman Conquest. After the conquest in 1066 occupation continued, but looks more like an ordinary farming community. This may be the result of a major local change. William Malet was one of the new Norman landowners given extensive estates by William I. He established his centre at Eye where he built a new castle of the motte and bailey type which became the focus of his wide reaching holdings 'The Honour of Eye'. This was protected by being on an island, the meaning of the place name Eye, in a large area of marsh, most of which has since been drained. Domesday Book records in some detail the complaint from the Bishop, whose see at that date was based at Thetford but had extensive property holdings in the Waveney valley. Bishop Herfast complained that Malet's new market at Eye had destroyed the value of the market on the bishop's estate at Hoxne[50]. Hoxne is about as far east of Eye as Thornham is west of Eye, so it is reasonable to suppose that any market or similar commercial activity at Thornham would have been affected in much the same way. Domesday records only a very small urban community of 25 burgesses at Eye[51], who presumably traded through the market held in front of the castle gate, where the outline of the market place can still be traced in the modern street plan. However the protection and encouragement of the Malets and their successors established it as a viable market town with which its neighbours would be unable to compete. The other family that was powerful in the region, but not in Thornham, was that of the Bigods whose castle dominated Bungay on the Waveney and who founded a great priory at Thetford. Bungay is generally linked to the four adjoining parishes called the Ilketshalls, which place name Ekwall derives from Ulfketill (Ulfcytel) who was famous as a military leader and perhaps alderman (earl) of East Anglia in 1004[52]. Perhaps this was an ancient traditional holding of the earls as at one time the Bigods certainly claimed the title Earls of Norfolk and Suffolk.

The loss of status for Thornham seems to date from before the Norman Conquest and we might look to the predecessor of Malet as owner of Eye: this was Edric of Laxfield who had large holdings including Laxfield, but he also held Dunwich. It seems that Dunwich was growing as a port between 1066 and 1086, and we might wonder if this development started under Edric and if he may also have been the instigator of the commercial centre at Eye before Malet took it over. Edric was the most important lay landowner in East Anglia and one of the richest in the country. We are told that at some time in the reign of Edward the Confessor Edric was outlawed but was later reconciled to the king, recovering his lands, and those of his freemen under commendation who wished to do so were allowed to return to his patronage[53]. It may be that he developed the commercial possibilities of his holdings in Suffolk after recovering them. James Campbell has remarked about Dunwich that 'no other English town of remotely comparable importance had a secular lord other than the king (or the king with the earl)'[54]. The compilers of Domesday Book may also have been conscious of an anomaly as they specifically stated that while there was no moneyer (the word 'cambitor' literally suggests money changer but may refer to a mint) in Dunwich in 1066, there was one in Blythburgh, which was a large royal manor[55]. This would be most easily explained if Dunwich as a town and port was a new creation in the eleventh century developed by Edric as an entrepreneur on his own land. We might suggest a similar development of Eye as a new town. There is an enigmatic statement in the entry for Eye that Edric had held the jurisdiction (soke and sac) of the episcopate, which is glossed as 'that is what the bishop ought to have had'. Edric certainly seems to have established a power to rival the church which was generally zealous in preservation of its rights and privileges.

Apart from the power of the Malets as lay magnates based at Eye, Thornham was on the interface between two great clerical landowners. The Benedictine abbey of Bury St. Edmunds had extensive properties to the west, including jurisdiction over the whole area that was to become the county of West Suffolk, and this 'Liberty of St. Edmund' touched the western edge of Gislingham. In succeeding generations the abbots of St. Edmund strove to maintain their independence from the authority of the bishops and increase their power in the region. The Bishops of Norwich and their Cathedral Priory had their holdings along the Waveney valley to the east. Herbert de Losinga, who replaced Herfast as Bishop of the see which covered both Norfolk and Suffolk, moved the seat of his bishopric from Thetford to Norwich in 1096. He strengthened the status of his Hoxne property where the church of Saint Ethelbert was said once to have been the seat of the bishopric for Suffolk. He changed the dedication of this church at Hoxne from the earlier martyred East Anglian king St. Ethelbert to the later, and by then more famous, St. Edmund. He claimed, perhaps for the first time, that this was the site of Edmund's martyrdom although recent research has suggested the true location was in the Bradfields closer to Bury St. Edmunds. The chapel was later taken over by a small priory established as a cell of the great Cathedral Priory of Norwich that had been founded by Losinga in 1101. The long standing story that this was the scene of St. Edmund's martyrdom is the product of the aspiration of the bishops to claim a direct link with him, and reflects the rivalry between different elements of the Church conducted on this neutral territory well away from both Bury and Norwich.

Although much of the property that became Malet's great 'Honour of Eye' had been held by Edric before the Conquest, one group of holdings came from a different owner. This was a lady called Wulfeva. She held parts of the Thornhams including the patronage of 36 freemen, with three quarters of a church in Parva, one carucate in Stoke Ash with its church, Braiseworth, including 60 acres and half the church (the other half of the church belonged to a holding of 140 acres shared by 15 freemen, which might have been part of the single manor before they received their freedom), Thorndon (including 3 carucates and the church with 50 acres), seven freemen in Occold and 220 acres in Rishangles with the church and some holdings in Gislingham. She is sometimes said to be under the patronage of Stigand the former Archbishop of Canterbury who had once been bishop of Elmham. This block of holdings in contiguous parishes does look like a single large estate (Plate 10). The original church at Braiseworth stands in a large circular churchyard in a dominant position above the River Dove, looking across to Clint Farm at the southern end of Eye Park. That a fine church stood here at an early date is shown by the carved stonework of two Norman doorways moved by the Victorians to a new church built on a different site, but itself now converted into a private house. Beside the ruined church the remains of two stone coffins testify to wealthy former residents. We have suggested that the quality of some local finds of the Saxon period, particularly those near Stoke Ash church, indicate a royal holding, which would also help explain the dedication of the Thornham chapel to Eadburga with her royal connections in Kent. Perhaps Wulfeva had acquired a royal estate, or part of one, after many of its tenants had been given their freedom when it was given up by the king, and it may be that Stigand was involved in this. Certainly the Earl of East Anglia had owned an estate nearby. In Domesday Book at the southern edge of Hartismere Hundred Mendlesham and Cotton formed an estate of eight carucates with some additional holdings in neighbouring parishes[56] which were held for the king by his steward Godric, having been the property of Earl Ralph with Burghard as tenant[57]. Earl Ralph, in succession to his father who was also Ralph, had been Earl of East Anglia until he rebelled against King William in 1075 and went into exile in Brittany after which the king dismantled the earldom. If we are right about all this we can see Thornham and Stoke Ash, having been a local focus of authority and commerce since long before the Roman period, losing their status as both a royal and commercial centre in the years before the Norman Conquest of 1066.

Notes

1   Although Paul Blinkhorn (Anderton, M (ed), 1999 *Anglo-Saxon Trading Centres: beyond the emporia*, Glasgow, 9) prefers to date Ipswich Ware *c*.720–850.
2   *Proc. Cambridge Antiq. Soc.* **50**, 1957, 29–60.

3   *PSIAH* **29** (1963), 233.

4   Dallas, C, 1993 *Excavations in Thetford by B.K. Davison between 1964 and 1970,* EAA **62**.

5   Lucy, S, 2000 *The Anglo-Saxon Way of Death: burial rites in early England,* Stroud, 133 and map 5.5d.

6   West, S, 1998 *A Corpus of Anglo-Saxon Material from Suffolk,* EAA **84**, plate VI 5.

7   West, S, 1998 *A Corpus of Anglo-Saxon Material from Suffolk,* EAA **84**, 35.

8   West, S, 1998 *A Corpus of Anglo-Saxon Material from Suffolk,* EAA **84**, 98.

9   West, S, 1998 *A Corpus of Anglo-Saxon Material from Suffolk,* EAA **84**, 38.

10 West, S, 1998 *A Corpus of Anglo-Saxon Material from Suffolk,* EAA **84**, 264.

11 West, S, 1998 *A Corpus of Anglo-Saxon Material from Suffolk,* EAA **84**, 104.

12 Chapter 3 and West, S, 1998 *A Corpus of Anglo-Saxon Material from Suffolk,* EAA **84**, fig.158.

13 Ekwall, B, 1960 *The Concise Oxford Dictionary of English Place-names,* Oxford.

14 See Stuart Boulter in *Current Archaeology,* 187.

15 *PSIAH* **50** (2001), 91 reports approximately 6500 Roman sherds and 7000 Saxon sherds.

16 Excavation by Stuart Boulter of Suffolk Archaeological Service at Handford Road, Ipswich in 2003.

17 Scarfe, N, 1986 *Suffolk in the Middle Ages,* Woodbridge, 28.

18 Stenton, F, 1971 *Anglo-Saxon England,* Oxford, 380.

19 M. Hardy; report of field walking in *PSIAH* **36** (1987), 233.

20 Rigold, S, 1961 The Supposed See of Dunwich, *J. Brit. Archaeol. Ass.* **24**, pp.5–59, and 1974 Further Evidence about the Site of Dommoc, *J. Brit. Archaeol. Ass.* **37**, 97–102.

21 Rigold, S, 1980 The Bishops of the re-established See at Elmham, in Wade-Martins, P, 1980 *Excavations in North Elmham Park 1967–1972* EAA **9**, 7.

22 Domesday Book (Suffolk 18.1) says Hoxne church was the seat of the bishopric of Suffolk before 1066.

23 Herfast had experience of the royal court as, before being appointed Bishop in 1070, he was head of the King's secretariat as chancellor from 1068, if not before.

24 According to Stenton (1971, *Anglo-Saxon England,* Oxford, 667) Herfast signed as *Tetfortensis episcopus* in the decree of 1072 about the primacy of Canterbury.

25 For a detailed discussion see S. J. Plunkett in West, S, 1998 *A Corpus of Anglo-Saxon Material from Suffolk,* EAA **84**, 349.

26 Whitelock, D (ed), 1955 *English Historical Documents. c500-1042. Vol.1,* London.

27 Hart, C, 1966 *The Early Charters of Eastern England,* Leicester, 65.

28 Scarfe, N, 1986 *Suffolk in the Middle Ages,* Woodbridge, 25.

29 Anglo-Saxon Chronicle tells us that St Botolph set up his monastery at Icanhoe (Iken on the River Alde) in AD654, the same year that King Anna was killed at Bulcamp and buried at Blythburgh.

30 Bede *Ecclesiastical History of the English People,* III, 25.

31 After destruction by the Danes it was restored in AD960 and refounded by King Canute in 1020.

32 BM Add. Mss 14847, the Liber Albus of Bury St.Edmunds, quoted by Tom Williamson (1993 *The Origins of Norfolk,* Manchester, 144. This should probably should be BL Harl. 1005 White Book, folio 195).

33 See Chapter 5.

34 We might note that one pupil of Eadburga at Minster was Leofgyth who was appointed abbess of a German monastery by Boniface and was a close associate of Boniface. Did another of her pupils serve in East Anglia bringing reverence for Mildred and Eadburga herself in the eighth century?

35 Scarfe, N, 2002 *The Suffolk Landscape,* (3rd edition) Chichester, 74.

36 Webster, L, and Backhouse, J (eds), 1991 *The Making of England: Anglo-Saxon art and culture AD600-900,* London, nos.52a and 52b.

37 Fletcher, R, 1997 *The Conversion of Europe; from paganism to Christianity, AD371-1386,* London, 458.

38 Doomsday Book, Suffolk, 6.218.

39 See Edward Martin Hundreds and Liberties, in Dymond, D, and Martin, E (eds), 1999 *An Historical Atlas of Suffolk,* Ipswich.

40 Scarfe, N, 1987 *The Suffolk Landscape,* (2nd edition) Bury St Edmunds, 113.

41 Hart, C, 1992 *The Danelaw,* London, 77 quoting Domesday Book, Norfolk 1.51.

42 Bede *Ecclesiastical History of the English People,* III, 18.

43 Scarfe, N, 1987 *The Suffolk Landscape,* (2nd edition) Bury St Edmunds, 118.

44 NGR. 077756.

45 Domesday Book, Suffolk, 35.5 & 7.

46 *PSIAH* **36**,198.

47 Domesday Book, Suffolk, 6.199, 200, 213, 214, 215, 216, 218.

48 Domesday Book, Suffolk, 14.127, 130, 147.

49 Domesday Book, Suffolk, 62.5. For other Thornham entries see 1.81 (the King) and 35.7 (Aubrey de Vere).

50 Domesday Book, Suffolk, 18.1.

51 Domesday Book, Suffolk, 6.191.

52 Scarfe, N, 2002 *The Suffolk Landscape,* (3rd edition) Chichester, 81.

53 Domesday Book, Suffolk, 6.79 and see Hart, C, 1966 *The Early Charters of Eastern England*, Leicester, 68.

54 James Campbell Domesday Herrings, in Harper-Bill, C, Rawcliffe, C, and Wilson, R, 2002 *East Anglia's history: studies in honour of Norman Scarfe,* Woodbridge, 14.

55 Domesday Book, Suffolk, 6.89.

56 Domesday Book, Suffolk, 1.76, 77, 78–87.

57 cf.Domesday Book, Suffolk, 14.146 for a dispute between Godric and the Abbot of Bury St. Edmunds over 14 acres in Stoke Ash.

Plate 1 *A view across the Waveney Valley.*

Plate 2 *The Dove Valley at Stoke Ash.*

A

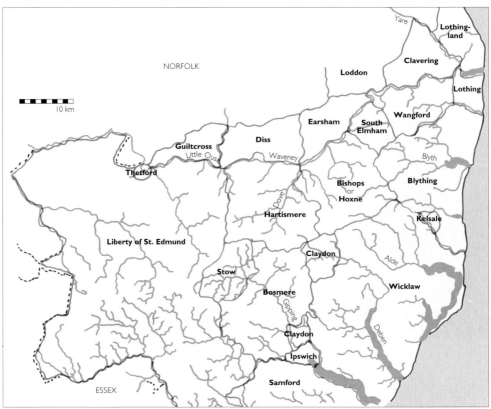

Plate 3 *The Hundreds and Liberties in relation to the river systems. South Elmham was a ferthing of Wangford Hundred. Kelsale was a detached portion of Hoxne Hundred.*

Plate 4 *The colour of Roman tiles varies considerably depending on the conditions of firing, as seen in these fragments of tiles rejected at the kiln.*

Plate 5 *Cowpasture Lane, part of an ancient long distance route. This stretch has probably changed little in the last two thousand years.*

Plate 6 *Roman pottery: an early piece of samian ware from a fine table service imported from France: fragments of similar vessels have been found at Thornham and Stoke Ash.*

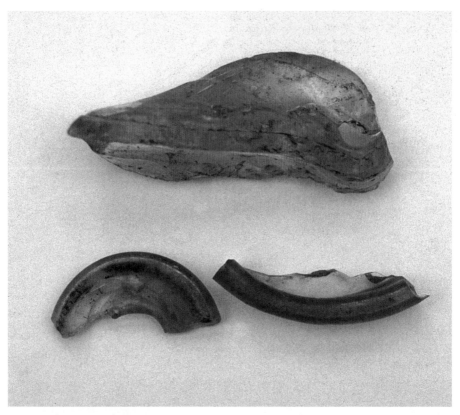

Plate 7 *Roman glass found at Thornham.*

Plate 8 *Two broken Anglo-Saxon girdle hangers or keys from Thornham. As worn out and broken objects they suggest an area of settlement rather than burials. They were probably worn at the waist and used as keys.*

D

Plate 9 *(top) Anglo-Saxon gold shilling or "thrymsa" found at South Elmham St Margaret; (bottom) A fragment of a silver penny of King Baldred of Kent (AD 823-825) found at Stoke Ash. Few of his coins are known so this find strengthens the argument for strong links between our area and Kent. The Moneyer DAN is a variant of DVNNVM the best known of his moneyers.*

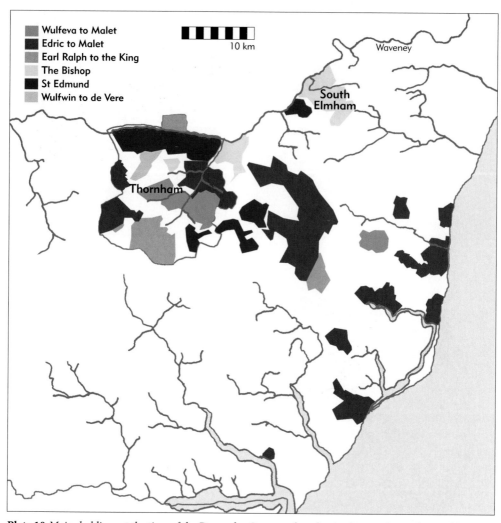

Legend:
- Wulfeva to Malet
- Edric to Malet
- Earl Ralph to the King
- The Bishop
- St Edmund
- Wulfwin to de Vere

10 km

Waveney

South Elmham

Thornham

Plate 10 *Major holdings at the time of the Domesday Survey referred to in the text. It is only possible to give an approximate idea of the locations, but the block of property that had been held by Wulfeva stands out clearly.*

Plate 11 *Part of the series of wall paintings of St Edmund in Thornham Parva church. In this scene King Edmund rides out from a castle or town gate wearing his crown.*

Plate 12 *Grims Ditch near Thornham Parva church where it has changed from boundary ditch to sunken lane.*

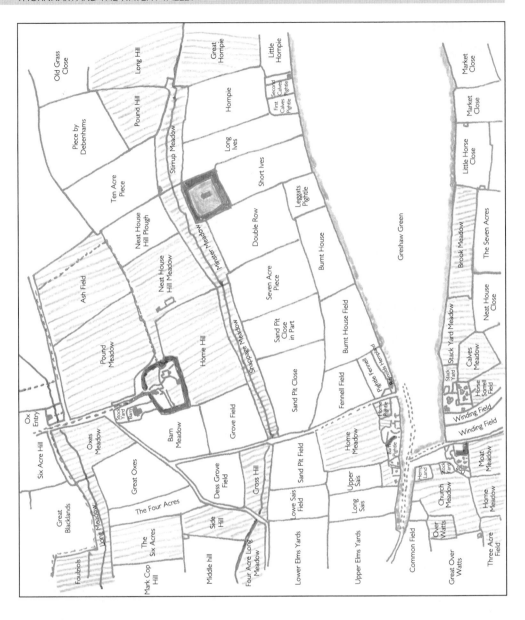

Plate 13 *Greshaw Green and South Elmham Hall. When the park was created it included the "minster" down by the river.*

Plate 14 *A rare seventeenth century beadwork plate showing Thornham Hall as it was in the time of the Killigrews .*

Plate 15 *Thornham Hall in the seventeenth century. The earliest picture of the building that survives.*

Plate 16 *Thornham Hall in the nineteenth century as painted by John Ward in the twentieth century.*

Plate 17 *A portrait of John, first Lord Henniker by Arthur Devis (1712–1787).*

Plate 18 *A portrait of John, 8th Lord Henniker by John Ward.*

Plate 19 *Elaborate decoration inside Flixton Hall to Salvin's design. It looks incongruous against the clutter housed there when the photograph was taken.*

For Master Henniket
25 August 1769
father

the Chandos Sloop —
Her Colours are always
Flying Whilst the Duke
is at Southampton --
Her bottom is Black —
Her Side Yellow with a
Strake of Green at the
Top — ———

the Chandos Sloop
going from You
her Stern painted
Green with a
Corronet on each
Side the Rudder
on the Stern and
a Yellow C —

the Rudder is
painted Red — but
it all wants new
Paint --

Plate 20 *The Duke of Chandos' yacht based on the "Dear Major" letter written in 1769. The colours are based on the description in the letter.*

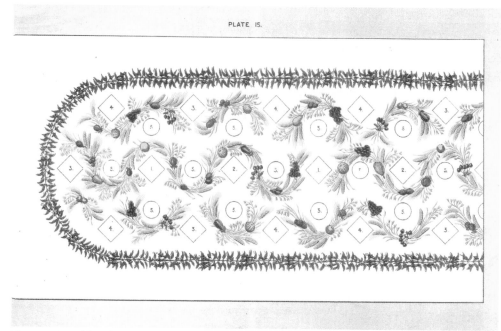

PLATE. 15.

Plate 21 *One of the table decorations by John Perkins for the harvest taken from his book.*

Plate 22 *The entrance to the Walled Garden at Thornham Hall today, showing the site of the Conservatory. The bases for the iron framework and the sill for the door are visible and changes in the colour of the bricks show where they were protected by the glass building.*

N

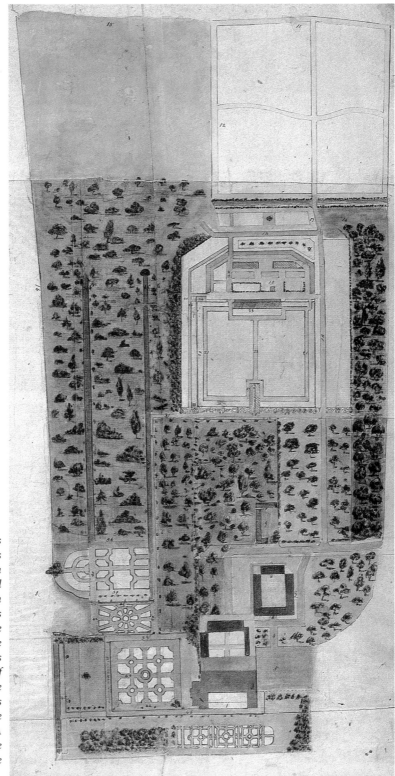

Plate 23 *The Gardens at Thornham Hall as shown in a nineteenth century plan. The Hall is coloured red, with the servant's quarters behind and the stable block in black. The walled garden stands out with the glass of the conservatory, vine house and frames marked in blue, as is the water of the "canal". A grass path leads to the "summerhouse" where the folly now stands.*

Plate 24 *Thornham Hall today showing the modern Hall built in the 1950s in front of those older buildings that have survived.*

P

Chapter 5

Churches, Hermits and Landowners

The victory of William of Normandy over King Harold of England at Hastings in 1066 brought a new administration to the whole country and its impact was soon felt in East Anglia. The Normans were North Men, descendants of Vikings who had moved through Europe from their Scandinavian homelands to settle in the part of France now known as Normandy. William as the new king of England claimed control of all the land and allocated it to his leading Norman followers. Many received large estates from which some of the previous owners were evicted, or in many cases required to pay rents and provide services to their new overlords while continuing the day to day administration of their holdings. Below these levels most of the population presumably continued farming the land or working at the same trades they performed before the conquest. One of the new magnates, given large estates centred on Eye, was William Malet who died in 1071 fighting Hereward the Wake in the Fens, when the value of his possessions is said to have been the equivalent of forty-six billion pounds in modern terms. As a powerful baron William built a substantial castle at Eye. Within its enclosing

Figure 5.1 *The motte of Malet's castle at Eye, where it dominated the town and demonstrated the power of the new Norman landowner to control the Saxon residents of the town and surrounding countryside. It was originally surmounted by a wooden tower.*

bailey, still a significant feature of the town, the tall earth mound of the motte would be topped by a tall timber keep towering over the new town below it. This gave the new lord military security but also symbolised his dominance of the surrounding country. At Ilketshall St. John a motte, 23 feet high with surrounding ditches and rampart, was constructed in the early 1100s by the de Ilketshall family. It was enlarged with additional moats to form Inner and Outer Baileys. Pottery collected from the enclosure suggests occupation until the fifteenth century when a new manor house was built outside the enclosure. By this time the manor was held by the de Norwich family and in 1326 Sir John de Norwich built a new castle at Mettingham. At Bungay the Bigod family developed their great stone castle as one of the key strongholds in their extensive estates in Norfolk and Suffolk. Across the Waveney at Denton in Norfolk the d' Albini family, who came from Normandy in the reign of William Rufus (1087–1100), constructed a motte and bailey castle about 1138. Pottery found here suggests occupation from the twelfth to the fourteenth century, and nearby are mounds for a rabbit warren and a windmill as well as a series of fish ponds, revealing their concern to manage the resources of this landscape as well as to dominate it. The family had large holdings in Norfolk, including Rising and the Buckenhams. To the west of our area at Thetford it was William de Warenne, Earl of Surrey, who built the early motte and bailey of Red Castle, planned the new town with his manor house and also endowed the priory at Castle Acre.

Coming closer to Thornham, in the last chapter we noted the remains of an early castle at Burgate. Another motte may survive in Gislingham, close to its border with Walsham leWillows. The origin of this earthwork in Cromwell's Plantation has yet to be verified but is said to be all that survives of a motte and bailey castle[1]. No doubt both represented new landowners marking their personal territory and ensuring protection from disgruntled locals. When the Domesday Book was compiled as a record of taxable property holdings throughout the country in 1086 William Malet's son Robert held much of the land in both Thornham Magna and Thornham Parva. Robert Malet later founded a priory of Benedictine monks at Eye, as a daughter house of the Abbey of Bernay in Normandy, and gave them his property in Thornham and Stoke Ash. In Domesday Book smaller properties in Thornham were held by the Abbey of Bury St. Edmunds and by a man called Isaac. The priory of Eye in due course received other properties here as Henry I confirmed their right to the land and the church, probably a share in one of the Thornham churches although it is not clear from Domesday Book which one, and all the things Isaac gave them on the day he became one of their monks[2]. It is interesting to see a man with a Jewish name entering a Christian monastery, although it was not uncommon at this time for wealthy men to decide to become monks for the last years of their lives. Because Eye Priory was an alien house subject to the French Abbey of Bernay its income was taken over by the King when England was at war with France, so it suffered severely during the Hundred Years' War. Its income declined from £160 to £20, but it was saved by Richard II who declared it an English house. The prior's right of free warren was confirmed by the king in 1396[3]. This gave him the right to hunt game and to take rabbits which were a valuable commodity in the Middle Ages. At the suppression of Eye priory the King granted its property to Charles Brandon, the Duke of Suffolk. In 1538 he was forced by the Crown to exchange his landed interests in East Anglia for estates in Lincolnshire, presumably to get him away from this area where he had become too powerful and perhaps to avoid conflict with the Duke of Norfolk in East Anglia.

It is clear from Domesday Book that many churches already existed in Suffolk, and most probably occupied the same sites as our parish churches today, but little of the original fabric survives. In many cases the early churches were probably built of wood and even the stone ones have often been rebuilt more than once. At Thornham Parva the round window with its splayed opening at the west end of the church may date from before the Norman conquest, while the decorated south door and plain north one are both Norman in style, as is also a small Norman window which has survived later alterations that removed other features of the twelfth-century structure. The south door appears to be in its original position but the north door may have been inserted into a blank wall and it is notable that the lower section is made of Barnack stone from quarries west of Peterborough while the upper section is Caen stone imported from Normandy. Much of the coursed flint stonework of the walls of the nave appears to date from the twelfth or early thirteenth centuries so this is a very old building which may be on a site of even earlier religious importance. The coursed flints in the nave walls of Thornham Magna church also suggest twelfth- or early thirteenth-century work. The survival of a simple font, found near the folly in the Park but probably displaced from this church in the Victorian alterations, strengthens the argument for an early church or chapel here. The north and south doorways of Stoke Ash church with their plain arches and simple pillars suggest early Norman work, if they are not reused from an earlier building. One might even wonder if these doorways, lacking any Norman decorative features, could have come from a surviving structure of the Roman town, but this must remain conjectural. The priest's door on the north side of the chancel also has a round head. Broken pieces of lava quern are visible in the walls, low down in the north west end of the nave and in the east end of the chancel towards the north corner. Volcanic lava from Niedermendig in the Rhine valley was popular for making millstones from the Roman period to the later Middle Ages. The grey to black colour and honeycomb appearance make this a distinctive stone whether built into church walls or turned up on a ploughed field. There is some long and short work at the top of the north east and south east corners of the nave, which is generally seen as a sign of early, possibly pre-conquest, work. We have already noted the more elaborate decoration of distinctive Norman type on the arched stone doorways preserved from the old church at Braiseworth, which still has a small Norman lancet window in the north wall of its ruined chancel. In neighbouring parishes the churches at Wickham Skeith, Gislingham and Yaxley were extensively rebuilt in the fourteenth and fifteenth centuries, leaving little evidence of earlier structures in their later medieval grandeur. It is interesting that the last two also had active religious guilds as Gislingham had a separate building recorded as the Guildhall in 1524, which is still visible to this day, and in the same year the return for 'Yaxle' includes 'in goodes of Saynte Thomas Gylde £10'.

We can see early stonework in the churches of the South Elmham parishes as these did not see the total rebuilding caused by the later enlargement of many churches elsewhere in Suffolk. There were originally seven churches in this group which formed a Ferthing or quarter of Wangford Hundred, but St. Nicholas became derelict and was

Figure 5.2 *The guildhall building at Gislingham was the home of a medieval religious guild. The guilds were social organisations similar to the later friendly societies, but their religious connections meant they were closed down in the 16th century dissolution.*

Figure 5.3 *Braiseworth church doorway relocated to the new church which is now a private house. It is a fine example of Norman work surviving after its move.*

Figure 5.4 *Braiseworth old church showing the small Norman lancet window to the left. The ruined building retains a number of original features.*

Figure 5.5 *South Elmham All Saints church with its round tower. The lower part of the tower is Saxon or early Norman work but the upper section has been rebuilt.*

pulled down in the seventeenth century. All Saints, which sits in an isolated position close to the boundary with St. Nicholas, is the only church in this group to have a round tower. This tower has early work in the base which is Norman or earlier although it has been heightened and restored in later years. The doorway visible in the west end of the church above the later arch into the tower may well be a restoration of the original Saxon entrance. Other churches nearby that have round towers include Ilketshall St. Andrew and St. Margaret and Mettingham. These all appear to have been built at an early date either before or soon after the Norman conquest. There has been much argument about the origin of these round towers, many of which are found in north east Suffolk and in Norfolk. There is no doubt that it would have been difficult to build a square tower entirely out of local flints and importing suitable stone for cutting square quoins to create sharp corners was expensive. However we might note that round towers built with finely dressed ashlar masonry are a feature of early churches in Ireland. These are said to have been designed to protect church books, plate and vestments from fire and theft, with the added precaution of having the entrance high above ground accessible only by a ladder. This feature is also found in some East Anglian towers, as is still visible inside All Saints church and is reported at Wissett. Given the early connections between the Christians of East Anglia and Ireland, we could see them seeking this as a solution to the threat of piracy and Danish raids on our coast. Whatever their purpose we should be mindful of the cost of building church towers. They need massively thick walls to carry the weight and this weight means that they could only be built in stages. A significant delay had to be allowed between stages to give time for the lime mortar binding the flints to dry and set before the weight of more flints and mortar could be added without the whole structure collapsing. Early work at All Saints is marked by two Norman lancet windows in the north wall of the nave and its Purbeck marble font. An engaged column on the outside at the north west corner of the nave appears to be the side of a Norman west doorway shortened by one block, perhaps when the stairway to the tower was added which might be using the original door opening in the corner of the nave wall. St. Cross church also sits on the edge of its parish overlooking the stream called the Sconch Beck. North and south doorways show evidence of Norman workmanship, with roll mouldings, volute and flower capitals. It is not clear when or how this parish became known as St. Cross. Early references speak of the parish of St. George of Sandcroft or Sancroft and this continues as late as 1515. It appears as Sandcroft in the taxations of 1254 and 1291. The parish might have taken its name from the sandy soil and was itself the origin of the family name of local freeholders the Sancrofts. Robert of Sandcroft was patron of this church in 1319–1329, while William Sancroft, Archbishop of Canterbury in 1685, was born and buried in nearby Fressingfield where the family also owned land. At St. James the base of the square tower shows some evidence of Norman work and the north doorway has fragments of re-used billet decoration. The remains of a Norman window are visible on the north wall and the square font is Purbeck marble with five flat blank arches with flat tops, but unfortunately it is in a very poor state. The church is in the centre of the parish with a road system radiating out from it. In St. Margaret the church is situated close to the northern edge of a dispersed farming community, on a crossroads leading to Flixton and St. Cross. The south doorway is well preserved with Norman roll mouldings, zigzags, shafts and volute capitals. A lancet window is evident on the south side. Both this church and Homersfield were often used for the bishop's court. The church of St. Peter stands between the former medieval community, which is now only marked by thousands of fragments of pottery that show on the surface of the field, and the properties rebuilt in the later sixteenth century that are situated on the brow of the hill overlooking the Sconch Beck. Early Norman work is evident in the south doorway with colonnettes and block capitals, while the blocked north doorway is also Norman. The small church of St. Michael stands on the edge of the green which butts up to the church land. This green was created in the thirteenth century, but the church is certainly older as it has a well preserved Norman south doorway with colonnettes, roll moulding, a frieze of scallops and a hood mould. Churches were noted in Domesday Book at Homersfield, where the church of St. Mary has a Norman south window, and at Flixton, where the ancient church of St. Mary was largely rebuilt between 1856 and 1895 to designs by Anthony Salvin. They make the total up to nine parishes in the modern 'Saints' or South Elmham group.

Of the three other churches in the Waveney group of parishes only St. Mary Magdalene in Withersdale still shows evidence of Norman work. This is visible in two windows of the nave and a blocked north doorway, while the font has been recut from an earlier version and early, perhaps Norman, decoration is visible on three sides carved with arches and a tree of life. In the church of All Saints at Mendham we can only see evidence of the rebuilding in the fourteenth century. However five entries in Domesday Book represent two and a half churches here, so it is likely that the foundations of an early church lie beneath the present structure. There was certainly a chapel in later years attached to the manor of Shotford Hall in Mendham, which included property on both sides of the Waveney. The earliest mention of this building is in the Taxatio Ecclesiastica of Pope Nicholas in 1291 when Capella de Shotford was valued at four pounds, six shillings and eightpence, serving the Norfolk portion of Shotford Hall and endowed by Sir Miles de Stapleton. In 1347 the patron was Oliver de Ingham who held the manors of Thorpe Hall and Withersdale where he lived. At a manor court held in 1385, the year of Oliver's death, Thomas de Copham was presented by reason of his custody of the lands of the heir of Oliver de Ingham, being a minor, that is too young to manage them himself. The chapel ceased being used for services about this time and became a malt house. Many doubted the existence of this chapel but when mains drainage was introduced to the village in 1973 several skeletons were found. Then in 1982, when part of the church land here was being developed for the building of a bungalow, the missing chapel was discovered, confirmed by the finding of its footings with pottery ranging from the twelfth to the fifteenth centuries. Unfortunately the site was destroyed by the development before archaeological investigation could be carried out.

We cannot ignore the four parishes of the Ilketshalls which were held as a manor in the time of Domesday, together with All Saints Mettingham and St. Mary and Holy Trinity in Bungay. Ilketshall St. Andrew with its round tower has Norman north and south doorways, the former being plain but the latter decorated with colonnettes and zigzags, and there is a Norman window in the north wall. The church is situated towards the north east corner of the parish surrounded by the main concentration of settlement. At St. John the Baptist a single Norman lancet window survives in a mainly thirteenth-century building. It stands at the crossroads to Mettingham and Bungay, close to the line of the Roman road and in the centre of the parish where the main settlement survives. St. Lawrence church held 20 acres of land at Domesday, but the main structure of the present church is twelfth century. Reputedly it stands within a one acre Roman encampment close to the Roman road now known as Stone Street, but so far field walking has not revealed any evidence of Roman occupation in this area. The church was built close to the main manor house at the northern end of the parish which is a long one, echoing the line of the Roman road as it extends back from it on both sides. In 1154 this church was appropriated to the Prioress of Bungay by the Lady Gundreda, when she founded that Benedictine nunnery of which the church, St. Mary in Bungay, is now parochial. Ilketshall St. Margaret has a round tower with possible Saxon work at its base, and the body of the church is considered to be a Norman structure. All Saints at Mettingham also has a round tower, of which the base is claimed to be Saxon with Norman work above. The church has a Norman north doorway with colonnettes and scalloped capitals. It is situated on the main road from Bungay to Beccles, overlooking the valley of the Waveney with an early settlement clustered round the church. At Bungay itself the Domesday church of St. Mary was taken over by the nunnery, but Holy Trinity remained parochial. It has an early round tower and a Norman window in the nave. Three other Bungay churches were mentioned in Domesday but these might have been chapels. There was certainly a medieval chapel dedicated to St. Mary Magdalene on the road to Flixton, and another with a hermitage attached stood until 1733 near the east end of the bridge on the south side of the River Waveney. Two other religious houses, which were believed to be hospitals, were dedicated to St. John and St. Margaret.

These churches were endowed and alterations funded over the years through the generosity of people from many walks of life. We can see the results in the different architectural styles represented in side chapels, porches and towers added, in the words recorded in many wills, 'to give glory to God and for the saving of our souls'. These enlargements of the original churches reflect the growing size and wealth of the medieval population. Although there is much argument about the real numbers represented by the Domesday figures, it has been estimated that in 1086 Suffolk had 108,000 people living in 639 townships and Norfolk had 149,000 in 730 townships. However the total population might have been significantly higher if we have failed to allow a large enough factor for the size of households and the numbers who were of no significance for taxation purposes. In any case there is no doubt that East Anglia was more densely populated and its landscape more intensively farmed throughout the Middle Ages than most other parts of England.

Much more expensive than building a simple church was the endowment of a monastery. It is likely that early foundations in East Anglia fell victim to the Danish or Viking raiders and it took some time for replacements to be established. One example seems to be Mendham which is recorded as a monastery in AD 951. It would have been vulnerable to later Danish raiders entering the Waveney, and sometime between 1140 and 1156 a new foundation here was given by William de Huntingfield to Castle Acre Priory. They created a cell of Cluniac monks on the Isle of St. Mary in the River

Waveney at Mendham. He also gave them Ulordage and the Granges there together with certain land in Crodustune, and Dugdale mentions a second charter being a gift by Roger de Hommesial and 'William, the son of Hosoetel and Sigar, bequests to provide the monks with a church of stone'. Additional gifts followed and Roger de Huntingfield gave all his rights in St. Margaret and St. Peter of Linstead and in the church of Mendham. This priory was a popular visiting place for Queen Eleanor who died in 1204 at the age of 82. She had received Kingshall Manor in Mendham from her husband King Henry II and this abutted the priory land. The first prior whose name we know was John de Lindsey in 1170, and his seal is in the British Museum along with his footstool, chair and slipper. By 1204 there were eight monks and several new buildings had been erected, including a landing stage on the river for the delivery of supplies and for imported stone to be used in the new buildings. The Waveney Valley survey has recorded evidence of the priory including medieval tiles from the church and the use of some of their land for osier beds. This was confirmed when test digging for gravel extraction in the area revealed the root systems of many willow trees, which would have been cropped for use in making baskets and other wickerwork. In 1291 it was valued at £11. 15s. 9½d. All the Cluniac priories had problems in the fourteenth century as they were 'alien priories' subject to the French abbey of Cluny at a time when England was at war with France. Mendham finally achieved security in 1373 when it gained the right to be considered 'denizen not alien', making it an English establishment. Its valuation was still included with that of Castle Acre. The Priory continued providing priests for local parishes although sometimes it required serious prompting. Thus in 1411 the parishioners of Needham complained to the Pope that their chapel was not being served by Mendham Priory, although they paid their tithes, so the Bishop of Norwich, Alexander Tottington, responded to a Papal Bull by requiring the Prior of Mendham to provide a chaplain resident in Needham to serve the chapel there. Mendham Priory was finally closed by Henry VIII in 1536 as part of the suppression of smaller monasteries and it was granted to Charles Brandon, Duke of Suffolk. He was Henry's brother in law and placed in either side of the great west window of the church the arms of his wives, one being Mary Tudor daughter of Henry VII of England and widow of Louis XII of France. Fragments of this window are preserved in the British Museum.

Another of the priories in the Waveney Valley was the 'minster' in South Elmham St. Cross, mentioned in the last chapter. Its origin has been much discussed, but it is now considered most likely that the existing ruin is part of an early Norman church built for a priory created by Herbert de Losinga who was Bishop of Norwich until 1119. He also endowed a new priory at Hoxne. The evidence from excavation at the minster certainly revealed a section cut from a Saxon tomb slab being used to support part of the church wall, which suggests that it came from an earlier church here. No other material was found when Dr Stanley West directed the latest excavation to be carried out within the enclosure[4]. The rectangular enclosure has a substantial ditch and bank on three sides, although the fourth side towards the beck appears weaker. The enclosure is much larger than would be needed just to accommodate the church, supporting the idea that it was designed to house a large community, perhaps a religious one as the traditional minster name suggests. Roman pottery found during a previous excavation of the ditches[5] was almost certainly re-deposited after being disturbed when the ditch was cut through a

Figure 5.6 *The carved stone from South Elmham Minster showing part of a panel of interlace and a diagonal bar. This is part of a tomb slab or coffin lid and the carving might have been the foot of a cross.*

large area of Roman occupation known to spread well beyond the enclosure. We can only say for sure that the enclosure was constructed late in the Roman period or at some later date. Why anybody chose to expend the considerable effort needed to create this large ditch and bank and the large church within it remains a mystery. The surviving masonry shows that the west end was a self contained room with access to the nave at north and south sides but no central arch to view the altar. This can be interpreted as the narthex used in early churches to assemble the unbaptised. Edward Martin has suggested that this very solid western unit might have housed a private chapel for Bishop Herbert Losinga at first floor level placing him above the congregation, much as his throne in the apse of his cathedral at Norwich gave him a prominent position. He suggests Losinga was trying to imitate the style of continental work from the days of Charlemagne and consciously used earlier traditions. If so the lower level might have created the dark feel of a crypt on a site which was certainly too wet to allow an underground crypt. At Norwich cathedral the group of eastern chapels at a lower level than the bishop's throne also suggests a type of crypt similar to the earlier one at Brixworth church, and related to a space for relics below the throne. At the east end of South Elmham minster excavation revealed an apse based on the full width of the nave. The church was probably never finished as the putlog holes, which housed the ends of the timber beams supporting the builders' scaffolding, were never filled in. Fragments of rotted material, which was probably the remains of this wooden scaffolding left in place, has stained the flint. This is true inside as well as outside the building, making it almost certain that the inside faces of the walls were never rendered or plastered which confirms the failure to complete the work. It seems that the community failed after a short period of time and this church was abandoned unfinished. Perhaps Herbert de Losinga planned a grand priory here, possibly on an old minster site, but the project was given up in favour of the priory at Hoxne, and a chapel at South Elmham Hall where

Figure 5.7 *Looking west inside the ruins of South Elmham Minster. The block of masonry in the centre obstructed a view of the altar from the west. Access to the nave in the foreground from the western chamber seems to have been by wide arches in the north and south ends of this blocking wall. There might have been a gallery above the enclosed chamber.*

John Ridgard has noted reference to an 'old cloister'[6], suggesting that a community of monks or priests was attached to the bishop's house itself. It still does not explain why he chose such a wet site for his 'minster' down in the valley.

Flixton Priory was founded by Margery de Creke on land held as a manor by her husband Bartholomew. On his death Margery moved to Flixton to create a home for gentlewomen following the Rule of St. Benedict. By 1252 this manor was listed as belonging to the Augustinian nunnery and in 1291 the temporal income of Flixton Priory is recorded as £41. Dedicated to St. Mary and St. Catherine its property was valued at £40. 15s. ½d. in 1534 but by then it had already been suppressed in 1528 by a bull of Pope Clement VII, which listed one abbess and seven nuns. This suppression had been intended to provide additional funds for Cardinal Wolsey's new school at Ipswich, but when he lost royal favour this collapsed and the Flixton property was finally sold in 1544 to John Tasburgh who was living at St. Peter's Hall. Much of the fabric from the priory was used in the refurbishment of the manor house of St. Peter's where it can still be seen. Close by is Abbey Wood which is presumably the wood for 20 swine recorded in Domesday, much of it still surviving until today.

Rumburgh Priory is remarkable for being mentioned by implication in Domesday Book, although its twelve monks are listed in the adjoining settlement of Wissett[7]. It is said to have been founded by Bishop Aethelmaer (Ailmer) (1047–1070), who was the brother of Archbishop Stigand of Canterbury, working with Abbot Thurstan of the Abbey of St. Benet of Holme in Norfolk of which it became a cell. Its dedication to St. Michael and St. Felix suggests an early origin and this may be another case of re-founding an ancient monastery. The name seems to appear in early sources as Romburgh and, although many place name experts will reject it, an obvious derivation might be Romanum Burgh or Romanorum Burgh meaning the Roman fort or fort of the Romans. There are no signs of a fortification here but much Roman material has been discovered in adjoining fields. It might be that when the community abandoned the Irish foundation of St. Fursey at Burgh Castle some of them moved inland seeking greater security at another recognisable Roman settlement conveniently close to the Bishop's seat at South Elmham. The priory was later made a cell of the greatest northern Benedictine Abbey of St. Mary at York. This is taken to explain the massive size of its tower with three tall lancet windows in its wide western end. A number of Yorkshire names in the list of priors confirms that they were sent from the mother house to manage this remote cell. The priory maintained as chapels the parish church of St. Andrew, Wissett with its round tower and Norman doorway, and St. Peter, Spexhall with a round tower (rebuilt in 1910). Wissett church, standing on the edge of the River Blyth close to its source, might be the oldest foundation as the inner face of the round tower is said to preserve the early, probably pre-Conquest, finish of round windows and the original first floor access door facing east. Wissett had been a property of the Ralph the Staller, a Breton nobleman who became a minister at the court of Edward the Confessor and whose son Ralph was made Earl of East Anglia by William I. This might explain its status and its decline after Earl Ralph rebelled against William in 1075.

The size of medieval monasteries varied greatly, depending on the gifts they attracted and the skill with which the monks managed their resources. The more successful houses had considerable impact on the landscape. Some of the monks, and the laymen they employed, developed farming skills to produce crops required to feed their communities and a surplus for sale. In some places on holdings far from the actual monastery their presence is still recorded in the naming of Priory Farm or Abbey Farm. The monasteries themselves employed builders and carpenters to maintain and extend their buildings. The larger complexes included a hospital for elderly and infirm monks and a guest house to accommodate visitors with enclosed space to graze their animals. Monks developed skills in water management as they were concerned to provide fresh water for their breweries, vital at a time when beer was seen as a safer drink than possibly polluted water, and to supply extensive fish ponds in which they farmed another essential element in their diet. Water had also to be directed to the kitchens, to washing places and to flush the toilets. They would direct water from springs or divert rivers according to their needs. All had herb gardens to provide medicinal plants vital to the medieval physician, who had access to illustrated herbals in the monastic library, and to enable the cooks to flavour the food. They also managed bee hives which produced honey, essential in the absence of other sources of sugar, and equally important wax for the candles needed in the church. Some had their own grape vines as is documented at the great Abbey of St. Edmund at Bury.

Contemporary records reveal sometimes complex relationships between the powerful monastery at Bury and the local priory at Eye. At some date between 1120 and 1138 an agreement[8] was made before the full chapter of the great abbey at Bury St. Edmunds between the abbot of Bury and the prior of Eye about a group of men of Thornham Parva over whom they had been in dispute. The men are named as Godric and his brother, Godwin, Cuithmann and his brothers, Lefstan who might be a fuller (fullo), Aldulph, who might be a weaver (telator) and Ulfus. The possibility that two men in Thornham were involved in weaving at that time is interesting. It may be that these are the holdings of nine free men attributed to St. Edmunds less than fifty years earlier in the Domesday Book of 1086[9] with 35 acres, one and a half ploughs and half an acre of meadow valued at six shillings. The editor of Domesday allocates the entry to Thornham Magna but the text only refers to Thornham without specifying Magna or Parva. These men, with their land and service, were granted by the abbot to Eye on condition that the prior should pay to Bury every year at the feast of St. Edmund a peacock and a crane or two pike suitable for a feast in acknowledgement of the abbey's lordship. Two large pike sound easier to find in Suffolk than a peacock and a crane. The dispute was not finally resolved then, as about 1203 they reached a new agreement[10] before the King's justices meeting at Northampton to change the payment to two swans at the feast of St. Edmund with the proviso that the bearer of the swans should have his meal. If this did mean a seat at the great feast we must wonder what discussions took place at Eye as to whose turn it might be in each year. It was also specified that Eye priory should pay to Bury two pounds of wax each year for the duty their tenants in Pelecoc (Thornham Magna) and Thornham Parva owed to the abbot's manor court at Brockford. Another link between the monastic houses is suggested by the record in the Pinchbeck Register of the great abbey of Bury St. Edmunds that a monk called Johannis Sudbury was transferred from the abbey to the Priory of Eye[11].

Later the Abbot of Bury St. Edmunds granted to Eye Priory a chapel with the land belonging to it. This grant by Henry, Abbot of St. Edmunds, to William, Prior of Eye in 1243 is recorded in the cartulary of Eye[12] for an annual rent of two candles of 2lb to be placed on the altar of St. Edmund at the feast of the Translation of St. Edmund in acknowledgement of the abbey's lordship. The chapel was in Thornham Magna 'at the place called Eadburgtre in the parish of Pelecoch', but on the boundary of Parva as land in front of it, part of its holding of over 42 acres, was in Parva[13]. A fourteenth-century list of the property of Eye Priory gives details of over 42 acres belonging to the chapel[14]. This chapel at 'Eadburgtre' or 'Atburctre'[14] was dedicated to St. Eadburga. This was probably Eadburga (or Eadburh) who died in AD 751 having been the abbess of Minster in Thanet after St. Mildred who died after AD 732. Eadburh was the recipient of letters from St. Boniface, otherwise known as Wynfrith, during his mission to Germany where he became bishop of Mainz. She might have met Boniface while he was teaching at Nursling monastery near Southampton in about AD 710. Boniface wrote to the Abbess Eadburh in about AD 735 'you have often comforted my sadness both with the solace of books and assistance with clothing. So I now pray you to add to what you have begun, namely to write for me in gold the epistles of my Lord St. Peter the Apostle, to secure honour and reverence for the Holy Scriptures when they are preached before the eyes of the heathen and because I particularly wish to have always with me the words of him who guided me to this course. And by the priest Eofa I send for writing this which I ask'. Presumably this last sentence meant that he was sending the gold for the writing. He thanked her for sending books as 'by sending gifts of sacred books you have consoled with spiritual light an exile among the Germans' and he prayed 'for an eternal reward in the heavenly court of the angels for all the kindnesses which you have rendered to me.'[16] When a nun called Leofgyth (Leoba) wrote to Boniface praying for his friendship and 'the shield of his prayers', she said she learned the art of writing poetry from Eadburh 'who continues unceasingly to search into the divine law.'[17] Tom Plunkett identifies our Eadburh with Ecgburh, the sister of King Aelfwald of East Anglia, who might possibly, but not certainly, be mentioned as abbess of Repton (Derbyshire) in the Life of St. Guthlac where she provided a coffin for Guthlac's burial in AD 714[18]. He suggests that she could have been educated in the royal monastery at Ely and might even at some stage have served as its abbess. If so she was certainly a royal lady with extensive monastic experience.

King Aelfwald of East Anglia (AD 713–749) himself wrote to St. Boniface between AD 742 and 749 promising that prayers would be said for him regularly at the seven canonical hours in the monasteries in his kingdom. This is the correct translation by Dr. Steven Plunkett of a passage that has been widely misread as a reference to seven monasteries. According to an account of the lives of certain saints[19] Eadburga as abbess built a new church of SS Peter & Paul at Minster and translated to it the body of St. Mildred (Mildryth) in the AD 740s. She was buried at Lyminge, near Lympne in Kent, beside its founder Aethelburga who was the sister of Eadbald, king of Kent and the widow of Edwin, king of Northumbria. It is interesting to note the dedication of the church in the centre of Ipswich to St. Mildred and wonder if there was a connection between the two Suffolk dedications. There is said to have been a major cult of St. Mildred at Utrecht where St. Willibrord had established his see and which is not far from Dorestadt, one of Ipswich's trading partners. There were close connections between East Anglia and Kent as St. Seaxburh one of King Anna's saintly daughters had married Eorcenberht, king of Kent AD 640–664 to become the mother of a dynasty of rulers. She later became abbess of Minster in Sheppey and then of Ely. Other links might be related to Boniface's activity in the eighth century in Frisia which was just across the sea from East Anglia, as well as the fact that Mildred had studied at Chelles where King Aelfwald's grandmother Hereswith had been a nun[20]. The Dictionary of Saints also gives St. Edburga of Winchester, died AD 960, the daughter of King Edward the Elder who was abbess of a nunnery at Winchester, but there seems no reason to link her to Thornham. Gelling[21] suggests tree place names may originate from trees used as boundary markers for large estates in which case this might have been the edge of a large royal estate linked in some way to Eadburga, and perhaps the tree itself was seen as holy, as in 'Hallowtree' names. Alternatively it might refer to a wooden cross in honour of Eadburga.

The chapel was occupied in the thirteenth century by a monk called Vitalis, and later by brother Hubert, living as a hermit away from the priory[22]. It attracted large donations but many of these which refer to the monk Vitalis date from the 1220s[23], so he was presumably originally a monk of St. Edmunds living here as a hermit on the edge of its properties who changed his allegiance to the nearer house of Eye. In the fourteenth century over 42 acres of land belonged to the chapel. Its site may have been close to Cowpasture Lane at the point where the parish boundary diverges to the east of the lane, as a number of documents granting land to the chapel in the Eye Cartulary refer to its location. One refers to 'one piece of land lying at Atburctre between my land and land of the chapel of Atburctre and abuts the road which extends in front of the door of the said chapel at an angle and is reckoned at one rood'[24]. Another describes 'two pieces of land of which one lies before the said chapel towards the east between the road which extends at an angle to the said chapel and land in the fee of William son of Nigel and is reckoned at one acre … the other piece lies between land pertaining to the said chapel and land of Adam Scopelot next to the same chapel towards the south and abuts the said road and is reckoned at half an acre'[25]. There are also 'two pieces of land in fields of Mellis with all the grass of a certain road lying between the said pieces … one piece lies beside the road which extends from the said chapel towards Mellis on the east lengthwise and abuts to the north on the meadow which is called Snaueregatemeadow; and the other piece lies beside the said road on the west lengthwise and abuts to the north on the meadow which is called Cotescroftmeadow'[26]. Another half acre of land, said to be near the chapel, is located between the road called Snaueregate and land of Adam le Snorte of Mellis[27]. It is notable that Cowpasture Lane which apparently passed the door of the chapel led directly to Redgrave and Botesdale. Redgrave had a large park belonging to St. Edmunds Abbey at Bury, which was acquired after the dissolution of the abbey by the Bacon family. Botesdale, meaning Botulph's valley, was a settlement within the parish of Redgrave but with a chapel (later incorporated in the Grammar School) dedicated to St. Botolph. Botolph was an important East Anglian saint who founded his monastery at Icanhoe, almost certainly Iken, in AD 654 and died on 17 June 680. When in 1227 King Henry III granted to the Abbot of Bury St. Edmunds the right to hold an annual fair for two days at Botesdale in his manor of Redgrave this was to be held on the eve and the actual feast day of St. Botolph (June 17th). As Botesdale took its name from the saint we can suggest that the chapel was there long before the market received its charter, and note that like Thornham's chapel of Eadburga it was dedicated to an early saint and located on the very edge of the parish. In fact it is significantly nearer to the two parochial churches of St. Mary at Rickinghall Inferior and Superior than to its own parish church of Redgrave. This area was certainly rich in medieval religious connections. The hermitage at Thornham was still receiving donations in the fifteenth century as in 1438 John Hobart, rector of Burgate church, in his will left two shillings 'to the hermit of Arborghtre chapel'[28].

Chapel Farm in Thornham Parva may mark part of the lands held by the chapel and the stonework in its buildings might have come from a barn belonging to the chapel. At the Dissolution of the Monasteries the holding of Eye Priory included under the Prior's Wood in Thornham, 'the farm of a grove in Great Thornham and a chapel called St. Arbory's Chappell'[29]. Tom Martin copied from a document in the papers of Charles Killigrew which recorded the sale in 1595 of 'that Grove called Priors Wood lyinge in Great Thornham' containing 16 acres with its herbage and pasture and 'also of a certayne Chappell there called St. Arboroughe Chappell with one acre of wood adjoining to the same.' This property was bought from Robert Smythson of London by Edward Honynge of Eye, but it was noted that it had been leased to Thomas Wiseman since 1537 at an annual rent of seventeen shillings[30].

The descriptions above show that the chapel was beside a lane, probably the one we know as Cowpasture Lane or a variation of it. It also has to be on the boundary between Magna and Parva which gives two likely places, one is where the modern lane changes direction as it crosses the boundary and the other is based on the possibility that at one time the lane took a line from here across the field to a point on the modern road near Villa Farm, which offers a possible site close to Villa Farm. Both deserve investigation on the ground.

In the twelfth and thirteenth centuries part of Thornham, possibly Thornham Magna as a whole, is called Pelecoch, or Pilecock. The earliest reference we have located is in a document dated some time between 1146 and 1174 by the Bishop of Norwich confirming the property of Eye Priory including the settlement (villa) and church called Pelecoch, as well as lands and a church in 'Thornham'[31]. The grant of the chapel in 1243 says it is in a place called Eadburgtre in the parish of Pelecock[32]. A number of fines on transfer of properties in the thirteenth and fourteenth centuries refer to Pilecock, Thornham Pylecok or similar variants[33]. In 1291 the Papal Taxation shows that the Abbot of Bury St. Edmunds still had interests in Pylecock in terms of rents and customary services assessed at £1. 1s. 2d. Compared to the Prior of Eye assessed at £4. 6s. 11½d. for land, rents and a mill, with another £1. 11s. 7d. for rents and land in Thornham Parva. The churches of Pylecok and Thornham Parva each paid 4 shillings to the Prior of Eye. Eilert Ekwall[34] suggests this Pilecok or Pilcock is possibly 'willow copse or hill' derived from Old Scandinavian pill = willow and Old English cocc = heap. The Old Scandinavian element is interesting in light of the proximity of Thwaite and Skeith, so might be a third item in this local group. Plenty of wet land offers suitable habitats for willow trees to grow. As it seems that part of Thornham Magna was held by the de Briseworth family it may be that from some time in the eleventh or twelfth century until the Dissolution of the Monasteries that part was called 'Briseworths', which is certainly the later name of the main manor, while the land held by Eye Priory was known as Pilecock until the two parts were united after the dissolution of the priory.

Thornham Parva church was dedicated to St. Edmund in the fifteenth century as John Skouthare specified in his will in 1450 that he should be buried in the chancel of the church of St. Edmund the king at Thornham Parva[35]. A version of the story of this last king of East Anglia, martyred by the Danes in AD 869, is shown in a series of paintings on the north wall (Plate 11), while the south wall shows the infancy of Christ and the church is now dedicated to Mary his mother. These 14th century paintings[36] have been damaged over the years and were covered with whitewash from the sixteenth century Reformation until the early twentieth century. Clearest on the south wall is the birth of Jesus shown round the head of the door and to the east of it an angel announcing the news to two shepherds. Parts of other scenes are visible as well as a pattern representing ashlar masonry, rosettes and foliage with large consecration crosses that were believed in the Middle Ages to frighten away demons and show the triumph of Christ's cross. On the north wall in the scene nearest the altar Edmund is wearing his crown, riding on a horse away from a castle to escape the Danes and his death by Danish arrows was probably shown where the later window is now. Next two tonsured monks are shown fitting Edmund's crowned head back on to his body, as after he was beheaded by the Danes his head is said to have been protected by a wolf and was miraculously joined back onto his body. Then his funeral procession shows a house shaped coffin with crosses carried by monks, accompanied by the wolf. Finally over the door is the miracle when Edmund's body was taken from Bury St. Edmunds to London for temporary safety during Danish raids about AD 1010 and a narrow bridge at Stratford, represented by the arch of the door, widened to fit the cart carrying the coffin. The two most famous surviving medieval versions of the life of St. Edmund are in illuminated manuscripts created at the abbey of Bury St. Edmunds, of which a twelfth-century Life of Edmund is now in New York and a fifteenth-century version of Lydgate's Lives of SS Edmund and Fremund is in the British Library. The wall paintings at Thornham are believed to have been created early in the fourteenth-century. This version of the story has some similarities to that painted in the mid thirteenth-century on the walls of the church of St. Helen at Cliffe-at-Hoo in Kent which is the only other known portrayal of this story in wall painting. The paintings at Cliffe are in three tiers in the north transept where the lowest scene shows the king riding out in similar fashion to the first scene at Thornham. This is followed by scenes of the shooting with arrows and the beheading; then the restoring of the head to the body and the funeral procession accompanied by the wolf. It is intriguing that an expert report[37] describes the headdress of one figure in a second series of paintings in the south transept showing the martyrdom of St. Margaret as very similar to one discovered at Ilketshall St. Andrew. The report also says that the St. Edmund sequence was drawn by Hamlet Watling[38]. One might wonder if it is significant that Cliffe-at-Hoo on the Thames estuary beside the Isle of Grain is on the coastal route to Minster in Sheppey and on to Minster in Thanet where St. Eadburga had been abbess in the eighth-century. Travel between Suffolk and Kent in the Middle Ages is most likely to have been by sea.

A remarkable piece of medieval art, the painted retable behind the altar in Thornham Parva church, was created in the fourteenth century but was not originally part of this church. It was found in Lord Henniker's stable in 1927, having been bought with the contents of Rookery Farm, Stradbroke. Of the nine panels two show Dominican saints, Dominic and Peter the Martyr, so it may have been painted for the great Dominican Friary at Thetford and formed part of an elaborate setting for the high altar of which another portion is now in the Musée de Cluny in Paris. Presumably it had been saved from destruction during the puritan destruction of such religious works and hidden at the farm in Stradbroke at a time when people still hoped to restore the decorative features and ancient rituals of the medieval Christian worship to their churches.

Not all medieval work proved to be of the highest standard. A Chancery document[39] records a complaint against two masons, John Tilley and Richard Cuttyng, who were building a new 'steple', that is a tower, for Little Thornham church. This can be dated to about 1486 as it was addressed to the Lord Chancellor as Bishop of Worcester who was presumably John Alcock, the first Chancellor of the new Tudor dynasty holding office under King Henry VII from October 1485 to March 1487. They had agreed to build a tower similar to that of 'Gasthorpe' in Norfolk, with certain amendments, for ten marks, three shillings and fourpence. They had already received five marks and a supply of 'lyme, ston and sand' but refused to repair the work when part of it fell down 'riven through'. We can see the actual terms on which a church tower was built at this time as the complete contract for building Helmingham tower in 1487 survives[40]. There the mason, Thomas Aldrych, was to be paid ten shillings per foot of height for a tower 60 feet high, exclusive of materials. He gave a 20 year guarantee subject to certain provisions, which included limiting the work to a suitable part of the year and agreeing not to install bells until at least four years after the building work was completed. We

Figure 5.8 *Hartismere Deanery seal and another medieval seal, both found at Thornham Parva. The image has been reversed to make the lettering legible. The hart (stag) is clearly visible facing to the left with the ripples on the mere behind it.*

do not know what caused the work at Thornham to collapse nor how the tower was completed as it stands today.

In a field near the church was found a medieval seal matrix of the deanery of Hartismere 'S. DECANATVS DE HERTISMERE', with a design showing a stag (the hart) and water (the mere). It was probably being used in the fourteenth century to authenticate official religious documents and we can only speculate how it came to be lost here. Remarkable evidence has turned up in the form of a small rectangular stone mould for the manufacture of medieval seal matrices which was found as long ago as 1756 'from Great Thornham Burying Ground' and is now in the British Museum[41]. It was bought in 1805 as part of the collection of Charles Townley (1737–1805). It is only 75 mm long but hollows have been carved out to create the backs of eight different types of matrix: on one side are three ovals and one circle, all enclosing circles; on the other a circle enclosing a cross and on one edge three oval hollows with crosses. They all include a central depression that would create a shallow 'handle' by which to hold the matrix. It may have been made in the thirteenth century according to John Blair and Nigel Ramsay who illustrate it in their book 'English Medieval Industries' (Hambledon Press 1991). It may be that a specialist maker of seals was working in thirteenth-century Thornham.

On the south side of the churchyard of Thornham Parva is a sunken lane which may be the remains of a long boundary called Grim's Ditch in the thirteenth century (Plate 12). Although we are not yet sure of its line it may have continued eastwards across the A140 towards Eye and westwards towards Mellis. At present its origin is unknown but it is likely to have been an important boundary marked out along the southern edge of the valley of the River Waveney some time, possibly a very long time, before the Norman conquest. It reminds us of the ancient importance of this area on the edge of the higher ground south of the Waveney. Grim is an alternative name for the god Woden, sometimes identified as the Devil, and in Saxon times people often described large earthworks of unknown origin as 'the devil's work' in this way. A document from the reign of Henry III refers to a field in Thornham called 'Grimisdich'[42]. One of the grants to the chapel of Vitalis recorded in the Eye charters refers to a field called Grimmesmor about 1230[43] and the list of the chapel's holdings given in the Red Book of Eye[44] includes two small pieces of land on 'grymmys dyche'. A field of four acres named Grimsditch in Thornham appears on an early nineteenth century estate map[45] and in the Tithe Survey of 1841. If we are right this boundary ditch later became part of a long distance cross country trackway which can be traced coming from Braiseworth or Eye to the east, crossing the A140 and continuing westwards, by tracks later known as Howe Lane and Cowpasture Lane to Mellis Green. From there it extended by Stonebridge Lane and Bugg's Lane in Burgate to the market at Botesdale and on across the watershed between the rivers Waveney and Little Ouse. In 1227 the Abbot of Bury St. Edmunds obtained a royal charter to hold his market at Botesdale in the corner of his manor of Redgrave as well as the grant of an annual fair which we have mentioned already. The weekly market was held on a Thursday and research by Redgrave History Group has enabled them to establish the layout of some of the shops and stalls. These were separated by lanes on a sloping site in front of the chapel of St. Botolph. They have also located both an 'old' and a 'new' Tolhowse from which the Abbot's officials regulated the conduct of the market[46]. In 1289 there were more than 52 stalls and 14 shops. This was clearly an important trading centre on the main road between Diss and Bury St. Edmunds so we can assume that lanes leading to it were busy with traffic to the weekly market as well as the annual fair. Another of these ancient lanes appears to run through Yaxley, Thrandeston and Palgrave to Diss. These routes had probably been in use since prehistoric times, long before construction of the Roman road from Colchester to Norwich. It is also notable that the sections of driftway marked on the current map as 'Broad Dock' and 'Green Lane' are part of a lane between Gislingham and Mellis destroyed by the railway line. Hodskinson's map of 1783 shows this as 'Park Way' running between the very large 'Alwood Green', which was apparently shared between Gislingham and Rickinghall Superior on the extreme western edge of Hartismere Hundred, to Yaxley and perhaps on to Eye.

One manor in Thornham was granted by Robert Malet to Eye Priory. In the twelfth century the Bishop of Norwich confirmed[47] that the property held by Eye Priory included the whole settlement called Stoke (Stoke Ash) with its church and tithes, the settlement which is called Pelecoch (probably Thornham Magna), with its church and tithes, some land in Yaxley, the church of Yaxley with its lands and tithes, the church of Mellis with its lands and tithes, and the church of Thornham (probably Thornham Parva) with its lands and tithes. The location of this manor in Thornham is unknown as Copinger traces a number of owners after the Dissolution of the Monasteries but finds no reference after 1597 when it was granted to John Athowe and Henry Becke[48]. Presumably its lands were acquired by the owners of Thornham Hall, although it is recorded as late as 1731 that Mr. Killigrew who was then lord of the main manor and lived in Thornham Hall held 'Chappell Yard, Chappell Field, Chappell ..., Chappell Close in Little Thornham ... copy [that is as a copyhold tenant] of Eye Hall alias Eye

Priory Manor'[49]: presumably the reference is to some of the lands of St. Aedburga's chapel, while another of Tom Martin's papers records that the chapel 'called St. Arboroughe chappell' with an acre of wood adjoining and the grove of 16 acres called Priors Wood in Great Thornham had been granted by Queen Elizabeth in the 36th year of her reign to Robert Smythson of London, skinner who in the following year sold it to Edward Honynge of Eye, although he would only hold it after the expiry of a lease granted to Thomas Wiseman for 80 years by Henry VIII in the 28th year of his reign at an annual rent of 17 shillings.

The tax return for the Lay Subsidy of 1327 reveals Thomas Gernoun (almost certainly Gernoun rather than Gernonn) as the largest payer in Thornham Magna at six shillings and sixpence. Two members of the family who gave their name to the main manor, the de Breseworthes, were assessed at three shillings and sixpence and two shillings and twopence. The manor which presumably included Thornham Hall, and was generally referred to as Bresworth in Thornham Magna[50], was held later in the 14th century by William de Briseworth. His daughter married Simon Blyant of Thornham Magna whose will[51] in 1450 gives his bequest to the Wisemans of a manor of 'Newton' which it is suggested might be in Thornham Magna, along with the manor of Bulls Hall in Yaxley. There is no obvious location for this manor of Newton but the list of manors held by Simon Wysman in 1485/94[52] includes Old Newton, a parish near Stowmarket, and this seems the best candidate. The reference to Bulls Hall, Yaxley is also interesting because it seems that in 1459 this manor named as Bulls Hall cum Blogate Hall belonged to John Herberd[53] who took the name Yaxley which was kept by his descendants. He was wealthy enough to pay for the magnificently decorated north porch of Yaxley church requesting in his will that he should be buried in the porch and the rest of it be paved at his cost. Simon Blyant's daughter married Nicholas Wiseman who thereby inherited the manor of Bresworth in Thornham Magna. It remained with the Wiseman family until the death of Edward Wiseman in 1561, whose sister Barbara married Edmund Bokenham of Thelnetham and it was then held by Bokenhams.

Less substantial than castles, but still making a significant mark on the landscape, were the moated enclosures of which many survive in our area. Digging large moats involved a lot of work and showed the wealth and status of the owner, as well as draining the site of his timber framed house and housing stocks of fresh fish. They provided protection from casual intruders or stray animals, although they were no defence against serious military attack. Really large moats were the mark of great wealth as shown by the moat of the country seat of the Bishops of Norwich at South Elmham Hall. This might have been created by Bishop Herbert de Losinga. It enclosed some three acres and from the account rolls we learn that the house had between twelve and fifteen main rooms with fourteen others; there was an inner court, outer court, the great bridge, the gate keeper's house, dove house, stables, herbarium and the King's arbour, as well as two cloisters and a chapel. Perhaps Edward II used this garden for royal visitors in 1326, when he stayed for a few days on his way from Hoxne to Norwich. The buildings changed many times over the years and the accounts record major refurbishments carried out by succeeding bishops. It may have been Bishop Scarning (1266–1278) who added the earliest surviving wall paintings in the Hall which have been dated to the 1270s and compared to those of that date in Norwich Cathedral itself. During the cleaning of the

Figure 5.9 *South Elmham Hall moat showing brickwork and timbers at the site of the great gatehouse, revealed when the moat was drained for cleaning.*

moat a large section of the foundation of the Great Gate House was exposed, as many of the cut oak timbers used to bridge the moat had been preserved in situ. A section of Early English coursed brick marked the span of the Gate House. This was several stories high as the Victoria County History and Copinger speak of six stories still being visible in the nineteenth century. In its high position this country seat or palace of the bishops must have been an impressive sight and was a favoured vantage point. Today all that is visible of the original buildings is some flint work at the base of the modern barn, some ruins on the western edge of the moat which could have been the site of the house for visitors as it stood outside the main quarters of the bishop, and some flint work in the modern garden. Several bishops spent many hours here, including Bishop Walter Suffield (1244–1257) who died here leaving a legacy of three marks to Gotle his steward. In 1278 Bishop Roger Scarning is listed as dying at his manor house at South Elmham and Bishop William Middleton (1278–1288) wrote to the king in 1286 from his seat at South Elmham. It was clearly a large establishment as an inventory of 1342 lists some of the main rooms and outdoor features as: Hall and porch, lord's chamber, private privy (perhaps the private toilet that survives with its wall paintings), resistereium (or pesistereium – meaning unknown), oratorary (presumably a chapel for prayer), bailiff's chamber and solar, marshal's chamber and solar, steward's chamber and solar, clerk's chamber and solar (so all the senior officers of the household had a pair of private rooms), old cloisters (perhaps for a resident community of priests), great garret, penthouse, high chamber, larder, dairy, King's arbour, herbarium, inner court, outer court, dovehouse, stables, porter minder (the gate keeper's house) and great bridge. The bricks at South Elmham were certainly made on the estate as we learn from the account rolls. There was one kiln inside the moat and another outside where we are

Figure 5.10 *South Elmham Hall guesthouse. These flint ruins are all that survive of an important part of the medieval complex that formed the bishop's palace.*

told that 3800 roof tiles and decorative ridge tiles were made in 1398–9, and that there was a firing of 14,000 bricks and corner tiles in 1444–5 with a further 8000 made later that year. On the east side of the drive approaching the Hall is a field full of earthworks which could have been one of the areas used for making the bricks. Norman Scarfe[54] mentions the production of 350,000 breketylls made here in 1464–5 and sent to Hoxne. Bricks were made here as early as the thirteenth century and are easily recognised by the cross, of St. Cross, marked on the surface. They would have provided a useful extra source of income for the bishops as well as enabling them to decorate the internal walls of their hall in the fifteenth century with designs similar to those that can be seen in Norwich Cathedral. In 1387 Bishop Henry Despenser obtained a licence from the king to crenellate the hall, that is to give it defensive fortifications. There can be little doubt that Despenser was taking precautions after the traumatic events of the Peasants' Revolt in 1381 during which he took the lead in suppressing the rebellion. The revolt is seen as, at least in part, a challenge to feudal authority when skilled men could claim higher pay and greater independence, because of the shortage of manpower in the reduced population after the great plague of the Black Death in 1348–9. Despenser's predecessor might not have endeared the bishopric as lord of the manor to the people of South Elmham if an example quoted by Christopher Dyer[55] is typical. He finds that in 1360 John Clench and John Soule claimed to be free but the 'whole homage' of the manor court stated they were serfs and they were put in the stocks. They had to do fealty as serfs to their lord, the Bishop of Norwich, and were also fined three shillings and four pence each 'for an unjust claim and rebellion'. Despite the apparent unanimity of the manorial court they were not alone, as another tenant who supported them was deprived of his lands until he submitted to the lord and paid a fine. Others no doubt noted this penalty, both public humiliation and significant financial loss, for opposing the manorial authority. It is difficult to be sure of the actual impact of both the Black Death and the Peasants' Revolt. It seems that the former did substantially reduce the local population, which might have been growing too large for the available resources, as it appears far above the figures at Domesday some 300 years earlier and did not rise so high again before the end of the Middle Ages. Some individual farms and cottages might have been abandoned at this time but no complete villages seem to have been lost through this cause. The revolt was probably just a stage in the relaxation of the feudal controls exercised by manorial lords, but there always had been variations in the way these were enforced and in some places the power of the great landowner faced little challenge for centuries to come. The archaeological evidence suggests that in the Thornhams a significant number of sites occupied in the years before and about the time of the Norman Conquest went out of use about then or before the end of the fourteenth century, while only two new sites were occupied later in the Middle Ages and went out of use in the fifteenth century. Presumably the other sites occupied by people named in the tax returns of 1327 and 1524 were those still occupied by farms or houses today. We might compare this loss of properties with the disappearance of the extensive Late Saxon town at Thetford where commercial prosperity seems to have been lost at this time, when at Thornham trade was being lost to the growing town of Eye. By contrast comparatively few of the sites we have studied in the Waveney Valley have produced the Thetford and St. Neots Ware pottery which belongs to the Late Saxon phase. A greater number of sites which were abandoned more recently produce quantities of medieval pottery. Here perhaps commercial activity increased as the Bishops invested in their estates in an area that might have been previously restricted to serving the religious needs of the South Elmham episcopal centre and the minster at Mendham.

Bishop Middleton also owned property nearby in Mendham. Here the earliest moated enclosure in Castle Field is shown by the pottery evidence to have been occupied from the thirteenth century to the sixteenth, when the new house was built which is known now as Middleton Hall. Another great moat is still visible at St. Peter's Hall which was originally called Tenement Tolls, after the Toll family who were merchants from Norwich. On the north side of the Hall fragments of pottery and lava quern reveal two sites that were occupied from the thirteenth century until the fifteenth but became deserted when the Tasburgh family took over the manor. Moats were certainly popular from the thirteenth century until the seventeenth, usually having a span of some 15 feet although some, such as South Elmham Hall, were wider. Eight moats have been found in Flixton. The largest enclosed the area of the Priory. Close to the edge of this moat six large fragments of lava mill stone indicate the probable site of the mill. A complete circular moat survives at the site of Boys Hall, the residence of the de Boys or de Bosco family, who also owned land in Thornham Magna and Parva. They were major tenants of Flixton Priory in the late thirteenth and the fourteenth centuries. Two moated sites, both occupied from the thirteenth to the fifteenth century according to pottery finds, were discovered off Park Lane which marks the southern boundary of the original manor of Newall. This was granted by Bishop William Bateman (1344–1355) to his brother Sir Bartholomew Bateman and is mentioned by Thomas Bateman in his will of 1485. Starknaked Farm had its name changed during the Victorian period to Sternacre but has recently reverted to its original name, which was clearly derived from its exposed position on high ground. Its moat has been filled in but late medieval pottery has been found there. At Heavyland Wood a single arm of the moat indicates the position of the former enclosure, marked by a group of withies still flourishing today on the bank, where they would have provided the medieval owner with material for basket making. There is clear evidence of moats at Hill Farm and Wood Farm. The latter took its name from a wood that once marked its northern boundary, and from the thirteenth century it sat on the edge of a three acre green. Today a converted seventeenth-century barn marks the site of the original farmstead.

At South Elmham All Saints two farms occupied by freeholders were moated and have produced lava querns, showing they too were doing their own milling. They both abut on the green known as All Saints Common, which became the main focus of settlement about a quarter of a mile from the isolated church, itself flanked by the moats of the manor house and the rectory. It is notable that this early church with its round tower and its churchyard enclosed by a substantial curving bank and ditch stands beside this solitary manor house, by whose owner it might originally have been founded, with no other sign of housing apart from the Rectory. Not all the Elmham churches are isolated in this way. St. James had at least 12 moated enclosures of which several were sited close to the parish church. Here the discovery of at least seven sites with occupation starting in the thirteenth century, one involved in milling and another

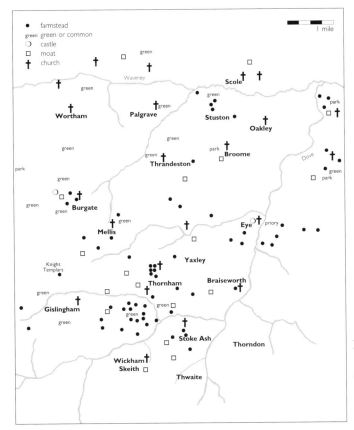

Figure 5.11 *Medieval sites at Thornham. This shows the many moated enclosures that have been identified, as well as the greens that developed away from the earlier village churches.*

119

Figure 5.12 *Medieval sites at South Elmham. This shows the number of greens and moated sites as well as the many scattered farmsteads.*

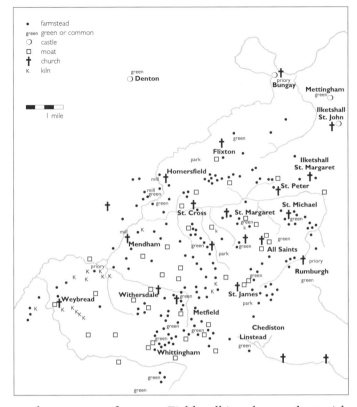

in pottery production, suggest the presence of a green. Field walking close to the parish boundary of Metfield and the Domesday parish of Whittingham, where the original Great Green was recorded, revealed 11 medieval sites. The earliest of these started in the thirteenth century and adding the present houses, of which three are moated, we had located this missing green. Metfield itself had 13 moats, some associated with the common, others more isolated. The largest are Willow Farm, on the northern edge of the common, and Metfield Manor House, which was listed as a quarter of a fee of the manor of Kingshall in Mendham in 1353. It was the home of the Jermy family from 1385 when it was a bridal present from Sir Roger Hales of Harwich, whose daughter Joan married a Jermy. The family lived there until 1652. Rookery Farm has a well preserved moat on three sides of an ancient building and an aisled barn. Eventually it became one of the holdings of the Thornham Estate. Six moated sites were located at Mendham and there was an opportunity for a small scale excavation at one of these, Withersdale Hall. The corner of the original manor house was located within the moat which was 30 feet wide. There was evidence of thirteenth-century occupation and Ranulph de Arderne held this manor in 1275. The building had been destroyed by fire in the fourteenth century leaving scorched wood sockets still visible in the base of the building with other burned material close by, including the remains of a small wooden chest of which the metal fittings survived, although distorted by the heat. The present house was built outside the moat and its construction is recorded in the manor court records. William Sadd appeared at the court of Mendham Priory Manor in 1648 to take possession of this manor, and in 1650 he was given permission to fell 10 oak trees on the south side of the moat, then a further 20. By 1651 three acres of land were released here for the house. Another manorial holding at Thorpe Hall had its moated enclosure but a smaller moat close by was an original circular rabbit warren which survived to be recorded on a map held by the owners which shows a coney sitting on top of the mount. At Flixton 11 of the 20 medieval sites found so far have yielded pieces of lava quern stone, so presumably freeholders were milling their own grain. In the southern part of the manor of Newall in Flixton excavation of a prehistoric burial mound revealed the base of a medieval windmill, obviously using the height of the mound to enhance its position. The whole of the cross tree was marked out by stones as was the position of the central post, possibly the complete trunk of an oak tree trimmed for the purpose. How many other prehistoric tumuli were used for such a purpose in the Middle Ages?

At Thornham Magna the medieval Hall was surrounded by a moat, most of which has been filled in but one side survives as a wide pond and the remaining outline can be traced as an earthwork in the Park west of the present Hall. Several other moats survive on the estate. Some probably belonged to the main houses of separate manors as we have records naming several manors. Hemenhall or Hemenhales in Thornham Magna was according to Copinger[56] held by Sir Ralph de Hemenhale who died in 1329 and was in that family until at least 1419. The family held the manor of Hempnall in Cotton but they displayed their commitment to Thornham as their arms[57] are carved on a shield on the porch of Thornham Magna church which is in perpendicular style,

Figure 5.13 *The later medieval porch of Thornham Magna church, showing the two shields. The three shells are the arms of the Hemenhale family, while the birds might be those of Toppesfield.*

so was probably added to the church in the fifteenth century. They also had property in Wickham Skeith and it is there that Ralph de Hemenhall was assessed for the tax known as the Lay Subsidy of 1327[58] at the unusually high figure of ten shillings which makes him one of the highest payers in Hartismere Hundred. His grandson, another Sir Ralph Hemenhale, was granted free warren, the valuable right to hunt game and take rabbits on his land, by Edward III in 1367[59].

The other manor in Wickham Skeith was given in 1135 during the reign of King Stephen by Robert de Sackville to the Abbey of St. John in Colchester. Originally this was on condition that four monks settled at Wickham to pray for his soul, in order to secure a faster passage for his soul through Purgatory to Heaven. However his son agreed that the four monks should be added to the Abbey at Colchester. In 1258 the Abbot of St. John's at Colchester had right of free warren in Wickham. It seems that one monk from Colchester was based here to manage the estate as about 1260 Robert son of William Gernun[60] of Pylecot (Thornham Magna) appointed Walter, who was keeper of the manor of Wickham and a monk of the abbey of Colchester, as his attorney. He was to pay Sir Richard de Hecham 21 pence of annual rent from a tenement in Wycham (Wickham Skeith[61]). After the Dissolution it was acquired by John Freston of Mendham. Presumably it is the property now called Wickham Abbey Farm.

In Thornham Parva Roger de Bosco was the wealthiest man to be assessed for the tax known as the Lay Subsidy in 1327, so he may have been the owner of the moated site of Woodhouse, as bosco is Latin for wood. However in 1391 Woodhouse in Thornham Parva and Swatshall or Swatsfield Hall in Gislingham were held by Richard del Chirche of Gislingham[62] and they included subsidiary holdings in Thornham Magna and Parva, Gislingham, Finningham, Wyverstone, Mellis, Burgate, Wortham and Gazeley. When Richard Chirche died in 1428 his daughter was married to William Toppesfield and a magnificent window in Gislingham church includes the original fifteenth-century glass with shields of the Chirche and Toppesfield families surrounded by blue columbine flowers[63]. William Toppisfield was Lord of Swatshall Manor and patron of Gislingham Church in 1480 when he gave 6s 8d towards the repair of its chancel. This was a time when much work was being done on the church, probably by the 'school' of Master Mason Hawes of Occold. A documentary reference[64] suggests that William Toppesfield was also lord of Woodhouse manor, so could the birds on a shield on the porch of Thornham Magna church be those of the Toppesfield arms as seen in the window at Gislingham church? By 1555 these manors were also held by John Wiseman owner of Thornham Hall. It was presumably at this time that the manor including the Thornhams became 'the manor of Swatshall Woodhouse & Bresworth'. Once the property had passed to the owners of Thornham Hall the sites of Woodhouse, probably the moated site in Lady Henniker Wood, and of Swatshall, presumably the moated site known as Swattesfield Hall on the modern boundary of Gislingham and Thornham Magna parishes, were not required as main residences and were used for less prestigious purposes. However it seems that although the Thornham Manor retained the title 'Swatshall Woodhouse & Bresworth', at some date between 1555 and 1603 when Michael Bedingfield was recorded as patron of Gislingham church the manor of Swatshall in Gislingham was transferred to the Bedingfield family[65]. Edmund Beaupre of Yaxley (d.1567) married first Margery, daughter of Sir John Wiseman and second Katherine, daughter of Philip

Bedingfield and Anne Yaxley, whose cousin William Yaxley of Yaxley (d.1588) married Eva Bedingfield, daughter of Sir Henry Bedingfield of Oxburgh & Redlingfield and sister of Nicholas Bedingfield of Swatshall. Certainly Nicholas Bedingfield (died 1636) and his wife Elizabeth were commemorated with a stone memorial in the chancel of Gislingham church. His will of 1636 refers to his provision of almshouses in Eye and when he purchased the land for them in 1621 he was described as 'of Swattis Hall, Gislingham'[66]. The chancel is dominated by a large coloured monument to Anthony Bedingfield a London merchant who died in 1652. He purchased Swatshall and the other main manor in Gislingham from Henry Bedingfield in 1649 for £4000 and subsequently gave them both to his brother Sir Thomas Bedingfield. We do not know what lay behind these family transactions but it was Sir Thomas and another London merchant, Robert Lowther, who paid for the magnificent monument with the kneeling figure of Anthony above an elaborate inscription in Latin and Greek. The hall of Swatshall was said to have been rebuilt by Charles Bedingfield who died in 1750 and it apparently continued in the Bedingfield family until 1781. After this it was reunited with the Thornham estate as White's Directory of 1844 says that Swattisfield Hall in Gislingham was rebuilt by Charles Bedingfield early in the eighteenth century, but that in 1844 Lord Henniker was lord of the manor of Swattisfield Hall. By this stage the moated site certainly must have become redundant and the manor has been part of the Hennikers' Thornham estate ever since. So once again the manor of Thornham justified its title of 'the Manor of Swatshall, Woodhouse and Bresworth'.

The list of manors held by Simon Wysman in 1485–94[67] includes individually named Thornham Parva (presumably Woodhouse), Briseworth in Thornham Magna and Swattishaugh in Gislingham (Swatshall) but these became the single main manor, known in post medieval times as 'Swatshall Woodhouse and Bresworth'[68]. All the moated sites are now being surveyed in order to learn more about their origins. There are also a complex series of earthworks at 'Ben Hunt's Plantation' on Clay Street in Thornham Magna. One of these appears to be enclosed by a large curving ditch that is cut through by the lane which appears to have been created later to link the presumed Roman line of Clay Street to the road to Wickham Skeith at 'Corner House'. A structure here would have dominated both the presumed Roman road and the river valley below. The site is confused by later house platforms constructed here on the edge of a green and by the creation of the lane, so it needs more detailed examination to determine whether it does have a medieval origin.

Although some were short lived, we have evidence on the ground of six moated sites in Thornham Parva. This may reflect the presence of ten taxpayers here in the Lay Subsidy list of 1327, as well as the recovery of medieval seals in the parish, including that of the Deanery of Hartismere. The best preserved of these moats is now hidden in Moat House Wood where the complete enclosure survives and the pottery evidence on the surface suggests occupation at least from the thirteenth to the sixteenth centuries. This is thought to be the manor house of Woodhouse mentioned above. At Carters Farm the moat surrounding the present house, which was built in the sixteenth century, seems to have been a medieval consolidation of occupation, as we have found material in the area around it dating from the Late Saxon period to the thirteenth century but not later. At Park Villa the moat sits on the boundary between Parva and Magna and many fragments of mill stone have been recovered here, as they have been at Carters Farm. Chapel Farm and Chandos Farm both show signs of moated enclosures but their full outline is less clear. At New Wood field a section of the medieval moat marks a field boundary where pottery from the thirteenth to fifteenth centuries has been found. At Thornham Parva church areas both east and west of the church itself seem to have served as greens and there were later allotments in this area. Church Field, west of the church, was part of the Glebe and in its south west corner was a collection of lava mill stone fragments with medieval pottery, but this field has a complex history. We have found evidence of much activity here from Prehistoric to Early Saxon and from Late Saxon to the seventeenth century, so it seems always to have been a focus of occupation. Along the lane from here to the Thornham Magna boundary are two more medieval sites, after which the lane seems to have been diverted as undulations in the present road suggest it is crossing older field boundaries. The line of the original lane ends in front of School House in Thornham Magna, where fragments of a moat survive in the garden, while pottery from the thirteenth to seventeenth centuries and a medieval pilgrim's flask have been recovered from the adjoining field. This is one of six moats thought to have existed in Magna, of which the largest surrounded the original manor house at Thornham Hall. Other moats reflect the edge of the green known as Mill Common, now marked by one of the Estate Walks footpaths, and the line of medieval tracks. Evidence from field walking and observation of the landscape supports one reference to Mill Common adjoining Clay Street and extending from building sites now covered by Ben Hunt's Plantation towards the properties now known as the Old Rectory, Lambs Farm and Spaldings Farm. The houses represented by groups of finds located round this green probably mark the homes of artisans, with small holdings of land insufficient to support a farmer, who settled on the edge of the established village community in the twelfth or thirteenth centuries. A large collection of material dating from the twelfth to fifteenth centuries found west of Spaldings Farm marks the edge of a medieval trackway that led from Mill Common to Little Swattesfield Hall. Medieval occupation is also evident along Clay Street, on the presumed line of the Roman road

Figure 5.14 *Pilgrim flask used to carry holy water from a shrine visited on pilgrimage and also serving as a tourist trophy, found at Thornham Magna.*

marked by the footpath starting opposite Street Farm to join the modern lane at Ben Hunts Plantation. Here confusing earthworks in the woodland have revealed so far evidence of occupation from Late Saxon to the fifteenth century. A possible early site is also indicated at Oak Farm. Along what is now The Street in Magna it seems that people have moved their houses from plots facing Mill Common to face The Street. It is notable that several of the older houses along The Street were built on Glebe land, so they do not appear on the first map of the estate. We are left to speculate when people first built on these small plots of church land to form the core of the modern village. The estate map of 1765 reveals another green known as Clink Common in the Water Houses area of Thornham Magna where field walking has revealed an area free from medieval occupation except at its edge. The medieval material marks settlement along Water Lane between the crossroads and the river and at the bottom of Clink Common. Such greens are found elsewhere in our immediate area of study, those at Thornham Parva and Stoke Ash being close to the churches. So far we have no evidence for greens in Gislingham, Yaxley or Braiseworth but additional field work might change this picture.

In Stoke Ash the main area of medieval settlement is beside the church and the green where small sections of the original ditch survive. So far evidence of the earliest medieval occupation comes from south of the church, where there is also Saxon material, and on the northern edge of the green where a quantity of lava quern might mark the entrance. There are also surviving moated manorial sites at Stoke Hall and Woodhall in Stoke Ash which survive as the names of farms. The manor of Stoke Hall in Stoke Ash had been given by Robert Malet to Eye Priory and was one of its most valuable properties, but after the Dissolution of the Monasteries it was conveyed in 1536 to Edmund Bedingfield. A branch of this family lived at Coulsey Wood which is another moated site in Stoke Ash, where pottery suggests occupation as early as the thirteenth century. There is an unconfirmed report of a Benedictine monastic cell, possibly a nunnery, at Coulsey Wood in Stoke Ash. There is also a story of a tunnel and of a golden statue in the moat. However the story might be based on the fact that the Benedictine nunnery at Redlingfield was connected with the Bedingfields and was bought back from the king by Sir Edmund Bedingfield at the dissolution. Sir Edmund was an associate of Charles Brandon, Duke of Suffolk. In 1558 Bedingfield sold Stoke Hall to John Parker whose son, also John Parker, sold it in 1596 to Edmund Bokenham of Thornham Hall so that it too was added to the main estate. In 1206 Woodhall was held by Eustace de Gerardville, who was followed by William de Gerardville who granted the advowson, the right to choose the parish priest, to Eye Priory and later the manor was held by Sir John Gerardville. By 1397 it was in the hands of the Poley family who held Badley near Needham Market. It was held by Sir Edmund Poley in 1640 in which year it was transferred to Sir Henry Crofts. It then changed hands fairly rapidly by purchase; in 1646 to Edmund Harvey of Wickham Skeith, in 1705 to William Ellis of Cotton and in 1752 to George Turner. In 1874 it was held by Commander Henry Lewis Round-Turner RN. In 1580 Queen Elizabeth granted the advowson of Stoke Ash to Hutton and Dawes who sold it in 1599 to Henry Bokenham Esq[69] so he became entitled to appoint the rector of Stoke Ash church.

Thornham Magna church appears to have some early work of the later twelfth or early thirteenth century in the nave, but has been enlarged and much altered in the later medieval period. Surviving features include a decorated piscina in the Chancel for washing the holy vessels after communion and stone seats (*sedilia*) for the clergy beneath the south window of the Chancel. Built into the wall on the north side of the chancel arch are the stairs to the Rood Loft which crossed the arch above the screen which was similar to the present one installed in the nineteenth century. The loft ran in front of the beam that carried the great cross with its portrayal of the Crucifixion (the Holy Rood). The nave has a fifteenth-century hammerbeam roof. The church was altered again in the nineteenth century when Victorian features were introduced and some of the original stonework, including gothic tracery and the medieval font, was incorporated in the folly representing a 'hermit's chapel' in the park nearby. This folly, which was rebuilt again in the last decade of the twentieth century, should not be confused with the genuine medieval hermitage. The porch has high quality later medieval stonework and incorporates coats of arms carved on stone shields which appear to be those of the Hemenhale family who, as we have already mentioned, owned property here and in Cotton. The apparent lack of other significant expenditure on the fabric of the Thornham churches in the later Middle Ages might be the result of funds being diverted either to the mother church of the Priory at Eye or to the chapel of Eadburga, whose hermit certainly attracted substantial endowments. In the Middle Ages a road separated the church from the Hall but this was diverted some time after 1765[70] to incorporate the church into the Park. The original road system seems to have enclosed the church and an area of land south of it in a pattern similar to that at Stoke Ash and Thornham Parva. This is one of a number of alterations made in the eighteenth century to thoroughfares that had been used during the Middle Ages and many probably for much longer. There is no doubt these changes increased the privacy of the residents in the Hall, but they closed routes that had been public thoroughfares for many generations.

In the parish of Gislingham, but sitting on its boundary with Thornham Magna, is Swatsfield Hall, a complex site of Middle Saxon origin. As a medieval manorial centre the Hall was enclosed by a system of moats in which the outer court included the orchard. Pottery evidence shows continuous occupation until the Hall was demolished in the nineteenth century. Gislingham has a further six moated sites situated close to Little Green and Rush Green and a large enclosure in Moat-yard Plantation marks the northern boundary of the parish. Map evidence suggests that a missing Great Green might be marked by Green Farm and Green Lane and the unusual curves in the nearby road system, one of which bends sharply beside the relic of a moat, while the southern edge of the green would reach the river. Could the Swatsfield brick works be on the edge of this green? As we move onto the higher clay lands the number of moats increases and we find eight recognisable moats in Burgate.

In Gislingham there was a preceptory, a local manorial centre, of the Knights Templars which supported the work of that military order of Crusaders which was founded in Jerusalem. It is said to have been founded in 1222, and in 1305 Brother Thomas de Stamford was preceptor. They had other preceptories in East Anglia at Dunwich, Horsham St. Faith and Haddiscoe. The Templar order was brought to an end by royal command following an Apostolic Decree in 1312 on charges of heresy instigated by King Phillip IV of France. The property at Gislingham was transferred to the other crusading order, the Knights of St. John of Jerusalem known as the Hospitallers, who held it through their preceptory at Battisford near Stowmarket until the sixteenth century (the Hospitallers also had a house at Carbrooke in Norfolk). It was said to be devastated in 1338 but survived to be dissolved in 1553 when it was granted to John Grene and Robert Hall for three pounds and four shillings.

Traditionally the majority of people living within the territory of a manor owed service to the lord of the manor. Sometimes this could mean they were transferred to a different lordship away from their village community as was the case for a serf living in Mendham. In 1282, when the manor was held from the Earl of Lancaster by Roger de Huntingfield, the latter presented a woman to Bungay Nunnery by a deed saying 'Greetings from Roger de Huntingfield. Know ye all that I demise and concess and by this my charter confirm to God and the Holy Cross church of Bungay and the religious there serving God, Aelgifu wife of Roger Brunman and her son Thomas by him, with all her tenement which was held of me in the town of Medefeud [now Metfield] out of the appurtenances of Mendham in free and pure and perpetual alms. For the welfare of my ancestors' and successors' souls, saving the services to the Lord King of twenty shillings and two pence be it more or less, and that this gift be firmly established by my hand and seal are attached and tested by William de Huntingfield …'. The witnesses included Godfried de Linburn who, in his will, left his holding to the Bungay nuns who in turn gave it back to the parish of Homersfield for the use of the poor and for common grazing, hence the name of Linburn Common. Those owing service to the lord included copyholders, whose right to live as tenants in the property they occupied, generally a farmstead, depended on a copy of the record in the court roll. This only lasted for their lifetime and transfer to their heirs or any other person depended on the approval of the lord. As well as paying rent they owed labour services to their lord, although increasingly this was converted into cash payment, and they were expected to use the manorial mill to grind their grain. Freeholders were absolute owners of their property able to leave it to their heirs or sell it. Some of these freeholders, their rights going back to Domesday and earlier, were farmers but increasing numbers seem to have been skilled artisans. One specialist group were millers who had greater freedom with the introduction of stockmills or windmills. Fragments of lava mill stones, some datable by the style of dressing on the grinding surface, suggest these were being installed on greens. Greens began to appear by the thirteenth century, sometimes being called commons or tyes. In place of the previously open commons we find ditched enclosures, created at a time when the population was growing and good agricultural land was scarce. Constant field walking along the edges of the greens confirms this date and reveals interesting evidence about their origins. Finds suggest that small plots round the edges contained the homes of freeholders who were not reliant on farming for an income but were tradesmen, paying rent to the lord of the manor who still controlled the activities on the enclosed green and imposed restrictions on the occupiers. This is attested by the fines imposed at the manor courts and recorded on the court rolls. A fine could be levied for cutting branches from trees, but greens were used by inhabitants of the parish for collecting fallen wood for their fires, gathering wild berries and grazing permitted livestock. Certain animals were excluded from some greens, and this is particularly well documented for sheep in the reign of Henry VIII. Nobody was allowed to break the soil on the green, but dew ponds were created as shallow depressions in the clay surface where rain water would collect to provide drink for cattle and other animals.

The enclosed areas varied in size from Flixton, the smallest at three acres, to Greshaw Green at South Elmham and Mellis Green, both well over 200 acres. Some were linked by drove ways, easily recognisable by the wide verges that provided grazing for the livestock as they were moved from one green to another. Intercommoning between parishes was introduced by the Bishops of Norwich at Greshaw Green which was used by all the South Elmham parishes (Plate 13) and by the Bigods in the Ilketshalls. Greshaw Green was enclosed in 1853 and its outline is no longer easy to trace. We have found that the small plots of land, often called pightles or closes, around the edge of the green reveal evidence of the trades carried on here. We have already noted the presence of millers, but a find made while field walking on the edge of South Elmham St. Michael's green turned out to be a fragment of a small stone mould used by a metal worker. Sufficient survived to show that the mould was designed for the production of heraldic brasses and this particular example had carried the arms of a family called le Blund. On the southern edge of Greshaw Green a large cutting tool was found that looked like the head of a pike, but in fact with handles on both sides it had been used for cutting animal hide in the production of leather goods. The field name 'Wretting Pits' is evidence of linen weaving because the flax grown in small fields was soaked in these pits to separate the usable fibres from the core of the stem. Converting these into linen cloth was a labour intensive task that would employ a growing population. Potters also started to move in and we find the family of William Sterffe acquiring small areas of land on the edge of the greens at St. James, Chediston and Rumburgh where they produced a very recognisable style of pottery. So the pottery industry we observed in the Waveney Valley during the Roman period was re-introduced and continued throughout the Middle Ages, taking advantage of the presence of suitable clay. A stone mason lived on the edge of All Saints green close to Rumburgh Priory, where he might have found regular employment. Wills attest the presence of carpenters who would leave little visible evidence apart from saw pits dug into their plot, although they might have worked beside the green to produce the complete timber frame of a new house, marking each piece with numerals or symbols to guide assembly on site.

We have noted that wealthy families enclosed their houses with large moats. In the thirteenth century some smaller freeholders and free tradesmen built up enough wealth to create moated enclosures on the edge of the greens. In some cases the green edge ditch itself was widened to form one arm of the moat. These moats, though smaller than those round manor houses, gave their owners a degree of security and marked out the status attached to wealth, as well as providing water for the house on its dry platform. They also provided a breeding area for fish, including shell fish which were a popular food in medieval households. A circular or elongated extension might be added near a corner of the moat to accommodate the fish – fish farming on a small scale. Larger greens, like the 200 acres of Greshaw Green, were used for markets and fairs including animal sales which brought extra income for the lords of the manor. Some of these uses are marked by the names of certain greens and some still provide the setting for fairs or circuses. Lollards preached against the established church at Greshaw Green and one

Figure 5.15 *Evidence of medieval craft activities found in green edge ditches at South Elmham: a large two handed leather cutter with a wide blade, a mould for making heraldic horse brasses, a buckle and a spur.*

Figure 5.16 *Greshaw Green, with the later enclosure hedge planted when the large open space was converted into individual fields.*

Johannes Skylly, miller of Homersfield, was tried for heresy before the Bishop's court at Norwich in 1429. Two from Bungay were tried the following year and this public use of the green for free speech carried a high risk, as the Lollards' Pit close to the Bishop's Bridge in Norwich marks the place where those found guilty of heresy were burnt at the stake. Greens were not always near the church or manor house, but could become the main centre of a separate village community. Greens might also be used for the violent traditional ball game known as camping or accommodate the butts for archery practice before the introduction of gunpowder brought pistol and rifle training. The churchwardens accounts from Metfield record payment to 'John Norton ye Younger for makynge ye butts' in 1551 and three years later John Unketill was appointed for a 'sowgier'. At this time it cost 10d to provide 'two sogers cotes' 16d to make a dagger, 12d for a sword 'gyrdle' and 2d for 'a bowe'. Artillery was mentioned when the Commissioner visited Fressingfield and gunpowder became part of the supplies for soldiers. In 1598 thirty nine shillings was spent in setting forth of soldiers into Ireland. The town arms were taken to Mellis for 'skowring' and the cost of transport was paid. We are reminded of the town armoury still preserved in the church at Mendlesham with items of armour ranging in date from 1470 to 1630, and it is recorded that their villagers were required to parade on Mellis Green in 1627 for military training.

The results of field walking in the Thornham area suggest that there were fewer individual farms than in the densely populated South Elmham area of the Waveney Valley or on the neighbouring high land in Mendlesham parish where Roy Colchester has identified 70 separate medieval sites. This suggests that land use in Thornham was different and we might see this as supporting the view that part of it was maintained as parkland, presumably for the priors of Eye. Although all farmers probably combined cereal growing and animal rearing the predominant agricultural activity is likely to

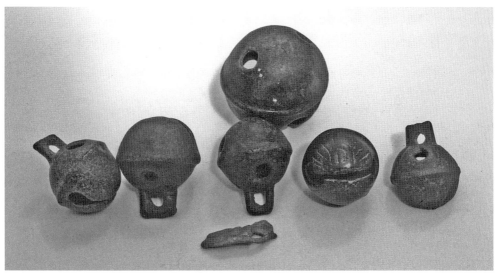

Figure 5.17 *Crotal bells worn by grazing animals, all found at Thornham Magna. They are clear evidence for the presence of many dairy cattle grazing on open grassland.*

have been pasturing livestock, including dairy cattle, and fattening animals for meat which required less labour than intensive arable farming for grain crops. The finding of a number of bells, so called 'crotal bells', of the type worn by grazing animals supports the view that stock grazing and particularly dairy farming was an important aspect of medieval agriculture here. This part of Suffolk was for much of its medieval and more recent history a dairy area producing butter and cheese. We cannot be sure about the park at Thornham, but we do know that William Malet and his successors as Lords of the Honour of Eye maintained a large deer park south of Eye. In the later Middle Ages the Cornwallis family had a park at Brome and Oakley, north of Eye. The holdings of the Bishops of Norwich in the Elmhams included a deer park that extended to 500 acres by 1316. This was situated beside their country seat at St. Margaret and reached the boundary between St. James and Chediston. Its presence is marked by the name of Park Farm. Thirteenth- to fourteenth-century pottery found at the medieval settlement marks the line of the pale or boundary ditch and fence at the south east edge of the park. A triple moated enclosure stood where the parker lived in order to ensure the safety of the deer from poachers. Poaching of deer was a problem for all park owners and the Bishops of Norwich did seek the help of Bury Abbey in combating it. After the Dissolution in 1536, when the Bishop lost these estates, it is documented that Edward, Lord North removed the pale and started the destruction of this park.

Some of the pottery used in Thornham was made in the Waveney valley but other examples came from further afield. Silver coins suggest successful commercial activity. A pilgrim badge is a reminder of the travels of those prepared to visit distant shrines. Part of a rare medieval reliquary was found in 1999 at Thwaite[71] by metal detectors and is now in the British Museum. It is a silver cross about 80 mm long engraved with a figure of the crucified Christ below the hand of God, comparable to eleventh or twelfth century examples from Denmark. The cross had been gilded and traces of niello show that the figure of Christ had been outlined with this black silver paste. It is the upper

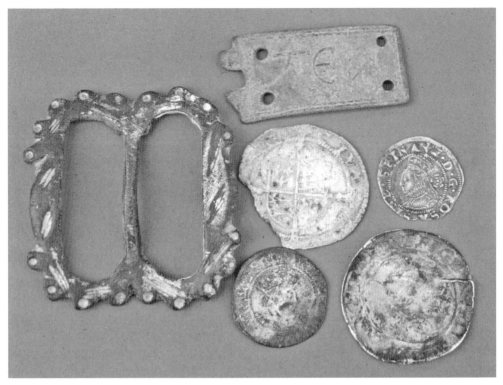

Figure 5.18 *Medieval silver buckle and silver groats found at Homersfield. The silver coins with a nominal value of fourpence and the ornate buckle are evidence of wealth here.*

part of a reliquary that would have held a sacred relic in the lower part attached by a hinge and clasp, with a loop so that the owner could wear it round their neck. The detail highlighted in black niello on the gilded silver background would have made this a very striking pendant. Unfortunately neither the bottom of the reliquary nor the relic have been found. It is always possible that the badge and reliquary had been lost by pilgrims travelling to the chapel of St. Eadburga at Thornham, but if the reliquary did come originally from Scandinavia we might associate it with those who gave Thwaite and Wickam Skeith names derived from a Scandinavian language.

Unusual finds such as this remind us of our area's contacts with the wider world. More mundane collections of medieval pottery show that in the Middle Ages there was a larger group of houses near Thornham Parva church and it was the focal point of a more important settlement than we see today. Although Thornham Magna village spread over a wider area than it does now, its centre probably lies under the houses of the present main street. Further searching for evidence of occupation on the fields and detailed study of manorial records preserved in the County Record Office should reveal more of the medieval history of these villages and their immediate neighbours.

Notes

1 Information from Gilbert Burroughes whose father lived at Mill Farm.
2 Brown, V, 1992 *Eye Priory cartulary and charters,* Woodbridge, no.13 dated *c*1107–1113.

3   Charter Rolls 20 Richard II.4.

4   *PSIAH* **36** (1985) 52 (excavation) and 325 (excursion).

5   Smedley and Owles in *PSIAH* **32** (1970), 1.

6   *PSIAH* **36** (1987), 199.

7   Domesday Book, Suffolk 3.14.

8   Brown, V (ed), 1992 *Eye Priory cartulary and charters,* Woodbridge, no.89 and Lord Francis Hervey (ed) 1925 *The Pinchbeck Register of Bury St.Edmunds*, Oxford, vol. I, 422.

9   Domesday Book for Suffolk 14.127.

10 Brown, V (ed), 1992 *Eye Priory cartulary and charters,* Woodbridge, no.366 and Lord Francis Hervey (ed) 1925 *The Pinchbeck Register of Bury St.Edmunds*, Oxford, vol. I, 421–2.

11 Lord Francis Hervey (ed) 1925 *The Pinchbeck Register of Bury St.Edmunds*, Oxford, vol. II, 334.

12 Brown, V (ed), 1992 *Eye Priory cartulary and charters,* Woodbridge, no.47.

13 Brown, V (ed), 1992 *Eye Priory cartulary and charters,* Woodbridge, no.251 of about 1260.

14 Eye Red Book, B. L. Egerton 3140.

15 Brown, V (ed), 1992 *Eye Priory cartulary and charters,* Woodbridge, no.47 of 1243.

16 Whitelock, D (ed), 1955 *English Historical Documents. c500–1042. Vol.1,* London, no.172 and 173, also Richard Fletcher 'The Conversion of Europe' Harper Collins 1997 p. 207.

17 Whitelock, D (ed), 1955 *English Historical Documents. c500–1042. Vol.1,* London, no.169.

18 See also Newton, S, 2003 *The Reckoning of King Raedwald',* Red Bird Press, 44 and Brewer, D, 1993 *The Origins of Beowulf,* Cambridge, 135n and Whitelock, D, 1972 *Anglo-Saxon England I,* Cambridge, 15n.

19 Vita Sanctorum Aetheldred et Aethelberti Martyrorum et Sanctorum Virginum, Mildryth et Edburgith

20 Scarfe, N, 2002 *The Suffolk Landscape,* (3rd edition) Chichester, 74 and 1986 *Suffolk in the Middle Ages,* Woodbridge, 43.

21 Gelling, M, and Cole, A, 1984 *Place-Names in the Landscape,* Stamford, 211.

22 Brown, V (ed), 1992 *Eye Priory cartulary and charters,* Woodbridge, no.198.

23 Brown, V (ed), 1992 *Eye Priory cartulary and charters,* Woodbridge, nos.197, 194, 195, 192, 191, 183.

24 Brown, V (ed), 1992 *Eye Priory cartulary and charters,* Woodbridge, no.184 dating from the late 1220s.

25 Brown, V (ed), 1992 *Eye Priory cartulary and charters,* Woodbridge, no.187 dated 1226–29.

26 Brown, V (ed), 1992 *Eye Priory cartulary and charters,* Woodbridge, no.188.

27 Brown, V (ed), 1992 *Eye Priory cartulary and charters,* Woodbridge, no.202 dated c 1240.

28 NCC wills, 52 Duke. We are grateful to Peter Northeast for this reference.

29 Said to be in PRO 'List of Lands of the Dissolved Religious Houses' vol. 3 (1964) 247.

30 Notes of Tom Martin, Cullum Collection, SROB: E2/41/9 – 11.

31 No.89 in Harper-Bill, C (ed), 1990 *English Episcopal Acta VI, Norwich 1070–1214.* (see also no. 215).

32 Brown, V (ed), 1992 *Eye Priory cartulary and charters,* Woodbridge, no. 47.

33 Rye, W, 1900 *A Calendar of the Feet of Fines for Suffolk,* SIAH: 53 Henry III no. 59 (1269), 56 Henry III no. 5, 15 Edward I no. 27, 17 Edward I no. 31, 5 Edward III no. 21, 23 Edward III no. 3 (1350).

34 Ekwall, B (ed), 1960 *The Concise Oxford Disctionary of English Place-name,* (4th edition) Oxford, 467.

35 NRO:NCC45 Aleyn, see also Northeast , P (ed), 2001 *Wills of the Archdeaconry of Sudbury 1439–1474,* Suffolk Records Society, note to no. 1014 will of John Wale of Thornham Parva 1454.

36 Details are given in a booklet by the Conservation of Wall Painting Department of the Courtauld Institute of Arts, Somerset House, Strand, London, 2nd ed. 2001.

37 In 2003 by Tobit Curteis.

38 At Christchurch Mansion, Ipswich R. 1951–26.36.

39 PRO:C1/76/30.

40 Salzman, L, 1967 *Building in England down to 1540,* Oxford, Appendix B, Item 97.

41 British Museum OA 7484.

42 MS.Harl.52A49 (Copinger, W, 1904 *Suffolk Records & Manuscripts,* vol. V, 185).

43 Brown, V (ed), 1992 *Eye Priory cartulary and charters,* Woodbridge, no. 195.

44 BL Egerton 3140. 15–16.

45 SROI: S1/2/300/29 and HA116/4861/1 page 57.

46 Sources include Redgrave Rentals of 1433 in BL Add 14850.

47 No. 89 in Harper-Bill, C (ed), 1990 *English Episcopal Acta VI, Norwich 1070–1214*..(see also no. 215).

48 Copinger, W, 1909 *The Manors of Suffolk*, London, vol. 3, 316.

49 Notes of Thomas Martin, Cullum Collection, SROB:E2/41/9, 10 & 11.

50 In the eighteenth century it is 'the manor of Swatshall, Woodhouse & Bresworth'.

51 Northeast, P (ed), 2001 *Wills of the Archdeaconry of Sudbury*, Suffolk Records Society, no.1169 and note.

52 SROB:HD1538/384/1 (from Iveagh collection).

53 John Blatchly refers to his will in his guide to Yaxley Church.

54 Scarfe, N, 2002 *The Suffolk Landscape*, (3rd edition) Chichester, 144.

55 'Dyer, C, 2000 *Everyday Life in Medieval England*, London, 210 quoting SROI:HA12/C2/14.

56 Copinger, W, 1909 *The Manors of Suffolk*, London,, vol 3, p. 316.

57 'Or, on a fesse, between two chevronels Gules, three escallops, Argent.'.

58 Hervey, S (ed), 1906 *Suffolk in 1327*, Suffolk Green Book.

59 Charter Rolls 41 Edward III, 2

60 In the Lay Subsidy of 1327 Thomas Gernonn was the highest payer in Thornham Magna at 6s 6d.

61 Copinger, W, 1909 *The Manors of Suffolk*, London, quoting Bodleian Library – Essex Charters 96: also note Feet of Fines, 15 Edward I no. 27 Richard de Boylaund v Richard de Hecham in Gyselyngham, Fynyngham, Melles, Wywardeston, Cortone and Thornham Pylecok. 1287.

62 Copinger, W, 1909 *The Manors of Suffolk*, London, Gislingham & vol. 3 p. 317.

63 This unusual survival is illustrated inside the back cover of Clive Paine's guide to the church (Gislingham Heritage Trust 2002).

64 IPM 20 Edw. IV, 31.

65 *PSIAH* **16** (1916), 1ff.

66 Paine, C, 1993 *The History of Eye*, Eye, 34 quoting SROI: EE2/M1/6/11, EE2/M1/9/26; EE2/M5/1.

67 SROB:HD1538/384/1 (from Iveagh collection).

68 Court Books 1727–70 and 1649–1917 are SROI:S1/2/18.1 & 3.

69 *PSIAH* **4**, 428

70 See 'A Survey of Thornham Hall . . . in 1765' by T. Skynner: reproduced as the first illustration in Chapter 7 below.

71 Hobbs, R, 2003 *Treasure, finding our past – exhibition catalogue*, London.

Chapter 6

Gentry to a Master of the Revels

The main manor in Thornham Magna was held by the Wiseman family from the fourteenth century when Nicholas Wiseman married the granddaughter of William de Briseworth, whose family name was kept in the title of the manor as 'Swatshall, Woodhouse and Bresworth'. The Wisemans owned large areas of land in this part of Suffolk. The manors held by Nicholas' grandson Simon Wiseman in the 1480s included, as well as Briseworths in Thornham Magna, Swattishaugh (Swatshall) in Gislingham, Thornham Parva (presumably 'Woodhouse'), Bulls Hall in Yaxley, Cranley in Eye and other manors in Wetheringsett (Rokelondes), Old Newton, Sturston, Fritton, Assington, Stanton and Badwell[1]. The Wiseman family certainly had wealthy connections as Simon's son Sir John Wiseman married Elizabeth the daughter of Sir James Hobart. Sir James was Attorney General to Henry VII; he died in 1507 and was buried in Norwich Cathedral. In 1490 he completely rebuilt the large church at Loddon in Norfolk. A painting on show in the church is of special historical interest as it shows Sir James Hobart and his wife and apparently reproduces the east window of the church as it was before destruction by puritans in 1642, as the churchwardens' accounts for that year say 'Laide out to Rochester the glaser defasinge of the images in the church £0 6s 0d' – where the reference to the glazier implies that the images were in glass. A Latin inscription at the bottom of the picture asks us to 'pray for the soul of James Hobart, Knight, who built this parish church of Loddon from the foundations at his own cost, and for Dame Hobart his wife who built the bridge of St. Olaves, together with the road leading to it at her own expense, for the public good.' The picture shows the church and also the bridge. This shows that the Hobarts also rebuilt the important bridge across the Waveney between Norfolk and Suffolk at St. Olaves. Another version of this painting hangs in Blickling Hall which was the later home of the Hobart family although Sir James had lived at Hales Hall near Loddon. Sir James Hobart had a close connection to Thornham as he owned the manor of Rushes and Jennies in Gislingham among his many properties in Norfolk and Suffolk.

The destruction of the window at Loddon is typical of the changes that followed the Reformation of the church in England. The early phase of opposition to the church of Rome had reached the Waveney Valley under the influence of Wycliffe and the Lollards, whose first martyr William Sawtry had been burnt alive at Smithfield in 1401. Lollard preachers were active in the Elmhams and at Bungay and they used a preaching mound on Greshaw Green. In 1428 William White and Hugh Pie who operated Lollard schools in the Waveney Valley were arrested, tried and executed in Norwich. At the same time those faithful to their established churches funded the addition of towers, new windows and side chapels, the latter being used by newly created trade guilds at Metfield, St. Margarets and St. James. Gifts to such works were mentioned in wills as part of the 'saving of souls'. The guilds at St. James and St. Margaret are mentioned in 1362 when Stephen Freeman made a gift to the latter. In 1482 three roods of land were given for the maintenance of a 'Guyeld' called St. John and St. James which also appears in a will of 1546. One is mentioned in 1527 as the 'Boston Guild' but its origin is unknown and we are left to wonder whether it reflects some trading link with the Lincolnshire port or an affinity with St. Botolph who was linked with Boston as well as Iken and Botesdale. There is also a Guild of the Image of St. Thomas. We have more details about the activities of guild members at Metfield who had their own Guildhall where a receipt was given in 1512 for money paid at the Guild. John Spynks made his will in 1490 including a gift to 'Ye Gylde of St. John ye Baptyste'. On 26th December 1556 Thomas Welton was paid for felling and ditching the Guildhall yard where stood the cottage for the clerk of the parish. During the same year as this ditching we are told that Richard Blythe and Thomas Skinner put into the Guildhall a timber chimney and plastered it. Such chimneys must have presented a fire risk but were not uncommon in local buildings. Ovens were another matter and in 1557 they provided 'fifty bryckes for oven at the Gyld hall'. It is notable that two masons are recorded at Flixton and two others in Rumburgh, both parishes having priories that would offer them a major source of income, although we can expect them to have been involved in all the building work at local churches. In the sixteenth century the Reformation and control of the church by Henry VIII brought changes as new bibles, in English, were placed in churches and parish registers were to be kept from 1538. In 1547 orders were given for the removal of images and pictures and whitening of church walls. Every church was to have a pulpit to support the new emphasis on preaching, a poor box to encourage the giving of money for the charitable relief of poverty rather than for building works, and a chest for the safe keeping of the register. The following year the celebration of wakes, church ales and Plough Monday were to cease and the use of holy water was banned as 'superstitious'. By 1550 the stone altars, with their consecration crosses, were ordered to be removed from the east end of churches and to be replaced by communion tables. The brief reign of Mary (1553–1558) saw the restoration of papal authority so the English books were burnt, while altars and rood crosses were restored. The accession of Elizabeth in 1558 reversed all this and it seems convenient that rood screens had been made easy to detach as close study of original examples shows that metal hinges had been fixed to the wall so that the screen could be slotted into place. Many images and fittings were removed before the official destruction and hidden by those who hoped the old order would be restored yet again. Images and elaborate fittings that had survived or been replaced under Charles I were targets of the extreme Protestants of Parliamentarian times so once again they were hidden or destroyed. A perfect example of preservation by concealment is evident at Thornham Parva where the retable is an original medieval screen from Thetford Priory. This had been hidden away and apparently all knowledge of its existence had been lost by the time that it was discovered in a stable in 1927. No doubt many images and paintings were hidden at the time, in the hopes of one day restoring the ancient features to the churches, but were later lost or sold without any knowledge of their true origin. One feature of the fear surrounding the mixture of religion and politics in the seventeenth century was the widespread use of accusations of witchcraft against unpopular individuals. In 1645 all constables were instructed to search for and arrest James More of Metfield who had escaped from Ipswich gaol on 2 October after being indicted for witchcraft and committed to James Rigges, keeper of Ipswich gaol on 9 August. Despite whatever happened to James the More family later returned to prominence in Metfield.

During the Middle Ages and later wealthy men who built up landed estates were never immune from the problems of high infant mortality and the lack of surviving sons to whom to leave their property. When there was no direct male heir great efforts were made by some families to find suitable marriage alliances for their daughters with men who were expected to inherit large estates. This meant the merging of different land holdings, sometimes in distant parts of the country. Often the manor houses of lesser estates were left without a role and might be used to house a managing bailiff or simply became tenanted farmhouses. Generally this meant a reduction in size and sometimes the building was abandoned entirely. Even the greatest local families were not immune from the problem and both the Bigod and de Warrenne families lost their dominance when only daughters were born. The same problems, on a smaller scale, affected the lesser freeholders, while the estate tenants might be left in impoverished circumstances or forced to follow their lords to distant parts.

We see some prosperous farmers acquiring additional land and consolidating their holdings by purchasing property that had been deserted, its buildings left to decay. They took to calling themselves yeomen or husbandmen. Some started to grow carrots and turnips in the Waveney Valley, while others reduced the acres of arable land, creating enclosures for dairy cattle. Increasing numbers of sheep required enclosure of open land for grazing. We find more references to weavers and fullers processing wool, while the inclusion of retting pits in the field names listed in estate surveys are evidence of the important linen industry. We know that flax and hemp were grown on a regular basis throughout the Waveney Valley. An important discovery was made during the renovation of a timber framed barn at Highfields in Withersdale. When the barn was stripped down it became apparent that the upper floor had been used for weaving as there were a series of mullion windows on either side to provide light for the looms. At the southern end was a gantry to lift the raw materials to the upper floor and supply the looms with flax, hemp or wool. Across the road that passed the barn a pond was discovered lined with tiles, some of which were decorated with a double eagle so perhaps removed from Mendham Priory after the Dissolution. This tiled pond would be ideal as a retting pit in which the flax and hemp were immersed in water to soften the fibres, and could also be used by a fuller to finish woollen cloth.

Farming practices varied during and after the Middle Ages. Sometimes more of the land was being managed in large open arable fields, but at other times some of these were converted into smaller closes particularly if more livestock were being kept. We know that in 1306 Flixton Priory had 150 acres of enclosed land and 50 acres unenclosed. An inventory of the priory in 1537 lists the garden lands and precinct, the great garden, inglos croft, church close, plumes field, plumes meadow, high field, cow pasture, pope lees meadow, song close, sheep cote field, horse croft and stock meadow. Tax returns for Metfield mention many enclosed areas such as 'in clauso vocat. Custys' (in the close called Custys), 'eodem per wodardes close' (to the same for Wodards close) and 'mylle close'. In 1391 cows and sheep grazed the enclosed area of the Minster at South Elmham. Changes in land use could mean that bond servants lost their jobs and homes so on occasion there were uprisings or riots, as when damage was done to Richard's woods in Eye. Incidents were reported at Stoke Ash and along the Waveney Valley during the Peasants' Revolt of 1381. During the reign of Edward VI (1547–1553) East Anglia saw a major rebellion led by Robert Kett who was a tanner. The enclosure of common land to provide grazing for more sheep caused resentment among those residents who had traditionally grazed their own stock there without obstruction. Real hardship was caused and some 10,000 protesters gathered together to blockade Norwich, many coming from the Waveney Valley and the Thornham area. They were unsuccessful and Robert Kett himself was hanged. It is interesting to note that use of greens was carefully regulated by many manors. In the fifteenth century a local regulation at Greshaw Green stated 'animals up to two years old only allowed to graze on the green' and by the end of the century no sheep at all were allowed to graze on the green. In manorial court records at Metfield we read that in April 1589 Joseph Watson was presented for digging a clay pit on Metfield Green, and paid a fine of three shillings and seven pence. On 7 May 1622 William Welton was presented for cutting down a great ash tree growing upon Metfield Green, being the free tenement of the lord of the manor, without licence from the lord of the manor and paid in court 15 shillings.

In 1524 when Sir John Wiseman, knight, had to pay the subsidy, a tax granted by Parliament to the King, he was assessed on lands at Thornham worth the substantial sum of £20 a year. The priest who had the clerical title of 'Sir' William Wiseman held lands worth £2 per year which were taxed as his own property rather than that of the church. Sir John also had three servants and Sir William one servant, all four being taxed on an income of £1. 6s. 8d. each. This marks them out as reasonably wealthy, although not on the same scale as the neighbouring Cornwallis family who were assessed on lands worth £90 per year. According to the records of the Star Chamber Court during the reign of Henry VIII Sir John Wyseman, knight, and Sir William Wyseman, parson of Great Thornham, were the subject of a complaint about tithe corn by Thomas Tyrrell, parson of Gislingham where he was recorded as parson in 1539. Apparently this was not an isolated incident as there were also complaints to the Star Chamber about an affray at Swatteshall and Thornham between Wiseman and Tyrrell[2]. Thomas Tyrrell might well have been a member of the Tyrrell family of Gipping, one of whom inherited the Thornham estate in the eighteenth century.

The manor remained in the hands of the Wiseman family, who added more properties in the area. In doing so they presumably took advantage of the opportunities offered by the suppression of Eye Priory in 1537. For example we have seen (Chap. 5) that from 1537 Thomas Wiseman, Sir John's son, leased the 16 acres of Priors Wood and the adjoining 'St Arboroughe Chappell' with another acre of wood. Another note in Tom Martin's papers records that in 1731 Mr Killigrew, who then owned the Thornham Hall estate, held Chappell Yard, Chappell Fold and Chappell Close in Little Thornham by copyhold from 'Eye Hall alias Eye Priory Manor'. These had presumably been part of the property belonging to the chapel of St. Eadburga which had become

Figure 6.1 *Medieval pillars of Eye Priory. Little survives of the extensive monastic buildings and the remaining evidence is now incorporated in the building and garden of a private house. They do show that it was a very substantial group of buildings.*

incorporated in the holdings of Eye Priory and might have formed the basis for the later Chapel Farm in Thornham Parva. Stones incorporated in the walls of buildings at Chapel Farm may have come from a barn belonging to the chapel as stone is rarely used in secular buildings in this area. A map of Mellis[3] shows a Chapel Field on the border with Thornham Parva and east of Cowpasture Lane.

After Thomas' son John Wiseman died, possibly in 1555[4], his wife Eleanor appeared as a plaintiff in the Chancery Court[5], being the guardian of Edmund (should this be Edward?) Wiseman son and heir of John Wyseman against Charles Wyseman regarding lands in Thornham Magna and Parva, Stoke (Ash) and Wetheringfield (?Wetheringsett) which had belonged to Thomas Wyseman (? died in 1544), the deceased father of John and Charles. Presumably Charles claimed all or part of his father's estate against his nephew, who had not yet come of age. No doubt the dispute cost the family a significant sum in legal costs.

As we have seen, the rector of Thornham Magna was William Wiseman so the family had secured the living of the larger church, although the right of presentation was still in the hands of Eye Priory. In 1535[6] William was paying four shillings to the Prior of Eye, while the glebe was valued at 30 shillings and the tithes at £6. 15s. 2d. After the suppression of the priory in 1537 the advowson of Thornham Magna, that is the right to present the rector of the church, was first recorded as being exercised in 1559 by Anthony Rushe and his wife Eleanor and by Anthony Rush in 1561 and 1573. Was Eleanor the wife of Anthony Rushe the widowed Eleanor Wiseman who had appealed to the Chancery Court on behalf of her son? If so, presumably the Rushes exercised the advowson of the church and administered the estate during the minority of Eleanor's children. Anthony Rushe of Thornham appears later in the Chancery records as defendant in a claim by J. Forde of Horkesley that he refused to complete the sale of a property in Essex[7]. Edmund Wiseman might have died in 1561 if he is the Edmund Wiseman of Suffolk who appears in the Register of Inquisitions Post Mortem, although there is a second entry for 1563[8]. In 1596 the advowson was held by Edmund Bokenham, who had married Barbara Wiseman and, although exercised by the Crown in 1599, it remained in the family who owned the Thornham estate being held by Edmund's son, Sir Henry Bokenham in 1601 and by his son Wiseman Bokenham in 1641[9].

In 1535 the rector of Thornham Parva, John Coundell, was paying five shillings to the Prior of Eye and his glebe was valued at 39 shillings and 8 pence, but his tithes were only 46 shillings and 1 penny (£2. 6s. 1d.). The nineteenth-century Tithe Apportionment[10] reveals that one small area of glebe in Thornham Parva belonged to Burgate, Gislingham, Mellis and Yaxley. David Dymond[11] suggests such situations probably result from a single benefactor leaving land as an endowment to be divided between different churches, which presumably shared the income equally between themselves.

If Anthony Rushe was exercising the advowson in 1561 and 1573 as guardian of the Wiseman children, Edward (?Edmund) Wiseman had not come of age before he died in 1561. Then the property went to his sister Barbara Wiseman who married Edmund Buckenham (or Bokenham) of Thelnetham. Once again the family were involved with the Chancery Court. We find the magnificently named Philologus[12] Forthe as plaintiff against Edmund Buckenham over the partition of property. Forthe had married Mary Wiseman, Barbara's sister, and their father had left the property in Thornham, to his daughters Barbara and Mary (as coparceners)[13]. There is also reference to properties belonging to manors of Brockford and Stoke Ash being claimed by Edmund. Whatever arguments there might have been, the ultimate position was that the Bokenhams became the owners of the estate.

About this time the hall was built in the form shown in a seventeenth-century painting[14] (Plate 15). This shows a brick house of typical sixteenth-century design; being E-shaped with a central porch two stories high surmounted by a large sundial and ornamental pinnacles with wind vanes. A structure in the eastern corner with windows on all three floors and an apparent cellar window might have housed the main staircase A stretch of water in which swans swim across the front of the picture suggests a wide moat. Queen Elizabeth is said to have stayed here during one of her regular journeys round the country staying with local landowners. However the known records of her travels do not support this story and Clive Paine, who has looked closely at such royal visits to Suffolk, says that in many cases stories that 'the queen stayed here' are based on visits by 'Mary, the French Queen' that is Mary Tudor sister of Henry VIII, dowager Queen of France who married Charles Brandon, Duke of Suffolk. From 1514 to 1538 Brandon was lord of the Honour of Eye, including a large house at Westhorpe, so was often at Eye. We can certainly accept that Mary Tudor is likely to have visited Thornham. In fact Charles Brandon himself had acquired land at Thornham as part of the property of Eye Priory, which he purchased from the king when the priory was dissolved but he sold all his extensive Suffolk properties to the king in 1538. It appears to have been part of a royal scheme to move Brandon from East Anglia to newly acquired properties in Lincolnshire, leaving the Howard Dukes of Norfolk as the most powerful nobility in East Anglia. By 1592 this Thornham property is recorded as being in the possession of Sir Nicholas Bacon of Redgrave, presumably the son and heir of the Lord Keeper, Sir Nicholas Bacon, who had died in 1579, but was held by John Athowe and Henry Beck in 1597.

Presumably at some stage Edmund Bokenham acquired this property in the Thornhams that had been held by Eye Priory but how and when is not apparent, as Copinger finds no reference after the grant to John Athowe and Henry Becke in 1597. It is said that in 1596 Edmund Bokenham bought Stoke Hall Manor in Stoke Ash from John Parker. Until the dissolution of the monasteries this had been part of the property of Eye Priory[15]. However another version (PSIAH IV, 417) records that Stoke Hall was acquired in or after 1574 from John Parker by John Bokenham Esq. of Thornham, the father of Edmund to whom it passed on John's death in 1609, but this might refer to a different holding, otherwise unknown, called Stoke Ash with Thorpe.

In the adjoining parish of Braiseworth the Subsidy Return for 1568 (Green Book) reveals the presence of one remarkably wealthy character as Alexander Newton was assessed on the unusually high figure of £70 in lands. He apparently held both the recorded manors of Old Hall and New Hall in Braiseworth and was married to Anne, daughter of Sir Humphrey Wingfield. Sir Humphrey, who died in 1545, was a successful lawyer with a large house in Ipswich which later became the Tankard Inn, from which part of a magnificent panelled room is preserved in Christchurch Mansion: he was custos rotulorum for Suffolk and Member of Parliament for Ipswich in 1523. Alexander Newton, who died in 1569[16], was one of those dismissed from his position as a Justice of the Peace at the beginning of Queen Mary's reign in 1553[17] along with his brother in law Robert Wingfield of Brantham. He was not favoured by the catholic faction in the county, as he had been appointed under the protestant king Edward VI in 1550. This seems to be an exceptional period when the parish had an important resident landowner. In the fourteenth century[18] Braiseworth had been divided between Sir George Thorpe at Old Hall and William Parker at New Hall, and later belonged to members of the Felbrigg, Tyndale and Playters families[19] although it is not clear if they were resident here. In the eighteenth and nineteenth century it became part of the holdings of the Cornwallis family and later the Kerrisons. The Cornwallis family built up considerable holdings in Suffolk from the fifteenth century. David Allen[20] has noted that in 1547 Sir Thomas Cornwallis, who was a supporter of Queen Mary still prospered under Elizabeth I. He rebuilt Brome Hall as his main residence and acquired the manor of Ampners in Thrandeston which had been held by the Almoner of Norwich Cathedral Priory of Holy Trinity (Ampners being a corruption of Almoner's) since at least the thirteenth century. A charter of 1373 by the Bishop of Norwich forbade the Archdeacon of Sudbury, the Dean of Hartismere, the Vicar of Yaxley and the chaplains of Yaxley and Thrandeston to punish crimes of the tenants of the Prior of Hoxne, then a cell of Holy Trinity, and the Almoner of Norwich in Yaxley and Thrandeston because all manors of the Prior and convent of the Holy Trinity were exempt from their jurisdiction. This manor of Ampners also had land in Thornham Parva, Mellis, Yaxley and Stoke Ash.

Presumably the Hoxne Priory holdings in Yaxley and Thrandeston descended from those held by the Bishop in Domesday Book, of which one carucate as a manor then belonged to the church of Hoxne[21].

We have seen in the last chapter that evidence from field walking shows throughout the Waveney Valley in the twelfth and thirteenth centuries a steady rise in new tenements, whereas at Thornham many of the early sites seem to have gone out of use, perhaps affected by the growth of the town of Eye. In all areas some properties were lost to fire. The typical open hall building with the fire always burning on the hearth in the centre of the main room must have posed a high fire risk. Most houses had a thatched roof vulnerable to sparks and walls of wattle and daub, all of which might be consumed once fire took hold. This was certainly the case at the Manor House of Withersdale where charred remains of the original house were discovered during excavation of the moated enclosure. It also happened at Metfield Hall at a much later date. Here documentary evidence indicates that during the rebuilding of the house the carpenters were instructed to re-use any of the timbers that were not too badly damaged. Another field at Metfield shows the repeated rebuilding of the house on slightly different spots. Occupation material was recovered from each corner of the field showing each site being used for about a century after the original building, dated by a silver coin of King John's reign, was lost possibly destroyed by a fire. The last new building here was constructed by the end of the sixteenth or early in the seventeenth century, after which a much more substantial house built in the adjoining field has survived to this day. The greater use of brick chimneys from the sixteenth century reduced the risk of fire but thatch remained vulnerable, and simple walls of wattle and daub or clay lump only have a long life, as some do, if their footings are well drained and the roof is kept weather proof. Buildings large and small can disappear leaving surprisingly little trace, particularly if re-usable materials were salvaged for use elsewhere. Throughout the sixteenth and seventeenth centuries changes were made to houses as in some cases new buildings replaced the old ones and in others extensions were added to the existing structure. Oak Farm at Metfield is one of the oldest buildings in the parish, still standing in its moated enclosure on the edge of Metfield Common. During its restoration the post holes of its original thirteenth century open hall house were exposed in the compacted clay floor. This building was widened during the fourteenth century and a solar added on an upper floor. Slowly alterations took place and by the fifteenth century an additional extension was built, and on its join a queen post was introduced into the roof as a support. This gives us some evidence of the wealth of the occupants. Unfortunately very few of the carpenters' marks survive in the roof structure. By the sixteenth century the well, that had originally been outside the building, was encased by a new extension, and at this time a back-house was added. This is a lean-to building which gave access to the newly constructed ovens that were fuelled by wood, as the stoke house was placed outside the building with the ovens opening to the inside. Stoking these fires each day to provide the heat needed to bake the daily bread was a task for the back-house boy. Throughout the elongated building the floors reflect the different periods of construction. They vary from compacted clay to paving to pamments and, in the final extension, plank flooring. This eastern end of the building had a small storage cellar which was entered from outside. At the Four Horseshoes in Thornham Magna extensions have been made to the original building of the fifteenth century so that the well, which was originally outside, is now situated in the centre of the restaurant towards the eastern end of the present building. Other properties that can be seen to be built in the fifteenth century style include Stoke Hall and the Rectory at Stoke Ash.

The fourteenth century was a time of change and sometimes violent disruption. In the Waveney Valley we see the creation of some seventy new households but 36 farms were lost. There were disastrous famines in 1314 and 1321 which increased the likelihood that children would die before reaching the age of 20. The great plague known as the Black Death struck in 1348 and reduced the population throughout Britain, with reports of particularly severe impact on Norwich and Yarmouth. Plague struck again in 1361 and 1369. The reduced population and disruption to production led to a shortage of labour and rising prices for basic goods. In 1351 the Statute of Labourers was introduced by Act of Parliament in an attempt to limit the wages for labourers and artisans, but it inhibited the mobility of those seeking work and tried to keep them subject to manorial discipline imposed locally by the use of stocks, whipping posts and gallows. After the attempt to impose a Poll Tax levied on every adult person regardless of income, frustration broke out in the Peasants' Revolt of 1381 when lesser gentry led the labourers in violent protest against the land owning nobility, destroying manorial records and attacking local centres of administration. One of those most determined in putting down the revolt was Henry Despenser, Bishop of Norwich, who ordered the execution of many rebels. Nevertheless this was a stage in the weakening of manorial control in many areas, which is already suggested by the occupations of some of those listed as liable to tax in the returns for 1327. When we come to the lists of taxpayers in 1500 and 1524 we find more freeholders and artisans, including labourers, who were in a position to make wills and pay taxes. They no longer gave service on the lands of the manor, could appoint deputies to serve on their behalf in times of conflict, and were able to pass on their tenements to male heirs.

The Dissolution of the Monasteries in the sixteenth century meant the end of their great estates which had been removed from lay control and placed 'for ever' in the hands of the religious communities owing ultimate allegiance to the Pope in Rome. Cardinal Wolsey had started this process in 1528 when he obtained a Papal Bull from Pope Clement VIII to suppress a number of smaller monasteries, including Flixton Priory, and use the proceeds from selling their property to fund his school at Ipswich and his college at Oxford. After Henry VIII declared himself head of the church in England he seized all the monastic property and sold, or in some cases gave, most of it to noblemen, existing gentry and rising merchants who aspired to become land owners on a grand scale. At South Elmham after the Dissolution of the Monasteries in 1536 the estates of the Bishop of Norwich were included in those surrendered to King Henry VIII in return for the estates of the Abbey of St. Benet. Henry made the abbot of St. Benet's, William Reppes or Rugge, the new Bishop of Norwich and for many years afterwards the Bishop of Norwich sat in the House of Lords not as diocesan bishop but as Abbot of St. Benet's, the only abbot in England to retain the title. The king transferred the diocesan estates into private hands and it is documented that as the new owner of South Elmham Hall Edward, Lord North started the destruction of the park by removing its pale. Later it passed to the Adair family. The Adairs also acquired the estates of Flixton Priory which had been obtained by John Tasburgh after its suppression by Cardinal Wolsey in 1528.

John Tasburgh[22] had been involved in the commercial life of Norwich when, on 5 January 1445, John Toll made over to him his manor house at South Elmham St. Peter. By 1509 his son, also John, had properties in Norwich, London and Flixton and was living in the manor house of St. Peter. When Cardinal Wolsey suppressed Flixton Priory John Tasburgh, the third of that name, purchased the priory buildings and transferred many of its architectural features to his house at St. Peters where in the summer of 1539 he employed a team of Norwich stone masons. Much of the stone work he transferred from the priory can still be seen in the south wall of the house which overlooks the moat. In 1544 he acquired the lands of the priory. He lies buried in the church yard of St. Peters towards the west end, under the steeple. The family constructed almshouses in the parish but unfortunately no trace of these remains. By 1600 the Tasburghs had purchased land at Ilketshall St. Andrew, Bungay and the manor of Boyse Hall in Flixton. In 1607 Sir John Tasburgh, who was knighted by King James, bought a further 500 acres of land at Flixton with five messuages (houses), a capital mansion house and a heronry from his cousin, Thomas Bateman. He created a new deer park here in 1611, removing the five tenements from his parkland, although traces of them were found during field walking and aerial photographs show their position, with the enclosures of three of them marked by what appear to be small moats. Flixton Hall itself was enlarged and improved between 1611 and 1628. In 1619 the household included a coachman, a kitchen boy, a foot boy and a cook named Lucas. He purchased the remaining manorial

Figure 6.2 *St Peter's Hall, showing the moat. The house incorporates much medieval stonework brought from Flixton Priory. An instance of recycled building materials.*

Figure 6.3 *An aerial photograph of Flixton taken by Bob Carr. It is possible to see the evidence of buildings enclosures cleared away to create Tasburgh's park.*

land of South Elmham from the Norths for £3490, but the parkland of St. James had already been sold in 1604 to John Lawrence who was resident in that parish. Later generations of the family became Roman Catholics and the costs of their recusancy led to financial problems. At the time of the popish plot of Titus Oates in 1678 Richard Tasburgh and his wife Margery being known Roman Catholics were imprisoned and tried for complicity but were acquitted. The last male heir of the Tasburgh family died in 1736 and the estate passed, through the marriage of the younger daughter Lettice, to John Wyborne and was sold eventually to the Adair family. A fire on 12 December 1846 destroyed most of the house built by the Tasburghs, but the semi-circular dovecote of red brick survived. It has an octagonal cupola with revolving ladder and revolving platform within.

Returning to the owners of Thornham itself, Edmund Bokenham was high sheriff of Suffolk in 1605 and died in 1618. He and his wife Barbara, the daughter of John

Figure 6.4 *Sixteenth-century work at Flixton Hall, including the dovecote. The young rock doves, called "squabs", were a luxury food of the wealthy.*

Wiseman, are recorded on one of the four ledger stones in the floor at the east end of Thornham Magna church[23] that record members of the Bokenham family. He was succeeded by his son Sir Henry Bokenham, knight, who was high sheriff of Suffolk in 1630; he died in 1648 and is recorded, with his wife Dorothy, the daughter of Guilford Walsingham, by a monument in the church at Thelnetham, his father's home parish. Pevsner describes this monument as two demi-figures in an arched niche, with books and a skull. There are looped up curtains left and right, and in the 'predella' are the son and daughter small, frontal in oval niches; 'The quality of the monument is poor'. The daughter was presumably Timothea who is named on another ledger slab in Thornham Magna church as having died in 1630 aged 24, being the wife of Francis Gardiner of Essex. Henry's son Wiseman Bokenham was high sheriff of Suffolk in 1649, marking the third successive generation of the family to hold this office. He died in 1670 aged 68 and was buried in Thornham Magna church where his tomb is marked by a ledger stone beside that of his wife Grace, the daughter of Paul d'Ewes. She had died a year before in 1669. Their daughter Dorothy was buried here in August 1654 and a son Henry in 1666 having died at the age of 40. The hall was assessed as having 17 hearths (fireplaces) in 1674 and was in the ownership of 'Cpt.' Bokenham, presumably Wiseman's son Paul. This conclusion is supported by Paul's will of 1677[24] in which he asked to be buried at Little Thornham with a gravestone inscribed in Latin 'Here lyeth the body of Captain

Paul Bokenham Standard Bearer unto the Great Duke, his Royal Highness the Duke of York in Anno Domini 1662'. James Duke of York was the brother of Charles II and became king as James II. Another four hearths were attributed to a Mr. Bokenham who might be the Richard whom Paul calls 'my loveing brother'. Apparently relations with his father had been less happy as his will continues 'An unnatural father giving away from me a great part of my estate caused grief in law which cost me near 600 pounds and am thereby indebted'. Paul's wife Frances was the daughter of Robert Bacon of Redgrave Hall. He is said to have been the son of Sir Robert Bacon of Redgrave Hall, so presumably he was descended from the Lord Keeper, Sir Nicholas Bacon of Redgrave. This shows connections with one of the wealthiest families in the county. Perhaps Paul Bokenham's contacts at the royal court when he was standard bearer introduced his family to Charles Killigrew who was to marry his daughter (Plate 14). Charles II is said to have stayed at the Hall, but there seems no firm evidence for this. Nor is there any indication as to whether it was part of his travels from Newmarket in October 1668 when he visited Viscount Hereford at Christchurch Mansion in Ipswich and inspected the coastal defences of Landguard Fort at Felixstowe. It was perhaps at this time that the king's travels in Suffolk took him past Flixton Hall, then the home of the Tasburgh family, which he admired and on being told it belonged to 'a popish dog' the king replied 'but the dog has a very beautiful kennel'. It is intriguing to note that a group of seven oaks trees a short distance from Thornham Hall on the edge of the open parkland, near the start of the modern Walks, frames an area of level ground reminiscent of the bowling green at Christchurch Mansion on which King Charles is said to have played during his visit.

Paul Bokenham died in 1681 leaving two infant children of whom the boy Guilford Bokenham died in the same year. In fact a memorial set up in Thornham Parva church by Paul's surviving brother Richard in 1685, apparently ignoring the request in Paul's will, recorded that Paul, his wife Frances and their son Guilford died in the same year of 1681. Their daughter Jemima, who inherited the estate, was described as the niece of Richard Bokenham mercer of London in 1687 when she married Charles Killigrew (1655–1725). He was a significant figure in royal circles having taken over the theatrical role of his father Thomas (1612–83) who was Master of the Revels to Charles II from 1673. He had been granted a patent to form a company of players and erect a playhouse in London at the Restoration in 1660 and was responsible for the revival of the theatre which had suffered from the puritanical disapproval of Cromwell's government. He features in the diaries of Samuel Pepys as manager of the Theatre Royal and Groom of the Bedchamber. Pepys notes his love of Italian music. Thomas had supported the king during the Civil War and went into exile with Charles II, so Charles was born at Maastricht in Holland in 1655. Thomas' elder brother, Sir William Killigrew, was also a courtier being knighted in 1626. Portraits of Sir William and his wife, Mary Hill, were painted in 1638 by the court painter Sir Anthony van Dyck and are now displayed in Tate Britain. He commanded a troop in the King's army during the Civil War and either because of his royalist connections or through a failed drainage scheme in the Fens he lost the family property in Lincolnshire after the Civil War. He was reinstated by Charles II after the Restoration and became a gentleman usher of the Privy Chamber. He too wrote plays. It no doubt helped the family fortunes that his sister Elizabeth

Killigrew, Lady Shannon, was a mistress of Charles II, by whom she had a daughter. His brother Henry was Master of the Savoy Hospital in London and Charles himself was to be buried at the Savoy on 8th January 1724–5.

The Civil War between the King and Parliament created many divided loyalties. Although Suffolk was largely seen as supporting the Parliamentary side, there were many in the Thornham and Waveney Valley areas who could be identified in 1642 as Royalists or 'Cavaliers'. When a levy was raised for the King in that year it was reported that Thomas Jermy Esquire of Metfield gave £20 and Lord Richard Baxter Gent. gave £30, although in fact Jermy was one of those who supported both sides during the course of the war! In June 1643 an order was received from the local Parliamentary committee, meeting at Cambridge, to raise a levy to maintain the Parliamentary forces of the Earl of Manchester for four months from January 1643 and the local representative, James Hubbarde of Mendham, raised £388. A further order was issued for £600, or 600 men, from the County of Suffolk. In 1644 William Dowsing, whose family came from Laxfield, was appointed Parliamentary Visitor to remove or deface 'superstitious' pictures and inscriptions in churches. His journal includes 'Item 146. To Metfield on August 30th. In the church was Peter's keys, and the Jesuits badge in the windows, and many on top of the roof. J for Jesus, H for Hominum, S for Salvator [Jesus Saviour of Men] and a Dove for the Holy Ghost in wood, and the like in the chancel, and the steps to be levelled by September 7th. Mr Jermin, the gentleman in the town, refused to take the inscription. As the churchwarden informed whose name is …'. He ordered the destruction of the Peter's keys and the Jesuit badges in the windows and the removal of brass memorial inscriptions and ordered that the steps up to the chancel be levelled. On the day he visited Metfield he also went to Hoxne, Eye, Occold and Rishangles.

The marriage of Jemima Bokenham to Charles Killigrew in 1687 brought to Thornham a character who was important at the royal court and gave Somerset House as his London address. Charles became a gentleman of the Privy Chamber to Charles II in 1670 when he was only 15 years old, Master of the Revels in 1680 and two years later was patentee of the Theatre Royal, Drury Lane which had been founded by his father. He was a friend of the poet and dramatist John Dryden. The Killigrew family originated from Falmouth in Cornwall[25]. They claimed to be descended from Richard Earl of Cornwall (1209–1272) the brother of King Henry III. Richard was remarkable for being elected Romanorum Rex, 'King of the Romans' in 1256, which entitled him to be crowned by the pope in Rome as Holy Roman Emperor, but the coronation never took place. However he was the only Englishman to come so close to the title of Holy Roman Emperor, who was seen in theory as the successor to Charlemagne ruling over Christian Europe. A brother of Charles Killigrew is recorded in Thornham Magna church as 'Robert Killigrew of Arwenack in Cornwall, son of Thomas and Charlotte, a Page of Honour to Charles II'. He held the rank of 2nd Brigadier General of Queen Anne's forces and was killed in 1707 in Spain at the battle of Almanza. In this battle during the War of the Spanish Succession (1701–1714) the army of the Grand Alliance, including English and Dutch forces, was defeated by the French and Spanish army commanded by the Duke of Berwick, a natural son of James II by Arabella Churchill sister of the Duke of Marlborough. Berwick was a marshal of France and by this victory established Philip V as King of Spain, contrary to English wishes. The list of paintings

Figure 6.5 *This painting shows Thornham Hall as it was early in the eighteenth century.*

in Thornham Hall in 1896[26] includes one of 'Robert Killigrew who was killed in Spain'. There were also two portraits with the Killigrew coat of arms, one of a lady and the other of a gentleman. Also of this period and possibly inherited from the Killigrews are two paintings of ladies by Sir Peter Lely (1618–1680) who was the leading court painter of the Restoration. There was also a circular panel painting of Thomas Killigrew. There were portraits of King Charles II and of Nell Gwynne which are most likely to have come from the Killigrews but were retained by the Hennikers when they added their own family portraits to hang in various rooms of the Hall.

An early eighteenth-century painting[27] shows that the Hall had been significantly altered in the late seventeenth century, probably by Paul Bokenham just before his death in 1681 as in his will he referred to his 'new house'. The tall central porch with conspicuous sundial was replaced by a straight front with a bell tower and large clock rising from the centre of the roof; tall windows were arranged symmetrically in relation to a central pillared doorway[28]. On either side of the front court were rectangular pools which may have been created from the moat; there was a walled flower garden with espaliered fruit trees to one side of the house and a walled plantation of trees on the other. Deer roamed in the park in the foreground of the picture outside the wall and railings that enclosed the front court with its curving carriage drive and central statue. This was the house to which Charles Killigrew moved on his marriage. His son, also called Charles, died a bachelor in 1756 and was somewhat eccentric as we are told that 'Mr. Killigrew was in the habit of making wills frequently, and every will appointed a different heir: he died suddenly and had sent a few days before to his lawyer to make another will'. His will included a bequest to Elizabeth Hailstone, born at Thornham in 1739, who was probably his illegitimate daughter, and he left the stewardship of his manor courts for life to his friend Thomas Martin of Palgrave, the great East Anglian antiquary[29]. He left the manor to his kinsman and godson Rev. Charles Tyrrell, a member of the Tyrrell family of Gipping near Stowmarket. Presumably the kinship was through his mother's family as in his will of 1677 Paul Bokenham had referred to his brother in law Edmund Tyrrell of Gipping. It was in Tyrrell's name as 'Charles Tyrrell Gentleman', the manorial court was still held on 4th January 1764[30], but he must have sold it soon afterwards to Sir John Major for whom a map of the Thornham Hall property was produced in 1765 by T. Skynner. Sir John Major had come from Bridlington in Yorkshire but already owned Worlingworth Hall in Suffolk and had been High Sheriff of the county in 1754.

149

In 1770 Sir John Major was holding his manor court in person 'at the House of Nicholas Goddard at the sign of the White Horse in the parish of Stoke Ash'.

When the Worlingworth estates were added to those already belonging to Thornham a very large area of countryside came into this one ownership. From this time Thornham Hall was frequently referred to as 'Major House'.

The estate map of 1765 shows farm buildings in several of the locations still used in the nineteenth century and we might suppose that these had for long been the sites of major farms on the estate. However it is interesting to note that most of the established timber framed houses along the Street, on either side of the free flowing stream, do not appear on this map. They were not built on estate land but on areas of Glebe land that belonged to the church and presumably provided the church with a healthy income from rents that could be applied to charitable or ecclesiastical purposes. This would be additional to the church's income from tithes. It meant that many local residents were not tenants of the lord of the manor but of the church. This was clearly the position before Major acquired the estate but there is no obvious explanation for the origin of the arrangement.

Meanwhile another branch of the Bokenham family had been here. Henry Bokenham had purchased the advowson of Stoke Ash church long before he inherited the Thornham estate from his father. It was treated separately from the estate as after the death of Wiseman Bokenham in 1670 it passed to Hugh Bokenham, whose position in the family is unknown but he was described as 'of the city of Norwich'. After him it passed to Walsingham Bokenham by 1710 and by 1729 it was held by Thomas Tyrell Bokenham. The use of the Tyrell name is interesting as it suggests this branch of the family also recognised the link between the Bokenhams and the Tyrells. As the family had kept the right to choose the rector of Stoke Ash and Thornham Parva parishes, when Henry Watts resigned as rector in 1712 it was Walsingham Bokenham of Hethersett in Norfolk who presented Joseph Bokenham (1688–1728)[32], presumably a relative, to the two churches. Joseph was already curate to Henry Watts at Stoke Ash but had started life as the eldest son of a Norwich weaver, going to Gonville and Caius College Cambridge as

Figure 6.6 *Glass label of 1741 from a wine bottle, found at South Elmham. This has survived where no paper label would last for long.*

a poor scholar and becoming a fellow of the college. He had married Bridget Gardiner[33] the daughter of a local gentleman and they christened a daughter Dorothy in 1721. Bridget married William Parke of Stoke Ash in 1730. Joseph was an antiquarian who built up a heraldic collection of over 1200 Norfolk coats of arms which is now in the British Library[34] and 730 Suffolk coats of arms. His Miscellaneous Papers, including topographical writings, are in Cambridge University Library[35]. It has been suggested[36] that Joseph put together a collection of early topographical drawings including one of St. Mary's Church, Walton signed Joh. Bokenham. One of these drawings is of Walton Castle signed by John Sheppard and dated 1623; so it is interesting to see that one of Sheppard's descendants John Sheppard of Ash High House Campsey Ash had property interests in Thornham in 1822[37] but these were probably of long standing as the John Sheppard (died in 1669) to whom the drawing is attributed came from Mendlesham. It might have been through this local connection with the family that Joseph gained access to the Walton Castle drawing.

If we can rely on the Hearth Tax returns of 1674 there were some 37 households in Thornham Magna, with 24 paying the tax and 13 'certified' as non-payers because they were too poor to pay. Thornham Parva had 18 households, of which 7 were taxpayers and 11 were described as 'poor that receive collection' because they were supported from the poor rates. The largest house in Parva with seven hearths was that of a Mr. Bruninge, but the village seems to have been very much the poor relation.

Thornham would have benefited from being served by the main road, originally

Figure 6.7 *The tollgate house on the A140 turnpike road in Braiseworth parish operated when there was far less traffic than streams past it today.*

constructed in Roman times, from Colchester to Norwich which presumably survived because of its solid base through the Middle Ages when lesser roads suffered from lack of maintenance which was left to local communities, so largely neglected. The main road itself was improved by a Turnpike Trust created in 1711. The trustees were authorised to make up and repair the road in return for charging traffic tolls which were collected at toll gates. Presumably this was the origin of 'The Tollgate House' on the A140 in Braiseworth parish close to the boundary of Thornham Magna with Parva, at the northern end of the former curving deviation. When traffic permits it is possible to see the window through which tolls could be collected. The maintenance of other roads remained the responsibility of individual parishes, each of which was obliged under an Act of Parliament of 1555 to appoint two parishioners as highway surveyors who had to inspect roads and bridges while the wealthier landowners were required to provide labour for repairs. The Turnpike Trust of 1711 for the road from Ipswich to Scole was the first in Suffolk and the northern continuation in Norfolk from Scole to Norwich did not become a turnpike until 1768. By 1836 this road was being used by the fast stagecoach service of the Royal Mail from London to Norwich via Ipswich and Scole, as well as providing a good surface for private carriages. Thornham Hall had a substantial stable block and coach house which are clearly marked on the plan of the Hall in 1845.

Away from the main roads travel could be perilous owing to the lack of maintenance of the king's highways. During the reign of Henry VIII (1509 – 1547) efforts were made to improve the position and one case in particular is highlighted by a communication from the king's court to the clerk of the town of Metfield levying a fine for non-maintenance

Figure 6.8 *A droveway in South Elmham All Saints. The wide verges provided grazing for livestock being moved sometimes over long distances. When animals were driven between markets and farms such wide tracks were essential features of the regular routes.*

of a way called Christmas Lane. It pointed out that this was a major route linking the valley of the Waveney to that of the Blyth, and there were many holes making it unsafe for legal travellers. Even the Highways Act of 1555, with its requirement that every able bodied man should give six days' labour per year without pay, did not eradicate the problem as complaints continued through the reign of Elizabeth with fines imposed again in 1580, 1582 and 1589. Another communication imposing a fine was recorded in 1650, while people would still complain today about the condition of some rural roads. In the past repairs to the highway meant that stones were collected from the fields for repair and maintenance of the roads. Farmers were happy to see some of the apparently inexhaustible supply of stones removed from their fields and the practice continued late into the nineteenth century when school records repeatedly note the absence of pupils for stone picking as this was generally seen as children's work. When larger quantities of gravel were needed pits were dug into suitable deposits and it was during one of these operations near the river crossing at Stoke Ash that big pieces of Roman pottery were discovered in the nineteenth century. Acts of Parliament also prescribed the clearing of verges on the sides of roads to remove the cover used by criminals who sought to waylay unwary travellers. This was often achieved by grazing animals on the verges or taking a useful crop of hay from the cleared strips. Modern highway authorities still struggle to control the growth of plants on the road-side verges seeking a balance between the safety of travellers and the preservation of wild life in a potentially rich habitat.

The importance of river transport and its potential for development was highlighted in 1656 by one Francis Matthew who proposed a navigation linking the Little Ouse to the Waveney as 'To His Highness Oliver, Lord Protector … is Humbly Presented a Mediterranean Passage by Water Between … Lynn and Yarmouth'[38]. This would have involved cutting a canal through the watershed between the rivers at Lopham, Redgrave and Blo Norton. It was never carried out but an Act of Parliament of 17 March 1670 pointed out that the Waveney had been navigable 'in former times' for lighters, keels and other boats of considerable burthen but was at that time so obstructed as to be unnavigable above Beccles, causing great poverty to the inhabitants of the surrounding district[39]. The Act empowered five Bungay men Thomas Walcott, William Barker, Robert London, John Gouche and John Girling, and John Saverie of Downham Market to improve the river so as to restore trade to Bungay Staithe. This was achieved by the construction of four locks between Bungay and Beccles. In the early twentieth century the navigation was operated by the local millers and maltsters W.D. & A.E. Walker whose wherry Albion appears in a photograph of Bungay Staithe taken about 1900[40]. The navigation to Bungay closed in 1934. In 1724 Daniel Defoe noted that 'the river Waveney is a considerable river and of a deep and full channel, navigable for large barges as high as Beccles'. Navigation below Beccles was further improved in 1831 to allow sea-going vessels to reach the town from Lowestoft. The commercial use of the river above Bungay by smaller boats transporting goods to Bungay or Beccles is not documented but references to staithes, even as far upstream as Braiseworth on the River Dove, confirm that such traffic took place. The advantage of river transport for bulky goods was too great to be ignored. It would not only be agricultural cargoes of grain and malt but also the products of the kilns making pottery, tiles and clay pipes that

Figure 6.9 *A wherry sailing on the Waveney at Beccles. The wherry with its large gaff sail on a single mast set far forward in the vessel replaced the old style keel which had a single square sail on a mast set amidships.*

Figure 6.10 *A wherry at Ellingham lock on the Waveney Navigation. This was one of the four locks on the Waveney that enabled vessels to reach Bungay.*

Figure 6.11 *The staithe at Bungay was the head of the navigation for the sailing wherries.*

were carried down the river, while we might expect manure from the towns and coal from Newcastle to find their way upstream. The rivers remained important highways until their role was supplanted by the railways in the nineteenth century. The ambitious scheme for a navigation between Lynn and Yarmouth was never achieved, although another attempt is said to have been proposed in 1818. An Act of Parliament of 1669 did authorise improvement of the River Lark from Brandon to Thetford. This was carried out by Henry, Earl of Arlington, in 1675–7 introducing a series of staunches (single, lifting lock gates). Less formal arrangements with dredging to remove silt that accumulated on the bed of the river and perhaps the introduction of simple staunches to maintain a depth of water could have improved the access by small boats to the higher reaches of both rivers and their main tributary streams. We should be looking out for any references to such activity.

The pottery industry we observed in the Waveney Valley during the Roman period had been re-introduced and continued throughout the Middle Ages. This was at its peak during the fifteenth and sixteenth centuries. The main reason must have been the presence of suitable clay. Analysis shows this clay contains phosphate, chalk and iron which can produce good terracottas as well as cream and grey wares. There was a particular concentration of production sites in Weybread, Mendham and Metfield. From documents we can recognise one family of master potters who came originally from Weybread where several of their kilns have been discovered. These were the Sterffes and one of their kilns was excavated in 1986[41]. In a will dated 19 February 1477, which was proved on 9 March that year, Robert Sterffe, potter, was a resident of Metfield, living at Docking Hall which had been built by the family. He left bequests to the churches of Weybread and Metfield and was buried at Metfield. He mentions in his will two sons William and Robert, both of whom are mentioned in the tax return

Figure 6.12a *Terracotta at Whittingham (1653) made from local clay.*

of 1515, when Robert was one of the tax collectors for Metfield. The family retained land in Weybread as testified by tax lists, so William Sterffe, potter, is listed there in the 1524 Subsidy Return, having 'In goodes two pounds in value' and Robert is assessed in St. James 'In obligacion and other goodes'. Two kilns were discovered in St. James, one close to the church and the other near to the parish boundary with Metfield adjoining Docking Hall. Here a kiln was excavated revealing a bee-hive type construction with a single flue, built on the edge of a deep clay pit. By 1568 a John Sterff was taxed on £3 in goods. Later the family purchased small tracts of land, 'pightles', to build additional kilns in Withersdale and Chediston, and kiln sites have been discovered in both these parishes. At Withersdale, close to a water source, remains of eight kilns were discovered set into the bank of a modern road. Water was supplied from a neighbouring river and clay pits survive in both banks of the river valley, their positions indicated by names on the tithe map and now marked by woodland. One of the kilns at Chediston was situated on the edge of the green and enclosure of the green gave us the opportunity for excavation. These master craftsmen experimented with early types of glaze, producing highly decorated and well made vessels. Their later products in the mid fifteenth to sixteenth centuries[42] are known to archaeologists as Late Medieval Transitional Ware. They included jugs, cisterns to hold ale, pancheons (large flat dishes) and skillets (three legged pans). Some were partially glazed in green with decorative black strips made with iron oxide. These strips seem to have been a distinctive trade mark of the Sterffes and are easily recognisable. Fragments have been recovered from the Thornham Estate. Eighteen kiln sites were operating at Weybread, Mendham, Metfield, St. James, Chediston and Rumburgh. The pottery became popular, being well made and highly decorated which no doubt accounts for its wide distribution. Fragments of these wares

Figure 6.12b *Terracotta at Mendham of the Freston Family.*

have been recovered on many sites along the Waveney Valley and at Thornham Magna and Parva as well as Stoke Ash, but their main market outlet was in the great city of Norwich and at Dunwich. They were certainly one of the reasons for the decline in the Grimston production centres at this time[43]. Now, as earlier, no doubt the River Waveney was a major highway for the transport of such heavy and fragile goods. While these 'Waveney Valley' products from Weybread and its neighbours reached a prestige market in Norwich, the products of the Wattisfield and Rickinghall kilns near the head of the valley seem to have served more local markets, being found only in areas closer to the centre of production. John Brabane of Syleham, potter, in his will made on 8 April 1634 and proved 3 May 1634, gave to his brother Robert his freehold tenement 'Dentons in Weybread' where he was producing his pottery as indicated by wasters and other kiln material found here.

Kilns were still operating throughout the seventeenth and eighteenth centuries, producing new types of glazed products at Weybread, Mendham, St. James and St.

Figure 6.13 *Late medieval transitional pottery, from the kiln excavated at Weybread.*

Figure 6.14 *Clay pipes with a bar from the kiln in which they were fired. These were all found at Weybread.*

Nicholas. Field walking of these sites has produced pots glazed in green, black and red. We also start to see a diversification of production with bricks and tiles being made. We know about the early records of brick and tile production by the Bishops of Norwich at South Elmham St. Cross, but now new centres were being established at Weybread and Mendham. Further kilns were introduced during the eighteenth and nineteenth centuries, but most of these brick making centres ceased production between 1930 and 1950. At least one manufacturer in Weybread took advantage of the good local sources of clay to meet a new demand created by the import of tobacco from America. He was making clay pipes, with heart-shaped bases, as early as 1610 to 1640[44]. These early pipes are marked by the very small size of their bowls, reflecting the high cost of tobacco when first introduced. It was very much a luxury commodity in those days. The area of production was steadily expanded and several of the kiln bars have been recovered together with a vast collection of pipe bowls and stems. As time went on the bowls increased in size and a spur was visible on the base. Some of these pipes, datable to 1650–1680, had the initials T B on them, but unfortunately no pipe maker with those initials is known to have lived in the immediate vicinity. However a Thomas

Figure 6.15 *Clay pipes with the maker's initials (TB for Thomas Browne) found at Weybread.*

Browne was listed as a pipe maker in Bungay so perhaps he owned the kiln. At this time a certain Thomas Parsley was trading from his market stall at Harleston, Norfolk, in 1692–3 and his initials have been found on fragments of pipe distributed throughout the Waveney Valley. We could possibly surmise that these two craftsmen might both have been producing their wares on the marshland of the river valley between Weybread and Mendham. Clay pipes are often found when field walking and no doubt some from remoter locations were discarded by shepherds living in their temporary homes near the flocks of grazing sheep during the summer months. In the eighteenth and nineteenth centuries pipes were decorated in various ways. Some had simple designs of barrels, acorns or baskets but others had embossed lettering along the stem to show the place of manufacture and advertise the pipemaker. Some reveal events or personalities of contemporary interest including representations of Nelson's ship the Victory, or the Relief of Ladysmith during the Boer War. Some portrayed individuals such as Mother Shipton from Yorkshire or publicised individual public houses. Although none are produced locally, the tradition was maintained by the manufacture of large numbers of pipes to mark the Silver Jubilee of Queen Elizabeth II.

Farmers are always affected by changes in the weather. Richard Muir in his book 'The Lost Villages of Britain' provides a simple graph of temperatures from the middle of the twelfth century onwards. This indicates a steady rise in summer temperature up to the thirteenth century followed by a decline in temperature to the seventeenth century when there was a 'Little Ice Age' between 1600 and 1750. The church wardens' accounts for Metfield contain many references to the weather, including a great flood of 20 January 1607 and severe storms on 19 December with much damage reported. A storm began on Thursday 24 November 1703 and carried on until the following Wednesday, being noted as the worst storm ever recorded. Just four years later, on Tuesday 17 July 1707, deaths from heat are recorded, and on 13 July 1808 ninety nine degrees were recorded. Many winters show long periods of snow and at Christmas in 1860 a temperature of 20 degrees below zero was recorded with five weeks of snow, but in 1868 a drought was recorded from May to October. As a result there were times when the population suffered from shortage of food and it is said that by 1810 the death rate had doubled with many starving to death in the villages. In some cases wives were sold and families broken up due to poverty. In 1816 ten people from Metfield took part in the 'Bread or Blood' riots when, on 6 June, a mob from Metfield and St. James, led by an armed man on horseback, assembled on Greazy Green but they were dispersed by the local militia without trouble.

We can see evidence in the landscape and the documents for changes in the size and shape of fields as the demands of farming varied. Study of survey maps show the creation of ditches and hedges, some of which lasted only a short time before the hedges were grubbed out and ditches filled in to create larger fields. Names of fields such as 'New Plough' or 'New Grazing' sometimes mark these changes. Field walking can reveal

Figure 6.16 *At Metfield a remarkable ancient clock survives in the church. This clock in a wooden case on the floor of the church tower is first mentioned in 1551. It was moved to the first floor of the tower in 1719 but returned to the ground floor in the 1970s.*

evidence of former ditches or filled in stock ponds. Such activity leaves signs visible to the discerning eye and on occasion datable debris is included in the fill so we can date the changes. Extensive and careful field walking surveys add to our stock of evidence and complement clues offered by field names and changes of ownership. Field names in the tithe survey of 1837 at Metfield reveal the regular practice of vicars claiming special respect, as the 45 acres of glebe farmed by the incumbent, who then lived in the parsonage about a mile away from the church, were all called 'Sir Edmunds', the style by which he no doubt expected to be addressed by his parishioners. Throughout the sixteenth century we generally see an increase in house building, which is certainly true of the Waveney Valley. At Thornham Magna this seems to be the time when some occupiers of properties fronting Mill Common Green moved away from ditched or moated enclosures on the green edge to build houses at the opposite ends of their plots adjoining the main thoroughfare, now known as The Street.

The Thornham Estate is within the area of High Suffolk that was the centre of dairy farming in the seventeenth and eighteenth centuries, producing butter and cheese from the Suffolk polled (hornless) cows. These cows, also known as the Suffolk Dun Cows from their colour described as varying between cream and red, were a local breed that became the ancestors of the later red-polls and were famous for the quality of their milk. They had a reputation for producing particularly fine butter although the reputation of Suffolk cheese was varied so that Daniel Defoe said Suffolk made 'the best butter and perhaps the worst cheese in England'[45] but the hard cheese, 'Suffolk Bang', kept well and so was favoured for use on ships. Daniel Defoe in his 'Tour Through the Eastern Counties' of 1724 describes the area round Debenham and Eye as being 'employed in dairies or in feeding of cattle. This part of England is also remarkable for being the first where the feeding and fattening of cattle, both sheep as well as black cattle, with turnips was first practised'. Farms generally had some arable fields and in many cases the proportion of arable was increasing by the end of the eighteenth century[46], although this was generally to provide fodder, including turnips, for the livestock. The turnips were important as providing a better means of feeding cattle through the winter and spring until there was sufficient growth of grass on the pastures, as farmers in this region had already discovered by the middle of the seventeenth century. During the nineteenth century the region seems to have turned increasingly to arable but now much of it was for growing corn. This expansion of arable farming owed much to the Napoleonic Wars with France (1793–1815) when demand for corn and so the price it commanded rose rapidly. Maps reveal that at this time more land in the Thornhams was being farmed as arable than is the case today, although it was divided into many more fields which were comparatively small. It is notable that Arthur Young in his 'General View of the Agriculture of the County Of Suffolk, 1813' selects for illustration a machine invented by Mr. Lionel Hayward of Stoke Ash Hall; this was an 'extirpator' for 'destroying weeds and clearing plough lands for seed'. It was a type of hoe which could be drawn by two or three horses depending on the soil. Young recommended that it should be used after an initial ploughing when it would easily work one acre per hour and reported that a farmer with three horses could work up to 60 acres per week. After the war the region maintained the large areas of arable and did not revert to a dairying economy. Apparently farmers continued with corn growing because they did not think they could establish new areas of good grassland in the dry climate of East Anglia with enough success to compete with cheap imports of butter and cheese from Holland and Ireland. However some animals were still kept as cows, bullocks and sheep provided manure for the crops. In fact the characteristic system of farming[47] at this time included a rotation of fallow or mangolds or turnips for fattening sheep and cattle; barley; clover or pulses; then wheat. Judging by the enlargement of Hall and Park, the estate escaped the worst of the depression that afflicted agricultural areas between the end of the war and the renewed prosperity of the 1850s. The area saw real prosperity when corn profits were restored by the outbreak of the Crimean War in 1853 and this lasted until farming entered renewed depression from about 1875 when things were made worse by a succession of bad harvests.

Notes

1   SROI:HD1538/384/1 bailiff's account roll (from Iveagh collection).
2   In Star Chamber records at PRO:STAC/2/23/206, 2/23/221, 2/29/83, 2/31/123.
3   SROI:HA 116/4676/40 (item 26).
4   Iquisition Post Mortem Register for 2 & 3 Philip & Mary gives John Wiseman of Suffolk, ref. Chancery Series II vol 106 no 59.
5   PRO:C1/1394/67–70 (a damaged document, difficult to read).
6   Valor Ecclesiasticus 1535, vol III, p.480.
7   PRO:C1/1427/70–71 re half manor of Dengewell in Wix and Gt. Oakley, Essex.
8   IPM Register for 3 Elizabeth refers Chancery Series II vol.131 no 171 & Court of Wards vol. 8 no 83 and for 5 Elizabeth refers Chancery Series vol. 135 no 40 & Court of Wards vol. 9 no 1.
9   Tanner's Index to the Bishops' Registers, per Peter Northeast.
10 SROI:FDA 256/A1/1a. plot 120 part: 3 acres of pasture in Broad Oak.
11 'The Parson 's Glebe' in Harper-Bill, C, Rawcliffe, C, and Wilson, R, 2002 *East Anglia's history: studies in honour of Norman Scarfe*, Woodbridge, 75, note.
12 From the Greek meaning 'lover of the word', presumably the Word of St John 's Gospel.
13 Chancery Proceedings of Elizabeth 's reign, volume I, 289.
14 It had been granted to Edmund Bedingfield in 1536 and acquired by John Parker in 1558, passing on his death in 1573 to his son, also John Parker.
15 Diarmaid MacCulloch gives the will of Alexander Newton as PCC 20 Sheffield (i.e. in records of the Prerogative Court of Canterbury).
16 MacCulloch, D, 1986 *Suffolk & the Tudors*, Oxford, 416.
17 Lay Subsidy return of 1327.
18 Copinger, W, 1909 *The Manors of Suffolk*, London
19 *PSIAH* 40, (2002), 145.
20 Domesday Book, Suffolk, 18.6 and 19.19,
21 For more details of the family see Evans, N, 1980 The Tasburghs of South Elmham, *PSIAH* **34**, 269.
22 IPM Register gives Edmund Buckenham of Suffolk 18 James I (Chancery Series II vol 384 no 138 and Court of Wards vol 60 no 245)and Barbara Buckenham 19 James I (Chancery Series II vol 449 no 3).
23 Copy in Notes of Thomas Martin, Cullum Collection, SROB:E2/41/9, 10 & 11.
24 See Appendix 2 for a family tree which includes the Killigrews.
25 SROI: HA 116/4861/10.
26 The apparent absence of the projecting porch may be artistic licence to emphasise the contemporary symmetrical straight front, as the porch is apparent in photographs of the remodelled Victorian house.
27 Information from Edward Martin.
28 Entry in Court Book for Manor of Swatshall Woodhouse and Bresworth, SROI:S1/2/18.1.
29 SROI:S1/2/18.1.
30 We are grateful to Dr.John Blatchly for details of Joseph Bokenham.

31 Court book, SROI:S1/2/18.1.
32 BL Add.MS 5522.
33 Cambridge University Library MS.VI.47.
34 Fairclough, J, and Plunkett, S, 2000 Drawings of Walton Castle …, *PSIAH* **39**, 419.
35 Court book, SROI:S1/2/18.3.
36 Williamson, T, 1997 *The Norfolk Broads,* Manchester, 140.
37 Malster, R, 2003 *The Norfolk & Suffolk Broads,* Chichester, 91 refers Act of 22 Charles II cap.16.
38 Malster, R, 1995 *Britain in Old Photographs – Suffolk,* Stroud, p. 26.
39 *PSIAH* **36** (1986), 156 excavation report by I. Perry and M. Hardy.
40 See Mike Hardy in *PSIAH* **36** (1985) 47-8 and Current Archaeology **115** (1989), 266.
41 Information from Sarah Jennings of the Norwich Survey Team.
42 Dated by Sue Atkin.
43 Dymond, D, and Northeast, P, 1995 *A History of Suffolk,* Chichester, 93.
44 Theobald, J, 1999 Changing Agriculture in High Suffolk 1650–1850, map 60 in Dymond, D, and Martin, E (eds), *An Historical Atlas of Suffolk,* Ipswich and 2001 'Changing Farm Sizes in Woodland High Suffolk 1690–1840' *PSIAH* **40**, 55.
45 For details see Thirsk, J, and Imray, J, 1958 *Suffolk Farming in the Nineteenth Century,* Suffolk Records Society.

Chapter 7

Timber Importing to Tree Planting

S ir John Major had a survey of his newly acquired park and adjoining farm land produced by T. Skynner in 1765, the year he was created baronet at the age of 67. The Hall stood in a substantial area of parkland (about 34 hectares) and was approached by a straight drive from the public road which then ran north of the church. The road has since been diverted to run some distance south of the church, which now stands inside the eastern edge of the enlarged park, although its line can still be traced as an earthwork partly visible from the modern road. The Park apparently contained a scatter of trees with more towards the northern boundary; it appears to be surrounded by a pale suggesting it might have held deer. The park appears to have been cut out of a series of fields aligned on the small stream from Gislingham which flows through Thornham Magna into the River Dove. These fields are clearly shown on the 1765 map and some of their boundaries survive today. It is notable that the fields along

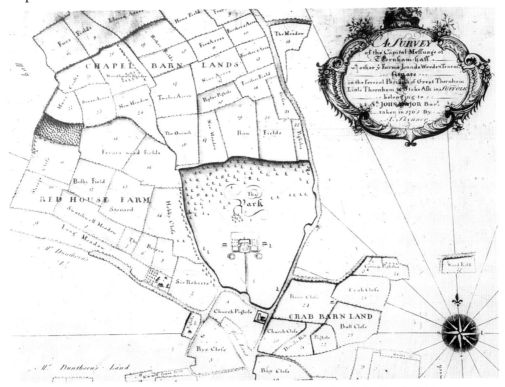

Figure 7.1 *This map of 1765 shows the Thornham Estate when it was bought by Sir John Major.*

Figure 7.2 *Worlingworth fire engine of 1760 preserved in the church. The long brass nozzle is resting on top of the pump housing.*

the northern boundary of the 1765 Park, now incorporated into the woodland of the modern Park beyond the Walled Garden, are on a different alignment which relates roughly to the line of Cowpasture Lane through Thornham Parva. It is possible that the western boundary of the Park in Skynner's map marks the line of a road leading to the moated site known as Woodhouse, now hidden in Lady Henniker Wood, as the northern section of this route survives as a substantial trackway.

Sir John retained Worlingworth Hall and was buried with his wife in a vault below the chancel of Worlingworth Church where a memorial, by Cooper of Stratford le Bow Essex, records that his wife Dame Elizabeth died at Thornham Hall on 4 September 1780 aged 76 and he died in London soon after on 16 February 1781 aged 82. He had presented the parish of Worlingworth with a fire engine in 1760 and this is preserved in the church with inscriptions recording that it was given by John Major Esq. in 1760 and that it was made by Newsham and Ragg of the Cloth Fair, London. The engine was hand pumped and stands on small wooden block wheels with iron rims. It has a lead lined box providing water to two pumps which forced the water under pressure into a copper cylinder to which the hose and nozzle are attached. The box could be filled by the pumps drawing water from a pond or by people using a chain of buckets. There are two lengths of leather hose each twenty feet long and a tapering copper and brass nozzle 46 inches long. If pumped steadily it could provide a powerful continuous jet of water. We mentioned in the previous chapter that buildings were vulnerable to fire and this machine, by a top London maker, was doubtless seen as a valuable local asset. We might wonder if he provided a similar engine for Thornham. According to the Churchwardens' Accounts the Worlingworth fire engine was tested and demonstrated every year on 29 May when it drew water from the Rectory moat and is said to have delivered a jet of water as high as the church tower which is 75 feet. It remained in use until 1927 and was restored to working order in 1953 so that it could be displayed at the west end of the church nave[1].

In the eighteenth century Sir John Major extended his land holdings elsewhere by acquiring significant properties. Sometime between 1736 and 1773 he purchased Rookery Farm at Metfield. This was a holding of 132 acres and the farmhouse was set on the edge of a moated enclosure, where material from the thirteenth century has been recovered. More was discovered in the garden area and from manuring scatters on the adjoining fields. The home complex is interesting as it has a large timber barn which is possibly of sixteenth century date, and in the back yard the stockmen's homes were situated above the stock barns. On 18 May 1800 the farm is listed as owned by Lord Henniker, but by 1900 it was no longer part of the Thornham Estate, as it had been sold to Joseph Barnard Dimmock of Shotford Hall. We gain an insight into the value of such a property in the nineteenth century from Yew Tree Farm, which is a farm of similar size adjacent to the Rookery. It also had a moated enclosure. William Briton insured this farm with the Norwich Union Fire Insurance on 29 September 1836, when a barn, stable, outhouses, building yards, gardens and orchards of one acre and one rood were valued at £350. The value of the house was £200 and was of stud, clay and tile, while the value of the barn, stable and cowhouse adjoining each other, being of brick, stud and tile, was £140 and the wagon shed of clay and thatch was valued at £10. The annual cost of the premium was eight shillings and ninepence.

Sir John Major was an Elder Brother of Trinity House, was High Sheriff of Suffolk in 1754, Member of Parliament for Scarborough in 1761 and was created a Baronet in 1765. He had been married since 1723–4 to Elizabeth, the daughter of Daniel Dale of Bridlington. They had no sons and on his death in 1781, aged 82, the estate passed to his two daughters. His older daughter Ann had married John Henniker, of Newton Hall near Dunmow in Essex, who took the title to her share and succeeded to the baronetcy. John Henniker was also active in politics as Member of Parliament for Sudbury from 1761 to 1768 and for Dover from 1774 to 1784. Sir John Major's younger daughter, Elizabeth, married Henry Brydges, the 2nd Duke of Chandos, in 1767. His father, James Brydges 1st Duke of Chandos who died in 1744 was from 1707 to 1712 Paymaster General for the Armed Forces, which proved extremely profitable for him and he built up a very large fortune. He built a magnificent mansion 'Canons' near Edgware in Middlesex[2] and rebuilt the church of St. Lawrence at Little Stanmore to include his own mausoleum. From 1717 to 1718 Handel was his composer in residence at Canons. He was the patron of the architect John Wood the Elder at Bath when he started the Georgian development there as well as being responsible for a major development in Bridgwater. According to a House of Commons report in 1721 he had lost £700,000 in the 'South Sea Bubble' but did not count this a serious loss. In the 1740s he was receiving substantial income from the Hanaper Office and the Sixpenny Writ Office and the rents of properties[3]. Henry Brydges, 2nd Duke of Chandos, had been attached to the Household of Frederick Prince of Wales as Gentleman of the Bedchamber from 1729 and as Groom of the Stole from 1742. He married his first wife in 1730 and she was the mother of his heir James, but she died in 1738 and in 1744 he married Anne Wells. She was said to have been his mistress for some time since he bought her from her husband, an ostler, at an inn in Newbury[4]. She died in 1759. Thus Elizabeth Major was his third wife and he only lived for another four years. After his death in 1771 she lived at Thornham Hall until her own death in 1813, initially with her sister and brother in law both of whom she outlived and then with her nephew and his wife. Her brother in law was clearly impressed by Chandos' sloop as on 25 August 1769 he wrote to his 16 year old son[5] 'My dear Major' that 'her colours are always flying whilst the Duke is at Southampton. Her bottom is black, her side yellow with a strake of green at the top. Her stern painted green with a coronet on each side. The rudder on the stern and a yellow C – the rudder is painted red – but it all wants new paint.' (Plate 20). He describes a masked ball and sailing at Southampton. He writes about shooting at Thornham with advice for his son about how to carry a gun, 'sparrow pye would be verry good indeed, if we had so good a marksman as you to shoot them for us – pray take care not to overcharge your gun.'

It was 'her ever affectionate and grateful nephew, John Lord Henniker' who in 1817 set up the memorial in Worlingworth church recording that the duchess died on 30th March 1813 aged 82. In fact the Manorial Court of 'Swatshall Woodhouse and Braseworth' in 1802 was held in the names of Elizabeth Dowager Duchess of Chandos and John Henniker Major, Lady and Lord of the Manor. Both had presumably subscribed at one guinea and a half each to the map of Suffolk produced by Joseph Hodskinson in 1783 as the Dowager Duchess of Chandos is named at Great Thornham Hall and Sir John Henniker Baronet at Great Bealings Hall. Early in the nineteenth century Lord and Lady Henniker and the Dowager Duchess of Chandos were among the patrons of the Eye Theatre[6]. A diary kept by John Henniker[7] reveals that in 1783 he attended the races in Ipswich with the Duchess of Chandos, arranging to hire lodgings in the town for the duration of the social events held during the races. The diary gives information about a number of journeys between Thornham and London, and through Hadleigh to a Sheldrake Farm at Stoke, presumably Stoke by Nayland. On Friday 3 October 1783 he records that he set out from London in his new chariot and four at 7 o'clock, broke his journey at Chelmsford at a quarter past twelve with a meal of whiting and veal cutlets costing seven shillings and sixpence, setting off at half past two, and reached Colchester at half past six. On the Saturday morning he resumed the journey at seven, reaching Copdock at ten for a breakfast break of an hour and a half, finally getting to Thornham Hall at a quarter to four. He recorded the total cost of this journey as £3. 3s. 11d. Given that he seems to have followed the main road all the way, it is worth noting that the journey took a full two days. In 1791 the family's London house was 19 Portman Square. This diary also records how Sir John Henniker made some of the appointments on the estate. On 15 June 1781 Mr John Orford was made gamekeeper of Crows Hall Debenham as were Mr Steptoe of Blood Hall and Mr William May of Worlingworth. A new lease was granted to a father and son, Stephen Thomas to become gamekeeper and Hammond to help shoot. Charles Coe 'living at Thornham Parva' has the key of the stables, the warehouse and the limehouse. On 7 August 1783 Sir John 'ordered Crows Hall [Debenham] brydge to be pulled down to the old width and a new parapet built upon it.' On the same day he held court at Debenham, presumably in the court house that stood originally in the grounds of Crows Hall itself.

The Henniker family came from Rochester in Kent where there are said to be family memorials in the cathedral. Memorials in Thornham Magna and Worlingworth[8] churches to 'Dame Ann Henniker, eldest daughter of Sir John Major Bart. & Elizabeth his wife' record that she died on 18 July 1792 at Bristol Hotwells and is buried in a vault in Rochester Cathedral. There is a fine memorial to her in Rochester Cathedral in Coade stone. Both the Major and Henniker families were Muscovy merchants trading with Russia and had business connections. John Henniker was involved in the supply of timber, particularly ships' masts, for the British Navy including imports from North America until the outbreak of the American War of Independence in 1775[9]. John Henniker's father, also John Henniker, baptised at Chatham in 1691 and granted the freedom of Rochester in 1712, was a Russia merchant and the greatest importer in England of masts from Norway, Riga and Petersburgh for the navy. He was buried in West Ham churchyard in Essex in 1749.

There are references to John Henniker bringing masts from Riga, Gothenburg and Quebec using special mast ships[10]. There is correspondence in the Public Record Office about both John Henniker and John Major being involved together in the provision of masts and other supplies, including Stockholm tar, to the Admiralty in North America between 1738 and 1741, which was the period of the 'War of Jenkins' Ear' fought against Spain to protect British trading interests with South America while Sir Robert Walpole was Prime Minister. John Major had a contract to supply Stockholm tar in 1740 and in the following year his ship The Prince of Orange, Samuel Harris master, sailed with stores for Gibraltar. In 1758 New England masts, yards and bowsprits as well as pitch, tar, turpentine and ash rafters were received by the navy from John Henniker who was operating mast ships called the Essex, the Tavistock, the St. George and the Scarborough. In 1766 Sir John Major and John Henniker were partners in the supply of victuals to the army in North America as they advised that two frigates were blocking the harbour at New York so troops in West Florida might be running short of flour. They also had a contract to supply salt pork and beef. Henniker was importing white pine and red pine masts from Quebec in 1767. He was also involved in fitting out commercial vessels as there was an Act of 1753 'to impower the Commissioners of the Treasury to direct the payment of the Bounty to John Henniker and others upon four Ships fitted out for the Whale Fishery, and lost in the Greenland Seas'[11]. The Greenland Whaling Fishery was a high risk business but one that could be highly profitable. Family letters are said to confirm John Henniker's interest in the mast business as he encouraged his son to apply himself in the dockyard to learning the timber trade, perhaps in the naval dockyard at Chatham[12] and records show that in 1781 Sir John Henniker asked that his contract with the War Office for supplying provisions be transferred to his son. In 1800 Sir John Henniker was created Baron Henniker of Stratford-upon-Slaney, County Wicklow in the Irish peerage (Plate 17). His daughter Anne Elizabeth was the second wife of Edward Stratford, 2nd Earl of Aldborough (1761–1800) whose papers are in the PRO of Northern Ireland[13] where correspondence with the Hennikers refers to the building

Figure 7.3 *A later generation of Worlingworth Volunteers assembled on Mellis Green in 1865.*

of Aldborough House in Dublin. This connection probably explains the presence of Irish portraits in the family collection.

The 1st Lord Henniker died in 1803 and was succeeded by his son John. The range of family properties is revealed when the 1st Lord Henniker is described as being of Worlingworth and Thornham Hall in Suffolk, of Stratford House and Newton Hall both in Essex, of Great Bealings Hall in Suffolk, of St. Peters in the Isle of Thanet Kent and of Stratford upon Slaney Co. Wicklow Ireland. In 1806 the title at Thornham had become John Lord Henniker and Elizabeth Duchess Dowager of Chandos[14], Lord and Lady of the Manor. By 1817 John Lord Henniker was Lord of the Manor while Sir Bridges Trecothick Henniker, Baronet, was trustee of the late Elizabeth Duchess Dowager of Chandos. The presence of the dowager Duchess of Chandos is marked today by the name of Chandos Farm in Thornham Parva and by her funeral hatchment still displayed in Thornham Magna church[15]. The 2nd Lord Henniker, who took the name Henniker-Major in accordance with a clause in his maternal grandfather's will, was a Tory MP and a Muscovy merchant with Russian connections – his journals survive. For the Napoleonic Wars he raised a Regiment of Volunteers at Worlingworth and was often painted in uniform. In a pamphlet 'Some account of the families of Major and Henniker' by John Henniker-Major, 2nd Lord Henniker, London 1803, written for the Volunteers, he included a list of them all and stated that from June 1798 to April 1802 he commanded 90 infantry for the defence of Worlingworth and eight adjoining parishes. Their colours, presented by Hon Mrs Henniker-Major in 1798, were 'now' placed in Worlingworth church. On the return of peace he presented the officers and men with a silver medal showing Worlingworth church and hall on one side and nine hands (for the nine parishes) on the other. We shall see that his father raised a similar force in East London. He clearly took a wider interest in public affairs as he was a Fellow of the Royal Society and was Member of Parliament for many years: for Romney 1785–1790, Steyning 1794–1802, Rutland 1805–1812, and Stamford 1812–1818. He died in 1821 at Stratford House in Essex aged 69, and he and his wife Emily were buried in a vault under Thornham Magna church as recorded by a monument on the north wall of the chancel, which is said to be one of the finest works of Joseph Kendrick. It shows that she had died at 'Major House' in 1819 aged 64. As they died without children, his nephew John Minet Henniker inherited the title.

A remarkable painting which hangs in Worlingworth church shows the feast held on 25th October 1810 to honour the 50th anniversary of the accession of King George III, which shows people seated in the open in front of the Church, the Guildhall and Worlingworth Hall. Others drink beer and dance, while the main feature is the roasting of an ox weighing 50 stones. The ox had been presented by the 2nd Lord Henniker and the spit of ash wood used for the roasting, which is fifteen feet long, still stands in the corner of the nave. The painting shows carriages in front of the Hall and the figures crossing the bridge to join the festivities are presumably Lord and Lady Henniker. Clearly the family maintained their interest in Worlingworth as well as at Thornham.

More ordinary activities in parishes can often be found recorded in the account books of the churchwardens. Those for Metfield survive from 1547 and give details down to 1785. They include details of income from land held by the church and regular expenditure on bread and wine for the communion. Costs include purchase of red and green silk, repairs to vestments and provision of frankincense. Under 'church plate etc.' in 1594 the churchwardens went to Sandcroft for a cloth for the Communion Table, which replaced the altar in the reformed church. It cost 11 shillings for John Liddilow to write the church creed and the Lord's Prayer in 1672, presumably so they could be displayed on large boards in the church. Two of the highest costs were for the Royal Arms to be displayed in the church which were painted by Lionel Baldrey of Framlingham in 1762 and then we have Mr Winter's bill for the King's Coat of Arms in 1826. The font received attention several times, mainly for being painted. In 1557 Richard Blythe was paid 18 pence for 'repairynge of the stooles' in the church, which payment included 'meate, drynke and wages'. We learn that in 1719 a gallery was set up in the church at a cost of £12. 7s. 3d. and through the following years singers were often paid to perform, while in 1805 two shillings and sixpence was spent on providing two reeds for the bassoon. There seem to have been several problems over the town chest, especially with the locks and keys, which would be taken seriously because the chest held money and all the parish records. An interesting series of payments relates to the ancient church clock. In 1551 Thomas Gydnys was paid fourpence for 'mendynge of the cloke', which was originally housed in a wooden case set on the floor of the church tower. In 1719 William Spendelow was paid for altering the church clock from a balance type to a 'pendeleum and removing itt into ye first chamber in ye stepell' at a cost of £2. 10s. Other costs were mentioned for 'lead wayts' and to John Betts, a mason, for making the 'stepell' ready for the clock. In the 1970s the clock was moved back from the first chamber of the tower to its original home in a wooden housing situated on the floor of the tower.

The accounts kept by the churchwardens included expenditure on books, the fabric of the church, bells and bell ringers, as well as listing baptisms, burials and preaching by the clergy and provision of food for guest preachers. Gifts for the poor are shown from 1547 when 'poore folke on Saynt Edwards Day given viiid' and this section includes some unusual items as for example in 1621 'given a gentleman which was ransomed from Turke xiid' and in 1623 'to travellers taken by the Turkes 6d' (there is no obvious explanation for Suffolk people suffering at the hands of the Turks but perhaps they had been engaged in the trade of the Levant or Turkey companies from the eastern Mediterranean through Turkey to Asia). Entries for 1641 reveal the impact of the start of the Civil War and of rebellion in Ireland against the English, so we find losses caused by fire and by the rebels when 20 women were paid 8d and 'given to Inglishe man driven out of Ireland 1s:6d'. The end of the Civil War was marked by more demands for relief in 1650 as 'all this year to many solgers and passengers and poore pepell cum from the Parliment with passes, some with briefs, 21s:10d'. Two years later one shilling was paid to two sailors taken by the French. Several entries deal with the health of the parish as in the payments to 'Mr Thorne for sogery and a Mr Rayner for fissicke and bleeding'. Mr John Carsey, surgeon, was appointed to look after the poor of Metfield 'in all sickness and distemper, the smallpox excepted'. Several entries mention broken limbs and payments to surgeons for repairing them. The churchwardens were also involved in the upkeep of 'the scole house, gildhall, townhouse and priest's house'. Almshouses had been built at St. Peter by the Tasburgh family in 1509 and in Metfield the 'towne houce' was rethatched in 1560. Children of the poor were often kept by other families who were paid for their care. In 1642 the inhabitants of Flixton maintained widows Carre and Kinge, and placed them in a cottage in St. Peter, possibly on the land of Charity Farm. Provision varied from parish to parish but by 1698 the Vestry meetings at Metfield were setting a poor rate for the whole parish, often charged at one shilling in the pound. On April 7 1698 widow Smith's son drowned and the resulting expenses were paid by the overseers of the poor: a Mr Wheeler was appointed to collect the body, William Harvey made the coffin at a cost of three shillings, woollen to wind him cost two shillings, and there was a shilling for making the grave and ringing the bell. The overseers could pay for food and clothing and sometimes for education, so Robert Cobling, schoolmaster, was paid to teach the poor children and see that they regularly attend divine worship. In 1794 a notice was displayed in the parish: 'All boys who are found at illegal play on Sundays will be set in the stocks'. We might see this as evidence of puritanical strictness or a sign of the difficulty in enforcing such regulations. How many boys were playing on the green when they should be in church or reading the bible and what attitude did their parents take? Many of those living in the townhouse were put out to work which brought revenue for the overseers, and we read about the delivery of children to various residents of the parish who put them to work. Records from 1801 to 1851 show most parishes had between 1 and 12 paupers but some had more. At this time the average life expectancy for a man was 30 to 32 years and for a woman 28 to 30 years, although there were certainly some notable exceptions, as we find that Mrs Susan Godbold, who was born in Flixton but lived in Metfield for 80 years, celebrated her 104th birthday on 13 September 1843 by walking round the village. Eight years after this celebration we learn that of the 68 paupers listed at Metfield 28 children were engaged in picking oakum, that is pulling apart old ropes to provide the loose fibres used for caulking wooden ships.

This was the time of the workhouses and the one at Thornham Magna was situated close to the parish boundary with the field behind it being called Charity. This is possibly the area of the town estate that was given in 1434 by John Bennett, being a tenement of four acres which had been let at £9, and was given for what were later called 'superstitious uses', no doubt intended to ease the passage of John's soul to heaven. The parish workhouses became redundant when the Union houses were established and the 32 parishes of Hartismere were served by workhouses at Eye, for adults and infants, and at Wortham for children. Already by the 1830s several families, especially those from the workhouses, went to the New World as they were given £5 to start a new life. Mr Samuel Noller of Debenham chartered ships, the Venus, the Lochiel and the Mary Stuart, to take emigrants to Canada, New York and British Honduras. To help with the plight of the poor farm labourers an Agricultural Union was created in 1872, and a year later an Act was passed to stop employment of children under the age of eight. In 1874 the farmers formed their own association at a meeting of employers held at Newmarket, so the plight of their employees worsened again as the farmers combined against the pressures from the Union. As a result many agricultural workers moved to the industrial Midlands, especially to the maltings at Burton on Trent where surviving records give the names and home villages of the employees. They were employed at the breweries from the end of September to early June when they returned to Suffolk to help with the harvest as much additional labour was required in the fields. Then they followed the grain back to Burton. Others who stayed in the county found winter work in the maltings and breweries at Bungay and Halesworth. Further attempts were made to ease the lives of children and reduce the exploitation of cheap labour, when a committee was set up to make it illegal to employ a child under the age of ten. Life had never been easy for the rural poor and their plight worsened when 1879, Black '79, brought failed harvests and the worst wet year on record, resulting in the death of three million sheep. This was followed two years later by outbreaks of Foot and Mouth disease and animal pleuro-pneumonia.

We saw in the last chapter that the Tasburgh family built up an estate at Flixton, which was acquired by the Adair family in the eighteenth century. While Major and the Hennikers were creating their estate at Thornham and Worlingworth, the Adairs acquired land in the Flixton, South Elmham and Metfield area of the Waveney Valley. The Adair family were of Scottish descent, but had been resident at Ballymena in Ulster, Northern Ireland, since the 1620s. We first hear of their presence in Suffolk in 1738 when they were in joint control of the manor of Cratfield le Roos. At this time they purchased additional land at South Elmham and Flixton. Over the next 150 years more land was steadily purchased, and by 1875 they held properties in Metfield, Withersdale, South Elmham St. James and St. Cross, Homersfield and Flixton. In 1753 the Adairs purchased the former home of the Tasburghs at Flixton and carried out many changes over the next hundred years, both in the house and in the great park. New woodland was created and some time after the tithe survey of 1844 the main road between Bungay and Homersfield, which marked the northern boundary of the park, was diverted to enable the Adairs to extend the land inside their park. A gate-house was constructed at either end of the former road in the parishes of Flixton and Homersfield so that access was denied to the public. In 1838 Sir Robert Shafto Adair, who was born in 1763, was made a baronet and the family's status was raised again later as Sir Alexander Shafto Adair had been created Lord Waveney by the time that he opened the Waveney Dock at Lowestoft in 1883. In 1856 the famous architect Anthony Salvin was employed to rebuild the family church at Flixton where the family monuments can be seen, including that of William Adair who died in 1783. Salvin created a chapel with a marble monument to Theodosia, Lady Waveney, who died in 1871. Sir Shafto Adair presented to the church two paintings of angels which are said to be of fourteenth century origin. Salvin was also commissioned in 1861 to undertake a refurbishment of the Hall that amounted to an almost complete rebuilding (Plate 19), and at this time new gardens were landscaped around the Hall and water features were created. The layout of the gardens, which might have been the work of the famous garden designer William Andrews Nesfield, can be seen from aerial photography[16]. The ice-house was constructed at much the same time the Hennikers were adding this facility at Thornham Hall. The Adairs were benefactors to the parishes that were part of their large estate. William Adair had left a gift in his will that enabled the churchwardens in 1782 to purchase New South Sea Annuities worth £1,704. 13s. 8d. which provided an annual dividend of £51. 2s. 8d. to support the poor and educate their children. Sir Frederick Adair, 4th baronet, was the author of 'Sport in Ladakh' and 'Summer in High Asia', and he gave specimens of rare Tibetan moths to the British Museum. High death duties and failing investments resulted in the Adairs selling all their property and returning to their estates in Ireland. Consequently the Hall was partially destroyed in 1950.

The Hennikers were involved in developing an area of Stratford in East London. In 1799 Sir John Henniker Bt. of Stratford House, Essex presented silver medals to members of the Loyal United West and East Ham Volunteers 'for preservation of internal peace, our King, and constitution'. In the following year he became the first Lord Henniker and in 1803 he was buried at Stratford. In 1821 his son, the 2nd Lord Henniker, died at Stratford House, which was demolished later in the century. Some time after the creation of the railway works of the Eastern Counties Railway in 1847 at Stratford a new town was built on Lord Henniker's manor of Chobhams, so now off Leytonstone Road in Stratford we find Chobham Road, Henniker Road, Brydges Road, Chandos Road, Newton Road and Dunmow Road and Leyton High Road becomes Major Road. There was also the Henniker Arms public house.

The 3rd Lord Henniker's wife is said to have planted a lot of woodland at Thornham in the early nineteenth century, including that now known as Lady Henniker Wood. A detailed record for the year ended on Lady Day 1824[17] shows total income from rents of £7554 of which £1195 was spent on disbursements to tenants. Most of the farms were let on 14 year leases with individual holdings ranging from five acres to 382 acres. Most of these farms are included in a book of maps of Lord Henniker's estates compiled in 1828[18]. He died in 1832.

The 4th Lord Henniker married Anne Kerrison the daughter of a neighbouring

Figure 7.4 *Silver medals presented to the West and East Ham Volunteers and in the centre one of the Worlingworth medals showing the nine hands.*

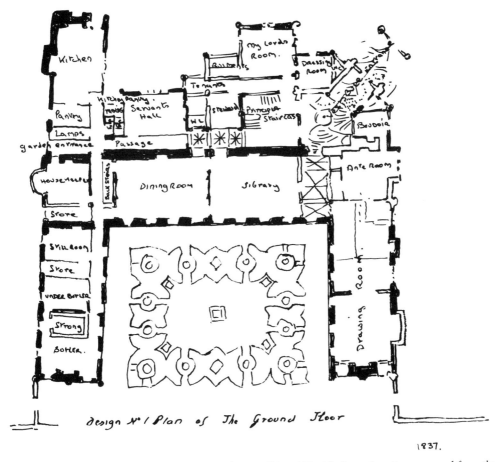

Figure 7.5 *Plan of the principal rooms at Thornham Hall in 1837 with the main entrance moved from the front courtyard to the north east corner (top right on the plan).*

landowner, Sir Edward Kerrison[19] of Oakley and Brome, in 1837. In the same year he made changes to the Hall to designs produced by Sydney Smirke[20] who had been the architect when Sir Edward Kerrison rebuilt Hoxne Hall (renamed as Oakley Park) in 1830, so no doubt he was acting on the recommendation of his new father in law to adapt the Hall for his bride. Major changes were made to the modified Elizabethan Hall and the plan of the ground floor with parterre flower beds in front of the windows of the principal rooms, Dining Room, Library and Drawing Room about 1837[21] appears to be another remodelling of the house shown in the eighteenth century painting. The entrance has been moved from the centre of the south facing block fronting the courtyard, now converted into a garden viewed from the windows, to the north east corner at what had been the back of the house. Here a covered carriage porch was added opening into an entrance hall which gave access to the principal rooms and the main staircase. The main approach to the Hall was now from the east, as it remains today, instead of from the south across the centre of the Park. A new extension was added on the west providing a New Drawing Room looking into the Park for which Smirke's design survives[22]. Plans survive[23] for later alterations including an undated

PLANS FOR BUILDING WORKS OF MAJOR HOUSE - 1837

1. Wood house
2. cinder and ash
3. Wash, baking and brewhouse
4. Passage to drying ground
5. Ironing and Laundering room
   A double sleeping room over
6. Goatpen
7. Yard
8. Maids privvy
9. Passage
10. Passage
11. Butchers meat larder.
12. Dressed meat larder
13. Game larder
14. For boots, vegetables etc.,
15. Scullery.
16. Kitchen.
17. Storeroom
18. Housekeepers room.
19. Still room.
20. Linen store.
21. Cloak, hat and stick room.
22. Butlers room. Plate store.
23. Under butlers Cleaning pantry.
24. Servants hall.
25. Drying and brushing room.
26. Knife house.
27. Shoe house.
28. Lamp house.
29. Yard.
30. Passage.
31. Tenants waiting room.
32. Antiroom.
33. Passages.
34. My Lords strong room.
35. Dressing room.
36. Best Bedroom.
37. Water Closet.
38. Force pump House.

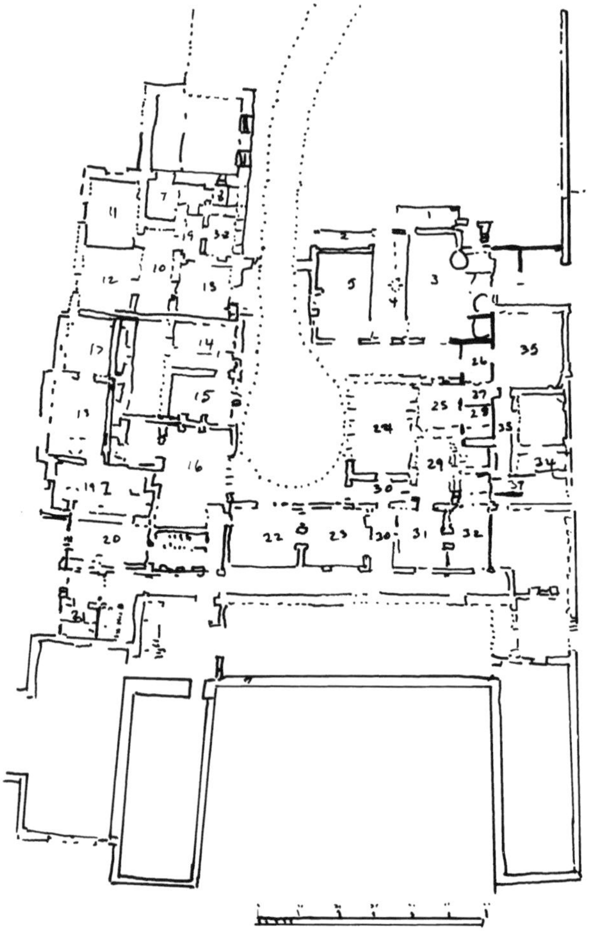

Figure 7.6 *The staff quarters at Thornham Hall in 1837, based on a plan for building works to extend round a courtyard behind the main building.*

design for additional 'offices' round two courtyards behind the house and more dated 1872–3 by James Colling, architect, for creation of nurseries and servants' bedrooms on the first floor apparently above the Servants' Hall on the north end of the west wing beyond the Dining Room. In 1844 White's Directory recorded 'a large and handsome mansion, which was considerably enlarged and improved about ten years ago, and occupies a delightful situation in a beautiful park which has recently been enlarged, and is finely shaded with full-grown trees and rising plantations.' It is difficult to date the different phases of extension of the park round the house which involved the diversion of roads, the lines of which survive as earthworks. In addition to the removal of the road round the north side of the church, which was replaced by a straight extension of the road from Gislingham, the road which had run straight up the side of the Park to Mellis was moved to link with the road to Thornham Parva. This was achieved by a circuitous route through woodland which took it eastward well away from the Hall making a substantial addition to the Park. This was carried out some time between the Tithe Award map of 1841 and the first Ordnance Survey map of 1884. Clumps of trees were scattered through the park with a variety of ornamental species mixed with oak and birch. Tom Williamson in 'Suffolk's Gardens & Parks' p.109 draws attention to an undated early nineteenth century notebook[24] describing the trees in clumps around the Park. He notes that one immediately north of the church had 'Ornamental plants Cedar of Lebanon Lucombe Fulham and Evergreen Oak thorn trees yews hollies junipers purple Beech' and another, to the north east of the Hall was planted with birch, common oak and Lavent oak, with 'the bottom ornamented with Ornamental plants such as Mountain Ash Laburnums purple beech and thorn trees.' As almost all the land in the parish was owned by the Henniker family in the nineteenth century it was a 'closed village' in which the one estate was the only employer so could exercise considerable power. According to John Glyde in 1854, 'Suffolk in the Nineteenth Century', Thornham Magna was then one of only seven villages in 'Woodland High Suffolk' to be completely owned by one individual. Jonathan Theobald[25] contrasts Worlingworth where in 1837 Lord Henniker was the largest proprietor but had barely a quarter of the total acreage of this parish in which there were 37 farms and 28 landowners, although most farms had less than a hundred acres.

The fields were much smaller than they are today, as they have since been opened up into larger units to suit modern machinery. In those days large numbers of people were employed as agricultural labourers working on the land, before farming was mechanised. Ploughing, sowing, weeding and above all harvesting the crops required a large labour force. In the village there was a shop, a blacksmith's forge and an inn and a windmill on the higher ground towards the crossroads at the Stoke Ash White Horse.

Some woodland was managed by coppicing in which blocks of woodland were felled at about 10 to 15 year intervals to produce poles, tool handles, firewood and other products as an important part of the rural economy. The trees grew again from the root system and the large 'stools' produced by this system are still visible in some of the woods. A number of trees were left to grow as standard trees until they were big enough to produce large timbers, which were more valuable but took much longer to mature. Apart from this were the ornamental trees grown to provide attractive visual features of the park landscape. The woods and clumps of trees were also carefully managed to provide suitable cover for the game birds that provided targets for shooting parties who were guests of the owner. It is notable that when the tithe survey was carried out in the 1840s there was very little woodland in Thornham Parva. There were only five tiny areas in the corners of fields which look like the remains of older woods that had been cleared to provide more arable fields. The extent of arable suggests a response to the profits to be made by growing grain crops during and after the Napoleonic Wars.

Figure 7.7 *The windmill at Thornham Magna was a typical postmill, standing high up on the field above the White Horse. The fantail at the back kept the sails facing into the wind.*

Also the reports of the assistant tithe commissioners[26] tell us that cultivation of the heavy lands in Stoke Ash and neighbouring parishes was being improved at this time by the introduction of drainage with underground field drains so that more turnips and mangel worzels could be grown which were fed to fattening sheep, thus more sheep were kept and their manure improved the arable for grain production, particularly wheat which was apparently the most important crop; they also reported large areas of vetch being grown of which some was mowed to feed the horses and the rest was grazed by sheep, while more sheep and bullocks were also being fattened in Wickham Skeith. Some of this land was later converted to woodland and remains such today but it is clear that many of these woods were only planted in the later nineteenth or the twentieth century.

The 4th Lord Henniker was MP for East Suffolk from 1832 to 1847 and from 1858 to 1866, and High Sheriff of Suffolk in 1853. The 1832 election was fiercely contested. A number of posters survive in which Henniker declared that he was against Free Trade, supported the farmers and was against a tax on carts. He was involved in the Great Exhibition of 1851 and some of the Victorian woodwork in Thornham Magna church was made for the Great Exhibition. The churchwardens' account book[27] shows that on 29 April 1856 £52-10-0 was paid to Mr. Ringham of Ipswich 'for Exhibition Screen', which was presumably the present chancel screen, and £1 to 'Stokes his man' for fixing it in the church. Henry Ringham (1806–66) of St. John's Road, Ipswich appears in the 1855 edition of Whites Directory of Suffolk as both carver and joiner. This work seems to have been funded by three payments in 1856 and the following year from Lord Henniker: £44 'from purchase money' and £3-1-6 for items 'sold from the church' which might reflect the stonework from the church, including gothic mouldings, incorporated in the 'hermitage' folly in the Park; then £6 'as a present to the parish', presumably to make up the balance. Thornham Magna church was certainly very much altered during a Victorian restoration programme about 1851. Cynthia Brown has pointed out that Henry Ringham began his career as a carpenter and taught himself to restore and replace Gothic medieval carvings by working on timber church roofs. He developed his carving skills through a close study of the original medieval carvings that survived high up in the open roofs. He found his services were much in demand for Victorian restorations of churches under the influence of the Oxford Movement. Inspired by John Keble preaching at Oxford in 1833, clergy moved from a Low Church emphasis on preaching focused on the pulpit to High Church worship focused on the altar. This required major remodelling of churches with a new emphasis on the chancel. At Thornham Magna some of the original stonework and the stone font which were removed during these changes were used to create the fanciful 'hermitage' folly in the ornamental area of the park. This has recently been rebuilt and the font returned to the church. Several windows were replaced during the 1850s alterations: they are believed to be the work of William Miller of London who was then aged about 45. About ten years earlier he had made heraldic glass for Worlingworth church commissioned by Lord Henniker[28] and he produced other work for him at Thornham Parva and Bedingfield. A note on Miller's work was produced by M Harrison and Birkin Haward. This was also the period when an entirely new church was built at Braiseworth in 1857 to designs by Edward Buckton Lamb who had just rebuilt Leiston church. He is regarded as a maverick who combined traditional gothic with Victorian eccentricity to produce his own version of Victorian High Gothic architecture, being called by Pevsner 'that arch-rogue'. The church has now been converted into a private house and is not open to the public.

Red House Farm was presumably always the home farm for the estate and an inventory of the contents of the Red House and farm, property belonging to Sir John Henniker, had been prepared in 1786. In 1864 Lord Henniker rebuilt the complex as a Model Farm with a large house for the farm bailiff, which is now Red House. He made further changes to the Hall itself, converting the front to the appearance of an ornate

Figure 7.8 *The Folly at Thornham Hall in the nineteenth century showing a more substantial building than survives today (photo by Cleer Alger).*

French 'chateau' using white bricks made on the estate. To achieve this he added new corner towers and an outer wall to the sides of the front courtyard which are said to have made the house dark and gloomy, although one of the rooms was now decorated in gold and white with panelling from a French chateau. In 1866 Lord Henniker was made an English peer as Lord Hartismere. He died in 1870 and this marked the end of the 'heyday of prosperity' for the estate. In Debenham church the east window is a memorial to 'John Henniker Major, IV Baron Henniker, Baron of Hartismere by his sons and tenantry 16.4.1870', a reminder of the family's extensive holdings in that parish. His widow Anne lived until 1899. They are commemorated in Thornham Magna church as are their two daughters. Mary died in 1902 and was buried here while Helen who died in 1907 was buried at Brookwood, presumably in the fashionable necropolis in Surrey served by funeral trains from Waterloo station, but both are recorded on a tablet in the church set up by their brothers Edward and Arthur. Arthur Henry Henniker (1855 –1912) was the third son of the 4th Lord Henniker and chose a military career. He rose to the rank of major-general after serving with the Coldstream Guards in Egypt in 1882 and in the South African or Boer War from 1899 to 1902 when he commanded the second battalion whose colours are still displayed where he hung them in Thornham Magna church. His wife Florence conducted an extensive correspondence with Thomas Hardy which forms the basis of the book 'One Rare Fair Woman' edited by Evelyn Hardy and Frank Pinion in 1972. Florence had married Arthur Henniker Major in 1882 when she was 27. Thomas Hardy recorded that Arthur Henniker said the only time he read poetry was when engaged to Florence, when he bought a copy of Byron and 'read him manfully through. He then got married and has never read any since'. In her thirties she published three novels and some short stories. She met Hardy in Dublin in 1893 when acting as hostess for her widowed brother Lord Houghton, Lord Lieutenant of Ireland. Hardy was 53 and she was 37. She became very close to Hardy. She died in 1923.

Lady Anne Henniker's brother Sir Edward Kerrison (1821–1886) inherited the Brome and Oakley estates from his father together with much property in Eye and Yaxley, amounting to a total of some 10,000 acres, so during this time the Henniker and Kerrison families between them owned a large proportion of the property in the area. On Sir Edward's death the estate passed to his, and Anne's, sister Agnes who had married Lord Bateman of Shobdon in Herefordshire. After her husband died in 1901 Lady Bateman moved to Brome Hall, living there until her death in 1918. Then the estate was broken up and Oakley Hall itself was demolished in 1930 and Brome Hall in 1958.

The 1861 Census offers a snapshot of the inhabitants of Thornham Magna. There were thirteen resident staff at the Hall headed by the housekeeper, Mary Cobb aged 58, and including John Perkins the gardener, then aged 37. The Rev James Farr Reeve occupied the Rectory with his wife, three children and four servants. The Farm Bailiff, John Wilby aged 64, was at Red House farm and a second farm bailiff, James Smith, may have been based at Street Farm as it does not appear by name but was part of the estate farmed in hand. Other farmers were Alfred Cracknel at Star House working 162 acres with seven men and four boys, Edward Dove at Dog House (later Grove Farm) farming 320 acres with ten men and six boys, and Daniel Lamb, presumably at Lambs Farm in the Street, having 65 acres with four men and three boys. The Lambs were also

Edith Jocelyn

Figure 7.9 *Staff at Thornham Hall in 1866. John Perkins and his wife are the first two on the top line.*

blacksmiths and their neighbour was John Grice the wheelwright (in the twentieth century the village blacksmith's forge was still at Lambs Farm, now the Street Forge Workshops). Charles Cubitt the schoolmaster lived at the Lodge and his wife is described as governess (perhaps to the children at the Hall) while a lady teacher lived at Star House Farm. The curate of Mellis occupied Park Villa. There was a woodman at Gate House and gamekeepers at Chickery (perhaps the Pheasantry where the chicks were raised for shooting) and Dormans Hall (now lost but presumably marked by Dormans Wood). We also find the innkeeper at the Horseshoes and the miller at Mill House, but

Little Swatsfield Hall was the home of a bricklayer and his wife. Apart from those listed as in the Village, presumably along the Street between Lambs Farm and Street Farm, there were four households at Water House, five in Clay Lane and two in Clay Street (although it is not clear how we should differentiate between Lane and Street) and in all of these 35 occupants are listed as agricultural labourers with ages ranging from 9 to 76. Other residents included a wash woman, a groom, three gardeners, gloveress, dealer, shoemaker, sub postmaster, tea dealer, brickmaker, carter, dressmaker and a carpenter whose son was also a carpenter. Three servants were specifically described as dairy maids.

By the nineteenth century many parishes had brickmakers, but we do have evidence of some centres making bricks long before this. In the Middle Ages the Bishops of Norwich had a long tradition of brickmaking on their estate in South Elmham St. Cross. At Gislingham between 1550 and 1559 a brickmaker is listed in the tax returns and this might have led on to the commercial manufacture of bricks on the Manor of Swatsfield, where much later they produced the cream bricks for the rebuilding of Thornham Hall. William Butcher and Son are listed as bricklayers at Thornham Magna. On 18 September 1779 Daniel Betts, a bricklayer, and Anne his wife were recorded on a Movement Order from Metfield to Withersdale, where brick ovens, possibly of this period, can still be seen built into the bank at Withersdale Cross. In 1839 the Godbold families were owners of brick and tile kilns at Mendham and Metfield. By 1874 Edward Godbold Senior was listed as brick, tile and drainage pipe maker, farmer and steam threshing machine owner. The census return of 1851 shows Metfield had seven bricklayers/makers.

Figure 7.10 *Photograph of Thornham Hall in 1886 showing how the front had been adapted in the style of a French chateau. (See page 194)*

For dating bricks a useful table was published in 1930 in 'The Moated Houses of England', written by a Suffolk born author R Thurston Hopkins. He gives the following sizes in inches:

Thirteenth cent. 9 × 4½ × 2;   Fourteenth cent. 9 × 4⅜ × 2 ¹/16 ; Fifteenth cent. 9 × 4½ × 2;
Late Fifteenth cent. 8¼ × 4½ × 2¼; Sixteenth cent. 10 × 4¾ × 2½;   Seventeenth cent. 9 × 4¼ × 2½;
Eighteenth cent. 9½ × 4½ × 3.

There will always be some exceptions in the days when bricks were produced by hand by many different makers, but this table gives a valuable indication.

Reference to the miller is a reminder that the postmill at Thornham Magna was said to have been built in 1750; it was featured with a photograph in 'Model Engineer' for 27 March 1947 but was burned down by vandals in 1959. It stood in a small enclosure on the large Common Field east of The Street with the miller's house beside the road from the Horseshoes to the White Horse. At one time there was presumably a second mill on another piece of exposed high ground west of the Street on Mill Green beside Clay Street. The postmill with a round house beside the village school at Stoke Ash is said to have been destroyed by fire in 1883. It does not appear on Hodskinson's map of 1783, but he does show a mill beside Stoke Hall. The early mill at Allwood Green, Gislingham, which was said to have the date 1516 carved on its crown tree, had disappeared by 1885. The location of a mill is indicated by Mill Hill in Wickham Skeith and another is shown on Mellis Green on Hodskinson's map of 1783. Today no mills survive in the immediate area, although at one time they were a familiar feature of the landscape and vital to the local economy before all the grain was transported to distant roller mills for processing. Some of these windmills had probably been built on the sites occupied by similar mills through the Middle Ages but finds of many fragments of small millstones suggest that some households had once used their own hand operated mills. Evidence of windmill sites can be more difficult to identify than watermills. The leat that supplied water to the mill wheel often survives even if the buildings have been lost or converted to other uses. We do have quite a lot of records of millers so at Homersfield, where the water mill is mentioned in Domesday Book, tax returns give us Johannes Skylly (the Lollard) as miller in 1429, C Barker (a non-communicant) in 1594 and others listed between 1650 and 1699. The windmill at Metfield is recorded when John Strobyly Junior paid tax in 1500 and a 'mylle close' was taxed 60 years later. Sometimes windmill sites are found by accident as when the excavation of a burial mound at Flixton revealed the base of a stock mill which had been placed to take advantage of the raised position. Our earliest record in South Elmham shows de Agn le Mellere paying tax in 1327 and details of tenements reveal mills at St. Nicholas and St. Margaret in 1350 so perhaps one of these was owned by de Agn. Reputedly a mill in St. Margaret was taken down and transported by ox cart to Chippenhall Green where it was re-assembled. This mill was later replaced by another with a wooden round house that was still visible in 1934. Today the only evidence of these mills are the mounds on which they stood at Chippenhall Green and at St. Margarets. Not all such enterprises were successful as at Withersdale a tower mill was built in 1802, but within three years it was for sale because it had become redundant and a few years later there is no record of a mill on that site. Post mills are recorded at Metfield plus a tower mill which lost its sails in a storm in 1916. The census of 1851 recorded five millers living in Metfield. Single mills were recorded at St. Cross,

Figure 7.11 *The site of the watermill at Homersfield is marked today by this weir in the river.*

at St. Michael and at All Saints. There were two mills at St. James and one of these had been transported in 1864 from Starston in Norfolk, but both had gone by the twentieth century. It was during the 1830s that the highest number of mills was built in Suffolk, but by 1926 only 48 were still working.

White's Directory of Suffolk records that in 1844 the ecclesiastical parish of Thornham Parva had been combined with that of Thornham Magna of which Lord Henniker was the patron and the rector was a member of the family, the Reverend Sir Augustus Brydges Henniker, although he was not resident having a home at Newton Hall, Great Dunmow[29] in Essex and renting Plashwood at Haughley in Suffolk. A tablet in Thornham Magna church records that his wife Frances Amelia, daughter of John Henry Stewart of South Ockendon in Essex, died in 1823 at the age of 25. He died in 1849 and was commemorated by a stained glass window in Thornham Parva church. The house known as the Rectory was occupied by his curate, Reverend Thomas Preston, who carried out the religious duties. However by 1855 the Rectory had a resident rector

Figure 7.12 *The site of the medieval windmill mound at South Elmham St Margaret marked by a tree.*

Reverend James Farr Reeve. Sir Augustus Henniker did involve himself in local affairs, as in 1837 he was chairman of the Board of Guardians for Hartismere Union. This was created under the Poor Law Amendment Act of 1834 to provide for the poor of 32 parishes with a workhouse for adults and infants at Eye but a separate one for boys and girls at Wortham. This arrangement, which significantly reduced the cost of providing relief for the poor, made individual parish workhouses redundant. In 1856 Lord Henniker purchased the former workhouse of Stoke Ash which was a brick house and cottage with two yards beside the road from the A140 to Stoke Ash church surrounded on the other three sides by Henniker's land[30]. A 79 year old farmer, Thomas Knights, testified that the property 'from my earliest recollection was held and possessed by the Churchwardens and Overseers of the Poor of the said Parish … and up to the time of the passing of the Poor Law Amendment Act it was always used and occupied as the poor house or Workhouse for the said parish and from that period up to the present time … let at small weekly rents … to poor persons belonging to the said parish'. The neighbouring Hoxne Union was dissolved in 1907 and merged with the Hartismere Union, so Hoxne's workhouse at Stradbroke became redundant. It was sold, and the documentation of this sale records that the site in Stradbroke had been purchased in 1836 from Lord Henniker being part of his manor and farm of Barle Haugh Hall. The five acres known as Pear Tree Piece were purchased for £274 in 1836 and sold for £560 in 1907, including at the latter date the buildings constructed for the workhouse. Elsewhere in the county White's Directory for 1844 shows Lord Henniker as lord of the manor of Great Bealings, although not resident there, but he was patron of the Rectory which was held by a relative, the Honourable and Reverend W.C. Henniker MA. Lord

185

Figure 7.13 *Parishes in which the Thornham Estate held properties in the nineteenth century. The light shading shows those that appear in the book of maps prepared in 1828. Additional properties mentioned in the court book of 1891 are given darker shading, and all those listed in the rental of 1824 (Appendix 3) are marked R.*

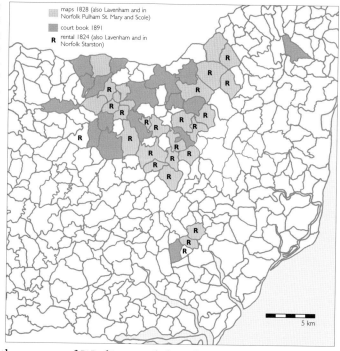

maps 1828 (also Lavenham and in Norfolk Pulham St. Mary and Scole)
court book 1891
R rental 1824 (also Lavenham and in Norfolk Starston)

5 km

Henniker was also lord of the manor of Worlingworth but the Hall was occupied by a farmer, probably William Spurling: the Reverend Edward Barlee was rector of the church of which Lord Henniker was patron.

John, 5th Lord Henniker, born in 1842, was at Cambridge with the future King Edward VII and became a Lord in Waiting to him when he was Prince of Wales. In 1868 he became Member of Parliament for East Suffolk, which had been his father's seat until he entered the English peerage as Lord Hartismere in 1866. He was chairman of East Suffolk County Council. According to the 1872 Return of Landowners Lord Henniker of Thornham owned 10,910 acres 1 rood 35 perches of land in Suffolk with a gross estimated rental of £15,158. There were another 130 acres elsewhere in the country. In 1891 he had 'copyhold hereditaments' in the manors of Brockford with its members, Chepenhall in Fressingfield, Mendham Hall, Mendham Kingshall, Skelton Hall, Thorpe Hall [is this Thorp Hall in Ashfield?], Yaxley Bulls Hall with Blogates Hall, Wilby, Woodhall in Stoke Ash, Ulveston [could this be Ulveston Hall, Debenham which was part of Tooley's Foundation, Ipswich (cf David Allen's Ipswich Archives p.403)?], Playford with Mitchells etc., Mendlesham with its members, Walsham etc., Earl Soham, Bedfield, Thorndon with its members, Rishangles with its members, Braiseworth Old Hall New Hall with Barnes, Hoxne Hall with the Priory, Wickham Skeith, Chickering with Wingfield, Horham Thorpe Hall with Wootten, Wetheringsette, Monk Soham, Withersdale, Cotton Hempnalls, Kingston, Winston cum Pulham, Pulham [Pulham St. Mary, Norfolk], Worlingworth, Eye Hall otherwise Priory, Eye Sokemere, Osmondeston in Scole, Palgrave, Pountney Hall in Mellis, Gislingham Goldingham otherwise Goldingham Hall, Stoke Hall with Thorpe [Stoke Ash], Swatshall Woodhouse and Braisworth [Thornham Magna and Parva], Debenham Butley, Great Bealings, Burgate, Mellis St. Johns, Heigham, Rushies and Jennies [probably the manor of Rushes &

Jennings in Gislingham], Westhall, Redgrave and Botesdale, and Gislingham. It is notable that by this date the family had extensive properties in and around Eye itself. Some of the workers on the Thornham farms lived in cottages in Eye and walked the two miles to their work.

At Gislingham according to White's Directory of 1844 Swattisfield Hall was the farm of Charles Cracknell, presumably as tenant of Lord Henniker, and Rush Green was farmed by Thomas Steggall. The dominance of the Hennikers in Gislingham is reflected by their control of the large square 'Squire's Pew' in Gislingham Church, known as the Henniker Pew, until its removal in 1933 with Lord Henniker's permission to make way for a new organ[31]. It stood on a raised base at the east end of the south side of the nave, numbered as one in the series of nineteen box pews, and was large enough to be used on Sunday afternoons for teaching the girls' Sunday School. Following the 1870 Education Act, Lord Henniker worked with the Rector, Reverend Thomas Colyer, to enlarge the Infant and Mixed Schools in Gislingham.

The estate was apparently still being expanded in 1884 as the printed map for the sale of the Yaxley Hall Estate by Biddell and Blencowe in that year appears among the family papers, so this was presumably when the Hennikers acquired it. It had been the property of P R Welch in 1855, but Lord Henniker already owned Bulls Hall in Yaxley, so presumably the family were consolidating their holdings in this parish adjoining Thornham. Yaxley Hall was certainly part of the Henniker estate in 1923 when proposals for alterations to the Hall were being considered, as revealed by detailed papers and a clip of correspondence with Philip Palmer of The Red House, Thornham who was Lord Henniker's agent at the time[32].

Lord Henniker was Lord in waiting to Queen Victoria from 1877 to 1880 and from 1885 to 1893. With the Duke of Grafton he was one of the governors of the Indian prince Duleep Singh who lived in exile at Elveden. There were big shooting parties and a large staff, but the estate was in serious decline by 1892. Declining income from farming was not enough to pay for the lavish lifestyle kept up by the family and the expenses of being in the social circle of the Prince of Wales. In 1889 John and his wife Alice celebrated their Silver Wedding Anniversary by planting the 'Silver Oak Avenue' of 12 trees, one for each of their 12 children. Most of the oaks are still growing, although two have been replaced by younger trees. In 1895 he became Governor of the Isle of Man, which provided an essential income, and he moved there with his family. He stayed there until his death in 1902.

The middle of the nineteenth century saw a change to the landscape caused by an intrusion unparalleled since the Roman road was built. The new feature cutting through field patterns and the established scene was the iron highway that would carry people and goods drawn by the latest steam locomotives. The railway line through the estate was opened from Ipswich to Norwich in December 1849 by the Eastern Union Railway which was incorporated into the Great Eastern Railway in 1862. The chairman of the Eastern Union at the time was John Chevallier Cobbold of Ipswich and the general manager was the engineer Peter Bruff who lived at Handford Lodge in Ipswich. They appointed as contractor for building the line Thomas Brassey who had been involved in the construction of many railway lines. He employed as his agent to oversee the work on the spot a Scotsman, Alexander Ogilvie who later settled in Suffolk, buying

Figure 7.14 *The Silver Wedding avenue of oak trees at Thornham planted in 1889 as they appear today.*

Sizewell House at Leiston from Richard Garrett. Work on the line started in February 1847 and one of the sub-contractors on a section near the estate, Alexander Cummings, completed his work by October 1848 as he advertised his equipment for sale at Mellis, including ten horses with their harness, a timber drug with six inch wheels, nearly new, 30 picks, 8 keying and adze hammers, 12 augers [to make holes in sleepers for the oak pegs (treenails) holding the chairs in place], 12 iron crowbars and 12 piles [stakes driven in to dislodge earth in cuttings], 6 beetles [mallets used to drive in the piles], 24 shovels, 5 levers, 5 spring bars, 15 lamps with irons, an 8-coomb corn chest, several mangers, racks etc., 7½ cwt cart grease, about 2 tons of nails, spikes etc., quantity of boards, planks etc[33]. The local farmers clearly sought to take advantage of any free assets as Peter Bruff had to complain to Lord Henniker that one of his tenants, Mr Cracknell of 'Swatchfield Hall' (Swatsfield), was taking topsoil from the works that was still needed for the railway company's own use. Bruff undertook to tell them which topsoil was surplus to their requirements as soon as he could[34]. Apparently the first steam locomotive travelled the section of line between Finningham and Diss in January 1849. It was the contractor's 0-4-0 engine with 5 foot diameter wheels, officially called 'Woodlark' but generally known as 'Mudlark', presumably a reference to the condition of the line's earthworks. In May 1849 it was transporting materials from Finningham for building the stations at Mellis and Diss. Lord Henniker had a private 'flag halt' on the line so that he could arrange for trains to stop on request. There was a drive through the woods directly from the Hall to the halt and a tower on the right of it from which a man signalled with a flag when there were passengers for the train. Lord Henniker complained to the railway company that poachers in his woods when chased by his gamekeepers took refuge on the line and he obtained permission for his staff to chase poachers along the line although the company refused to accept responsibility for the consequences. The nearest public station was at Mellis which became the junction for a short branch line to Eye. The branch line was created by the Mellis and Eye Railway Act of July 1865 supported by Lord Henniker and Sir Edward Clarence Kerrison. It was opened on 2 April 1867 in the ownership of the Mellis and Eye Railway Company but operated by the Great Eastern Railway who took it over in 1898. By the 1920s direct bus services were running and there were poor connections with main line trains so the passenger service to Eye ended in February 1931, although goods services continued until 1964 when the Beeching axe brought them to an end. An isolated stretch of embankment near Yaxley is one of the few surviving reminders of this short branch line. Mellis station was closed altogether in 1966 leaving Diss or Stowmarket as the nearest railway stations, while electric trains between Norwich and London now race past the edge of the estate and the site of Lord Henniker's flag halt.

The Adairs invested in transport enterprises in the vicinity of their estates, as the Hennikers did at Thornham. The Adairs supported the navigations on the Rivers Waveney and Blyth and the Waveney Valley Railway. This railway project began in 1851 to link the Eastern Union Railway's main line at Tivetshall to Bungay. It reached Harleston in 1855 and was eventually opened to Bungay on 2 November 1860, being extended to Beccles in 1863. As the railway ran on the Norfolk side of the Waveney the nearest station to Flixton Hall was at Wortwell, being reached by a bridge at Homersfield. The plan of the Adairs to improve this bridge is revealed in a letter of 16 December 1869 from the Iron Department of the Coal Exchange that a new bridge was to be constructed at Homersfield. This was to replace the old wooden bridge and

7.15. The arms of the Adair family are a conspicuous feature on Homersfield bridge.

would use the area of the wooden abutments for its construction and would be made in wrought iron and poured concrete, which would support to a strength of 200 tons, with an ultimate strength to withstand 1200 tons. Including decorations and a concrete road it cost £344. This did not include the demolition of the old bridge. The Ipswich architect, Henry Eyton, communicated to Sir Shafto Adair 'that he felt this was in his consideration a low price as other bridges built throughout the County were at a far higher cost.' Work was carried out and completed in the early 1870s, which enabled the Adairs to cross the river safely in their carriage to the railway station at Wortwell. For other users a toll of 2d was charged, but foot passengers were free. During a surveyor's inspection in 1907 it was noticed that a chain and padlock were fixed to the centre of the bridge on one day a year when the river was at full flood. Presumably the Adairs were enforcing their right to control the bridge as their own property. In 1990 it cost £85,000 to renovate the bridge, which is a notable example of the early use of concrete for structural purposes and is said to be the oldest concrete bridge in Britain, a forerunner of modern reinforced concrete structures. The middle of the bridge marks the junction of seven administrative boundaries, and when it was re-opened seven scissors were used to cut the tape and each section went to one of the seven authorities involved. The monogram of the Adair family and their arms, which feature the red hand of Ulster, are still visible on the ironwork. Most notable in the decoration are the painted 'bloody hands' which are said to originate from a local story about the punishment of a young ostler who was so badly beaten that he died from his wounds. In his dying moments he left a bloody hand print on the wall. In retribution for this act the Adairs were instructed to add the 'bloody hands' to their family crest. The more orthodox explanation is that all families with titles in the Irish peerage were required to include in their arms the red hand of Ulster. This was said to be the ancestral badge of the ancient O'Neills, the High Kings of Ulster, being the amputated hand of the legendary giant from whom they claimed descent. It also appears in the arms of the Hennikers as peers of the Irish creation.

Provision for education was always seen as an important contribution to the community. Back in the seventh century St. Felix, first bishop of East Anglia, set up schools in his diocese and through the Middle Ages village priests and the friars provided education for the poor. Gifts in wills often mention money being left for the education of the poor. In 1590 at Metfield we learn from the churchwardens' accounts of 'the scole house planchering'. At Gislingham the school was being repaired in 1636, and six years later four schoolmasters/ tutors are recorded. In the book of the overseers of the poor in Metfield we read that on the 20 April 1701 payment was made for 'learning of William Harper to read 27 weeks at 2d per week.' There are records that Thornham Parva had a schoolmaster between 1650 and 1654, and Stoke Ash paid a schoolmaster from 1704 to 1707. During the nineteenth century education became more widespread, although between 1801 and 1851 in Suffolk 143 parishes were still without a school, and only 8% of males attended those that did exist. At a time when many boys were required from a young age to work during the week, it is less surprising that Sunday Schools show large attendance during the early part of the century. We read of some fee paying schools for the better off and weekly boarding schools as with Schools for Young Ladies at Mendham, Metfield and Homersfield. Families like the Hennikers and Adairs supported schools for poor children. In Thornham Magna the Parish History Survey says in 1818 there was a day school attended by 12 pupils; that in 1833 a school was held on Tuesday and Friday and that two Sunday schools were attended by 33. Schools of Industry were established at Flixton, Homersfield and St. Cross and 70 pupils attended at St. Cross. In 1860 a new school was built with the help of the Adair family and to this day many houses and schools in the South Elmham area display the Adair crest as a mark of their concern for the living conditions and education of their tenants. In 1867 we first hear of National Schools, the one at Flixton being known as the Public Elementary School. As a result some of the smaller parish schools closed, so in 1867 children from St. Cross were attending the National School at Flixton. At Metfield the school situated behind the church, on the former site of the workhouse, was built in 1874–5 as a parish school supported by the church to provide for 124 children at a cost of between £560 and £600 most of which was raised by subscription from the landowners and occupiers of the parish. Captain Charles Rayley RN, who was lord of the manor but lived at Southwold, left an endowment of £500 which provided an annual income of £16. In 1912 it had a savings bank, library and miniature rifle range provided by the schoolmaster. The appearance of Reading Rooms in many parishes, including Thornham Magna, reflects the growing interest in improving the mind.

There has always been a tendency for independent thinking in East Anglia. We have already mentioned the activities of the Lollards, but their suppression did not lead to universal conformity in religion. In 1536 John Bale, curate of Thorndon, was accused of inflammatory preaching. At Homersfield in 1596 C Barker, a miller, was identified as not receiving communion. These are just some examples of non-conformity which was clearly extensive and led to the creation of dissenting groups with their own meeting places. At Withersdale in 1663 the Fox family built a Quaker Meeting House which included a two roomed cottage for the preacher. During renovation work on the cottage several items were discovered in the Meeting House, including a mirror placed at the corner of the altar to enable the preacher to watch the congregation while his back was turned towards them. It was also found that burials had been placed in the garden. Methodist chapels were built in many villages. A new chapel was built in 1866 at Metfield, and six years earlier a United Methodist chapel was built at Gislingham. At the same time a Baptist chapel was recorded at Homersfield and in 1874 in Metfield the Plymouth Brethren held their meetings in the barn at The Willows during the time of Isaac Youngs Miles. In Chapel Cottage, Metfield, a large basin was discovered below the floor of a room. It was the size of the complete room so a Baptist minister would be able to assist in the total immersion of candidates during the baptism. In Mendham a chapel belonged to an independent congregation formed in 1796 but was also used as a place of worship by the Wesleyans. The Baptist Chapel beside the old main road on the boundary between Stoke Ash, Braiseworth and Thornham Magna has a date plate for 1846 in its gable and burials in its graveyard had started by the early 1850s.

Notes

1   Cribb, N, 1955 The Worlingworth Parish Fire Engine, *PSIAH* **27** (1955), 51.
2   It was demolished after his death and the site is now occupied by North London Collegiate School.
3   SROI:S1/2/107.

4   Notes & Queries 1870, 4th Series vol 6 p. 179.
5   SROI:S1/2/502.
6   Paine, C, 1993 *The History of Eye,* Eye, 49.
7   SROI:S1/2/500.1.
8   By Coade of London.
9   Albion, R, 1926 *Forests & Sea Power – the Timber Problem of the Royal Navy 1652 – 1862,* Cambridge.
10 Admiralty records in PRO.
11 It seems that John Henniker, Henry Bird the elder, Henry Bird the younger and Conrad Lang, of London, merchants wanted a 40 shillings per ton bounty, despite the ships (Merry Jacks, Sword Fish, Revolution & Neptune) not being equipped with a set of sails of British sail cloth as required by law. Information from Caird Library of National Maritime Museum, Greenwich per Stephen Schwarz.
12 Information from Stephen Schwarz.
13 Ref. T/3300/13.
14 Entries in Court Book, SROI:S1/2/18.3.
15 Chandos Lodge in Eye (on the corner of Lambseth St. & Castleton Way) was built in 1811 by her great niece's husband John Wythe Jr.
16 Williamson, T, 2000 *Suffolk's Gardens and Parks,* Macclesfield, fig. 57 and p.133.
17 SROI:S1/2/105.
18 SROI:HA 116/486/1 with flat copies of many maps in S1/2/300.
19 His father Matthias Kerrison had bought the extensive local estates of the Marquis of Cornwallis in 1825 bringing his total property to nearly 10, 000 acres.
20 Famous for designing the round Reading Room of the British Museum.
21 Williamson, T, 2000 *Suffolk's Gardens and Parks,* Macclesfield, fig. 43.
22 SROI:S1/2/300.64–68 and HA116/4530/14.
23 SROI:HA116/4530/14.
24 SROI:HA 116/3.
25 *PSIAH,* 2001, p. 55.
26 Holt and Kain, 1982 Land Use and Farming in Suffolk about 1840, *PSIAH* **35**, 123ff.
27 SROI:FB 163/E1/2.
28 SROI:HA 116/4676.
29 Maps of the Henniker estate of Newton Hall, Great Dunmow are SROI:HD417/44 & 46.
30 SROI:S1/2/50.7.
31 Clive Paine's Guide to St Mary's Gislingham (Gislingham Heritage Trust, 2002).
32 SROI:HA116/4676/Box 40.
33 Moffat, M, 1987 *East Anglia's First Railways,* Lavenham, 33.
34 letter in SROI:HA116/4530/16.

Chapter 8

The Modern Estate

So far we have considered people and the landscape in detail, but one of the most important aspects of the estate was the house with its gardens and parkland. There was continuous occupation from the earliest building within its moated enclosure to the grand manor house of the Wisemans and Bokenhams. This was the main residence of the family, the Manor Courts were held at Thornham Magna and the records of these were being written at The White Horse by the eighteenth century. A clear impression of the house built in the seventeenth century comes from a painting of Thornham Hall, possibly as built for Barbara Wiseman when she married Edmund Bokenham (Plate 15). The building is a high status mansion in the Elizabethan or early Jacobean style, with decorated corner pillars surmounted by ornamental weather vanes and twisted chimneys. The main entrance has a decorative porch with a sundial above. The painting shows three floors and indicates a servants' wing on the west with its own entrance. The main doorway is approached by a central drive through lawns with formally arranged ornamental planting in the forecourt. This is entered by a bridge across an arm of the moat. In front of the moat are decorative gates and arches framing the approach. Doorways on the east and west sides of the forecourt probably led to the stables on one side and the garden on the other. The painting shows eight double chimneys and in the hearth tax of 1674 Captain Bokenham was assessed on 17 hearths. Another member of the family is also listed in the assessment for four hearths. Less than a decade later Paul Bokenham made his will in 1681 with a reference to his 'new house at Thornham'. Does this indicate that we are already seeing changes to the house in the seventeenth century? This is certainly the case later, as in a painting of the early eighteenth century we see major changes have taken place. The decorative work on the roof has now disappeared and the sundial has been replaced by a clock, but the entrance is still in the centre of the building although we now see an additional entrance to the east wing. On both sides of the house are walled gardens marked by coach houses on either side. These are also shown on the survey map of 1765 commissioned by Sir John Major.

Kellys Directory of 1892 describes Thornham Hall and claims that Charles II spent a night or more there as Killigrew was his favourite, and that the hangings of the king's bed could still be seen at that date 'and the chairs are worked on linen in beautiful old crewel-work'. If Charles did visit Thornham, and this remains unproven, his host must have been Paul Bokenham as Charles Killigrew did not marry Paul's daughter Jemima until 1687, two years after King Charles died. However it is useful to have this description of the house near the end of the nineteenth century. Kellys tells us that the old house was of brick covered with stucco and the 4th Lord Henniker had built a new outer wall around the court using white bricks made on the estate. The style resembled that of a French chateau. Inside was a salon of lovely old white and gold panelling of the Louis XIV period, which had come from a chateau in France. The mouldings represented some of Fontaine's fables. Hanging in the hall were portraits of Richard Cromwell, the Earl of Nottingham by Mytens, the Duke of Norfolk painted by Holbein, portraits of the Henniker and Major families by Sir Joshua Reynolds and Landseer's painting of Sir John Henniker aged 22 at Thornham. The sedan chair of Lady Chandos was still at the Hall, as was an organ built by the 3rd Lord Henniker. There was a collection of important specimen pieces of pottery from the factories of Lowestoft, Yarmouth, and Swansea, with examples of Wedgewood and of oriental china. Chippendale furniture could be seen in many of the rooms.

We have confirmation of the appearance of the building in a photograph of 1886 (Fig. 7.10). This shows the major changes to the front and reveals that the former main entrance had an even more elaborate tower with its clock above, surmounted by a cupola presumably designed to house a bell. The front garden layout had changed with decorative flower beds and specimen trees situated within a gravel surround and edged by grass walkways. The two coach houses seen flanking the front in earlier paintings, and in the survey of 1765, had gone. The tithe map of 1841 shows that by then they had been replaced with a large new stable block and coach house hidden behind the Hall. The main entrance was now from the rear of the original building in the north east corner approached by a new carriage drive. The new entrance hall is shown in the layout prepared by the architect Sydney Smirke in 1837. Alternative plans seem to have been offered as one shows a service wing with 38 additional rooms adjoining the main building on the north. This was a change from an earlier plan submitted that year which allowed for additional space for servants to be built on the north side of the house and reached by a separate drive. It included a brew house, ironing and laundering rooms with double sleeping room above. In the second version the grand vestibule and entrance hall seem to have been reduced in scale to make room for the washing, baking and brew house facilities. A force pump house was presumably linked to the water tower which is mentioned as a conspicuous feature at a later date. The tithe map of 1841 seems to show a compromise with the main entrance drive sweeping up to the north east corner, but the new service wing built along the west side of a northern courtyard behind the Hall. The stable block was built round three sides of a separate courtyard with its north side closed by the coach house. We also see a circular building which is the ice house, as is confirmed by the fact that the distance between stables and ice house on the map corresponds with the present position. The ice house is a red brick, domed structure covering a deep circular pit, tapering towards the base, with a round opening at its head covered by a mound of earth to keep it cold. The bricks were made on the estate and are of late eighteenth to early nineteenth century date. Further north are two more outhouses. North of these the tithe map shows the outline of the walled garden with its glasshouse. This whole area is listed in the tithe apportionment[1] as the park side of the mansion, gardens and ornamental plantations of 87 acres, 3 roods, 35 poles. In the 1765 survey the house, gardens and park are given as 79 acres, so obviously additional land had been included by 1841 and the reference to 'ornamental plantations' shows that the planting of specimen trees behind the Hall had already started by then.

A coloured plan of the gardens made some time after 1851[2] shows to the south and west of the Hall itself a formal layout of parterres, geometric patterns of beds for flowers and shrubs, defined by low hedges of box, thyme or hyssop (Plate 23). The plan mentions the summerhouse which appears to be the structure now termed the folly. This was created out of fragments of ecclesiastical architecture removed from Thornham Magna church during the Victorian refurbishment, and the medieval font was used here as a planter. The folly was much bigger than the present one as can be seen from an undated photograph and from the plan of its construction. It had a fireplace close to the main entrance in the northeast corner of the building. Just south of the folly is now the pets' cemetery which was created in the late nineteenth century and has a remarkable series of memorials to the horses of Major-General Arthur Henry Henniker. These start with 'Bob' his charger when he was adjutant to the 2nd Battalion of the Coldstream Guards, who served in the Egyptian Campaign of 1882, including the battle of Tel el Kebir, and survived to die at Thornham in 1894 aged 17 years. 'Mahuta'

Figure 8.1 *The Folly at Thornham Hall in 2004. It has been rebuilt several times over the years.*

is recorded as having 'retired on pension' in December 1886 and died at Thornham in April 1889. Also commemorated are 'Joll' aged 26 and 'Punch', born at Thornham, who served as his charger from 1891 to 1902, aged 17. They both died at Thornham. Finally there is 'Toto', present as his charger at Belmont and Modder, wounded in the South African War at Magersfontein, served at Driefontein and Johannesburg, but was killed at Pretoria in 1900. Also recorded are the dogs of Arthur and his wife Florence and some other later family pets. It is ironic that Arthur Henniker died in 1912 aged 57 after being kicked by a charger he was trying out in the Riding School of the Blues. At the time he was Major-General commanding the First London Division of the Territorial Force.

The plan shows the walled garden and indicates that the main entrance from the south, towards the Hall, was through a long conservatory that extended a little in front of the wall at the present entrance and stretched back into the walled enclosure. The outline of the front section is still visible, including the sills that held the door hinges and four bases that supported the iron framework of this large building. As the walls of the main part of the walled garden stand today, south of and including the main glasshouse, we can see that the bricks were made on the estate probably about 1700. Enclosing this area of formal kitchen garden provided a favourable area for vegetables and fruit trees and protected them from the deer in the park. One feature survives from an earlier garden as the large underground cistern in the walled garden is lined with older bricks of the type made in the 1550s when John Wiseman was living at the Hall. It was used to collect and store water and a drainage channel enabled rain water from the surface to fill the cistern ready for use in the garden. This cistern lies under part of the main glasshouse which was heated as the Gardener's Book of 1849 says it had a 'stov'. On the plan it is shown as the vinery and marks the northern extent of the

Figure 8.2 *The walled garden at Thornham Hall showing traces of the gardener's cottage. The fireplace on the first floor is just visible behind the tree which grows in the middle of the site of one of the rooms. The back wall is part of the main wall of the garden.*

walled garden. The walls enclosing the extension north of this were built at a later date, possibly before 1884 but after 1851. At the northwest corner was the Gardener's House, which is now part of the administrative complex but the old beams are still visible and the original dimensions are clear to see. At this time the working access to the walled garden was on this northern side with two main routes for the gardeners coming from the unenclosed top section, the frame garden, which contained two large glass frames. These had brick bases which were rediscovered recently when a water feature was introduced. The area of water now known as the canal is marked on the plan with a gravel track crossing it to give access to the nursery beds which were some three acres in size and divided into four sections.

The gardens were an important part of the estate and in 1848 a man arrived to join the staff who was to make a great impression on all aspects of the gardening at Thornham. John Perkins came from Astley in Warwickshire and was 24 years old when he was appointed Head Gardener, having served his time in the grand houses near Nuneaton. He probably lived in the gardener's house by the walled garden. Well educated, he could read and write well as can be seen by his neat hand in the garden books. He was responsible for the new designs and layouts as shown on a plan of the gardens, making them a positive feature of the Hall. Within a year he produced a list of the flowers and bedding plants at Thornham, mentioning the greenhouse with its stove. He listed fuschia, buddleia, roses, petunia, cacti, varieties of rose, gloxinia and new for 1850 were geraniums and gardenia. He listed the roses separately and included

Figure 8.3 *A view along the path outside the walled garden in the nineteenth century. The roof of the Conservatory is visible on the left and a statue marks the end of the walk (photo by Cleer Alger).*

HT, bush, climber, trailing climber, native basket, whites and dwarf crimson perpetual. He was reputedly responsible for providing flowers from the garden for Queen Victoria on a regular basis. One thing is certain – his expertise with flowers and plants. This is revealed in his book 'Floral Designs for the Table' and his love of beautiful things is apparent in his introduction to the book. The colour plates illustrate 24 coloured designs with the directions for ornamentation with leaves, flowers and fruit (Plate 21). They give suggestions for table decorations for the breakfast, luncheon and dinner tables, the wedding breakfast table, cricket luncheon, harvest home dinner or supper table, hunt breakfast and Christmas dinner table. This clearly reflects the variety of functions for which he was expected to decorate the table at Thornham. The book also includes generic lists of plants that produce berries, a list of plants from which suitable specimens may be selected to suit all tastes for dinner table decorations and also a generic list of plants which produce ornamental leaves. The book was published in 1877 by Wyman and Sons of London and became a best seller. It was dedicated to The Right Honourable the Dowager Lady Henniker. This was Anne, the daughter of Sir Edward Kerrison and widow of the 4th Lord Henniker who had died in 1870. We can be pretty sure that it was John Perkins who established the Lady Henniker apple which was awarded a Certificate of Merit by the Royal Horticultural Society in 1873 and still appears in some specialist catalogues of apple trees. This apple can be seen featured in one of his designs. He clearly stood in that tradition of Victorian head gardeners who gave loyal service to their employers but were keen to look beyond the immediate needs of the families for whom they worked.

John Perkins was still listed as part of the Thornham Hall household in 1861, but by 1867 he had married the widow Jane Childs whose former husband was the inn keeper and farmer at the White Horse. She had a child who was 6 years old at the time of their wedding. We see from the census of 1871 that the couple had a daughter of their own, Ada, who was born in 1868 and eventually we see the family listed as living at Park Villa, the former home of Reynold Hayward, the curate of Mellis. Of the many gardeners working at the Hall one was Susanna Wade, who at 52 years of age was listed as working in the gardens. She lived at Water Lane with her three children, the youngest Pamela 10, Edward 12, and Maria aged 14. John Perkins, who had been Head Gardener for 50 years, died on January 17th 1905 aged 80 and is recorded by a memorial tablet in Thornham Parva church, set up by General Arthur Henniker, the younger son of the 4th Lord Henniker.

There has been much discussion about the Park which is definitely shown on the survey of 1765, but not on Joseph Hodskinson's map of 1783 nor do we have any earlier references to it. Can this be an oversight as it seems likely there was a park here when the new house was built in the seventeenth century? Evidence of the extent of early woodland and other old trees on the estate comes from the tree survey being carried out by Stephen Schwarz, a member of our research team. He has used GPS to map the locations of the large standing trees and the remaining boles, and has taken measurements of them which give us a clearer understanding of the old plantings which have taken place. Woodland was needed to provide cover for deer and shelter breeding birds being reared for shooting. The oldest recorded wood is one of ten acres near the Hall, where the gardens are included as being 25 acres in extent. The park is mentioned as being between 300 and 400 acres in size. Northwest of the walled garden was an area called 'Old Wood', which had a line of trees that led to the parish boundary with Thornham Parva. There are several ancient trees in the area of present parkland and many can be seen illustrated here on the 1765 survey prepared for Sir John Major after he took possession of the estate. The ancient track-way called Cow Pasture Lane is highlighted by a series of single trees that mark its route, as is a former lane crossing from Thornham Magna church to meet the curving line of another ancient road joining Majors Lane and leading to Thornham Parva. A small section of this lane is still visible near School House and on the other side of the road it is marked by a gate. The lane originally crossed the fields at this point and the route shows on the tithe map of 1841, where it was called 'The Drift', another word used to indicate a trackway, and it can be seen that it rejoined the present road that goes to Parva just past Villa Farm. The undulating nature of the modern road linking these points shows the way it cuts across several old boundary ditches. The parish boundaries are also marked by old trees as is to be expected. The most interesting group are those behind Oak Farm on Clay Street, where they mark old field boundaries to the south of the present building, and indicate the edge of the new wood, then follow the line of the parish boundary with Wickham Skeith. Howe Lane has a single surviving ancient specimen situated close to the junction with Cow Pasture Lane. Further information on woodland comes from the tithe survey completed at Thornham Magna on 30 January 1841 and at Parva on 31st December 1841. We can see that the woodland recorded at Parva is all under an acre in size, and only four areas are shown, one of these being at the corner of the former allotments, in the pasture land now called 'Nora's Meadow'. Just west of the church new plantations are indicated, which were used to provide cover for shooting. On the map one of these appears as marking the corner of Cow Pasture Lane. It is from 1841 onwards that more plantations of woodland appear, some expanding from the older woods. This is especially true in Thornham Magna where new species were incorporated near the Hall. Some areas were planted with trees to provide cover for game shooting, which became increasingly popular during the reign of Queen Victoria. Hunting deer and using trained hawks to catch birds had always been much loved sports, and were prominent pastimes for the rich and powerful during the medieval period. The introduction of gunpowder and the development of accurate shotguns meant that shooting became the norm. This promoted the increase in plantations and certainly the 'pheasantry' listed on the estate map of the 1850s confirms that formal areas were set aside for breeding birds. The important links with the court of Queen Victoria and particularly with Edward Prince of Wales and his friends meant that special events were held on the estate. The extent and popularity of shooting is reflected in the vast amounts of lead shot found throughout the estate. The 8th Lord Henniker had an interest in preserving rare game birds. He introduced viewing pens to house unusual game birds from all over the world. These are situated just outside the north side of the walled garden close to the canal.

Woodland was important for the estate in many other ways. A woodman and sawyers worked on the estate and in 1861 it was Gaimwood Colling, who was 54 at the time of the census, and lived at the Gatehouse with his wife Maria. Perhaps it was he who was responsible for creating, or at least using, a sawpit that was indicated by the

Figure 8.4 *A sawpit with a log in place. The top of the two man saw rises above the tree trunk marking the spot where the sawyers stopped for a break.*

'Sawpit pightle' on the tithe map. Here timber was cut by hand, the tree trunk being set above the pit and sliced through with a long two handed saw, one person being down in the pit and the top sawyer standing above. We can safely assume that the person below was constantly covered in sawdust and was probably the apprentice! The accuracy of cutting by this method could be impressive and a working sawpit can still be seen in action at the estate of Cothele in Cornwall. The evidence for other such pits comes only from the names on early maps, as this method of processing timber was replaced when steam power was introduced to drive sawbenches. Posts, rails, gates and planks were always needed on the estate and any surplus could be sold to provide useful income. Woodmen, sawyers and carpenters were important to all estates from very early days.

The census lists give us a great deal of information about the household staff and their respective roles. In 1851 there were 20 staff living at the Hall. This included a Swiss butler and his English wife, a housekeeper, a nurse and nursemaid, a stillroom maid, a governess, a French gardener, a needlewoman, a housemaid, four kitchen maids, a lady's maid, a cook, a labourer and two footmen, who stoked the fires in all the rooms. Ten years later there were only 13 resident staff in the Hall on census day, but certain key personnel would travel with the family when visiting their other properties so we cannot make too much of this figure. The family was one of the largest employers in the area and many staff travelled from other parishes to work on the estate. A tenant farmer, Alfred Cracknell who lived at Dog House Farm which was later called The Grove, farmed 400 acres on which he employed 15 men and nine boys. Another tenant at Star House, farming 160 acres, had seven men and four boys. Daniel Lamb, of The Street, Thornham Magna, employed four men and three boys. All of this goes to show the numbers employed in that labour intensive age. It was soon to change with the advent of modern machinery. There were other key roles on the estate and just one that was important given the emphasis on shooting was gamekeeping. George Sturgeon, gamekeeper, lived at Dormans Hall, and another, Charles Warren, lived at The Chickery, presumably taking care of the newly hatched birds. Lists of Hall staff included seven gamekeepers until 1930. The Red House was usually home to the Farm Bailiff, who would have to settle disputes over tenancies and over the management of the land as well as collecting the rents from the scattered tenants. This seems to have been a short term position and many names are listed over the years, including Walter Coe who was at The Lodge, Thornham Parva and was also parish clerk in 1882.

During this era horses played an important part in the daily life of the estate. At one time 15,000 horses were listed in Suffolk alone. Working horses were used to carry out the main farming jobs. They pulled the ploughs and the early, relatively simple, machines, they hauled carts and wagons. They were also ridden on the roads and in the hunting field and pulled the carriages. In 1861 George Bloomfield, living in The Street, was recorded as a groom and ten years later James Goodenough was the coachman. He had married Margaret Mary Watson from Stoke Ash when she was 18 and he was 29. We get some insight from the family records into the use of horses for riding and for pulling the coaches in which they travelled long distances or made formal visits. With the advent of the railway we note from family letters and diaries that the train became a convenient way to travel. Reduction in the role of the horse continued with the introduction of steam power for some tasks on the land. We find evidence of steam threshing and steam ploughing when we are field walking. Coke, coal and clinker lies where it fell from the firebox when a steam engine was moved around the fields. It turns up in most of the arable fields. The woodman who lived in the Gate House at Thornham Magna and the sawyers working in the yards at the Model Farm would have found their work made easier by the introduction of new steam powered machinery. However, increased mechanisation meant more work could be done by fewer men, so this heralded the decline in the size of the work force on the land. Farming changed steadily with the introduction of steam engines and then tractors, although remarkably at least one of the practices from the old days survived until the 1970s when one of the authors witnessed at Metfield top dressing by hand. This laborious task was undertaken by a veteran farm labourer who from 6 am to 6 pm walked across the field at a constant pace without let. The interest in the old times and traditional ways of working has encouraged farmers like Paul Watkins, of South Elmham St Michael, to preserve old machines. He now attends many shows and can be seen on television demonstrating the use of the old threshing machines and the traditional farming methods, although at the time these were the cause of the decrease of the workforce on the farms.

Although the population of the Thornham estate felt safe from hardships, poverty was never far away, and some indication of this comes from the school registers where we see children missing classes due to work on the farm. This was very apparent during harvest time when women and children would glean the fields, gathering all the loose grain missed by the machinery. For some families this could make all the difference between enough food for the coming months or starvation. In many cases families were supporting large numbers of children. The National School, with an attached teacher's residence, was enlarged and improved in 1874 and again in 1904. On both occasions the cost of this was met by the Hennikers. At this time the school had an average attendance of 72 pupils and Miss Eliza Mary Storer was the schoolmistress. This village school which served both parishes of Thornham Magna and Parva was presumably located at 'School House'. In 1904 it was known officially as the Public Elementary School (mixed) and was enlarged to accommodate 99 children in accordance with national standards. In 1916 Miss Lydia Schofield was the schoolmistress.

The benevolence of the Henniker family was reflected in many ways and we read that 'at great expense to the family the church of Gt Thornham was restored, newly seated and beautified with stained glass, encaustic tiles etc.'. Thornham Parva church was also restored by the family at a later date. Elizabeth, Duchess of Chandos, who died in 1813 gave an organ to the church at Thornham Magna.

From the census of 1861 comes the first indication of a Post Office at Thornham Magna when James Hunt, who was 70 at the time, was listed as sub-postmaster and eight years later he was still at the Post Office. The very first inland postal system was organised in 1635 and soon became a state monopoly. The General Post Office was created in 1710 and escorted mail coaches replaced post boys by 1784. The first despatch of mail by railway was in 1830. From the family papers we have mention of the postal service in a letter dated 25 August 1769 despatched to Master Henniker at Thornham, who was 16 at the time, from his father who was at Southampton and wrote that he

Figure 8.5 *Local children at Thornham School in 1927. The building was destroyed by a fire in the 1930s.*

Figure 8.6 *The White Horse at Stoke Ash about 1886 (photo by Cleer Alger).*

had forgotten that the post 'did not go from hence on a Saturday'. In 1874 when Mr G N Miller was postmaster at Thornham he also served as the grocer and draper for the community – the advent of the 'corner shop'! The penny post was first introduced in 1840 and a year later the first adhesive stamp was issued. The mail arrived at Thornham from Eye at 7.30 am and 2.30 pm and was despatched at 5.30 pm and on Sundays at 10.30 am. At Stoke Ash letters were received through Stonham by foot post and there was a wall letterbox at the White Horse Inn which was cleared at 6 pm. It is still possible to see the mark on the front wall nearest to the crossroads where this box was attached until destroyed by a lorry that hit the wall in 1994. It was replaced by a Queen Elizabeth II box on a free standing post beside the telephone box adjacent to the nearby layby.

The 5th Lord Henniker had been at Cambridge University with Edward Prince of Wales and became a firm friend of the future King Edward VII. The prince visited Thornham Hall many times and it is said that Lord Henniker's sister, Helen, was a favourite of Prince Edward mainly because of her wit, although she was rather unkindly described as being fat. Many of the best game shots of the period stayed frequently at the Hall. Guests included Prince Freddie and Victor Duleep Singh, who lived at Elveden Hall. His statue can be seen at Thetford. Lord Henniker was one of the guardians of Duleep Singh, along with Lords Ripon and Walsingham on behalf of Queen Victoria. Bertie, the eldest son who was a godson of Edward Prince of Wales, was sent to Australia to learn a new career in politics and served as Private Secretary/ADC to the Governor of New South Wales. Albert Edward John Henniker Major 'eldest son of 5th Baron Henniker died on 2 March 1901 aged 35' is commemorated by a window in Thornham Magna church 'erected by friends in Australia'. It is the south west window of the nave with glass by Morris & Co. showing pre-Raphaelite figures by Edward Burne-Jones. He also appears on a memorial tablet on the north wall of the nave which includes Cicely

Anne Lucy Henniker Major who died on 24 June 1901. Charles, the second son, joined the Rifle Brigade and Gerald the third son had been destined to become a diplomat but unfortunately the family was unable to raise the £400 per annum which was expected of a prospective member of the diplomatic service. The fourth son, Victor Alexander who was a godson of Queen Victoria herself, trained as a parson and was to occupy one of the family's livings. We hear of him staying in the manor house called Plashwood, situated at Haughley near Stowmarket. The youngest son, John, was a page to Queen Victoria and earned sufficient to pay his school fees at Radley which his older brother Victor also attended. John, who would become the 7th Lord Henniker, went to Cirencester to train as a land agent, but as a result of a boisterous prank there, in which he painted a bronze statue of a horse pink, he was asked to leave. Despite this he eventually became the Land Agent of the estate during his older brother Charles' tenure of the title. The daughters lived at home and were to go with their father to the Isle of Man. It was said that they were sheltered from the world and their lack of knowledge was to prejudice their future happiness. This was often the case for rich and famous households where daughters were expected to make good marriages. In many cases when families faced financial difficulties this was seen as the only way to save homes and estates, so men newly enriched by commerce were considered good matches.

During the latter years of the nineteenth century we see a complete change of circumstances at Thornham Hall. In 1886 some of the outlying farms, which had originally been purchased by Sir John Major, were sold. These were situated at Metfield and Lavenham in Suffolk and at Starston and Pulham St Mary in Norfolk. Lord Henniker's wife Alice died in 1892 and in 1895 he was appointed to a paid post as Governor of the Isle of Man where he took many of the family with him, so the Hall was let. At this time many of the grand houses in the area had problems. The male line of the Kerrisons had died out, but their successors the Batemans left and both Oakley Park and Brome Hall were demolished. Fortunately Thornham survived, although at the cost of further later sales of land and property. The 5th Lord Henniker died in the Isle of Man in 1902, about six months after the death from pneumonia of his eldest son Albert (Bertie), so he was succeeded by his second son Charles Henry Chandos Henniker Major, 6th Lord Henniker. At the time Charles was serving with his regiment in India and was on a punitive expedition as part of the Afghan War. On his return from India he decided that with ten brothers and sisters to look after he would not marry, but would continue in the army. With the start of the First World War in 1914 he took his battalion to France, seeing action at Ypres and Arras on the Western Front, where there were dreadful losses. This is certainly reflected at the parish churches where memorials list those who fell in WWI. At Flixton we see that Alan Adair of the Hall served and, like Charles, survived the war. Of the 22 men who went to war from Flixton eight did not return, while two of those from Mendham listed as fallen served in the Royal Navy and were killed in the Battle of Jutland. We can recognise many names on the Roll of Honour at Thornham as forefathers of present day families such as Frank Gooderham and Thomas Spalding, whose family name is remembered in the name of a farm. John Henniker also served in WWI but he flew with the Army Observer Group, later to become the Royal Flying Corps. He was adjutant to a squadron based in France. After the war was over the scars of mental fatigue and the vision of dreadful slaughter had terrible effects on many of those who survived. On top of this Charles had serious family debts to contend with and this resulted in the sale of 21,000 acres of land from the estate. The Hall was still let with Lt Col Michael James Hughes as tenant. The herd of red poll cattle grazing in the former park where John's mother enjoyed overseeing 'the admirable animals in the park' had dwindled in size. During the Great Depression of the 1920s and 1930s many Scottish farmers moved away from their traditional stock farms and came to East Anglia. They introduced the Ayrshire herds and soon many local farmers switched to this new breed. They discovered that these produced good milk yields, so the more traditional breeds, such as the Suffolk red polls, became rare. However today a healthy herd of red polls can be seen grazing the parkland that surrounds the present Hall.

Despite the financial problems of the family, in 1924 the Parish Hall was built at Thornham Magna with help from the Hennikers. There had been a Reading Room further down the road opposite Street Farm since at least 1912. Reading Rooms were founded in many Suffolk villages in the late nineteenth century when there was a 'Suffolk Village Club and Reading Room Association'[3]. No details are known about the facilities available at Thornham, but generally Reading Rooms were supplied with newspapers and magazines, sometimes with books, and often with games such as billiards, chess and dominoes. As meeting places they were seen as offering alternative evening entertainment to the public houses and as providing some opportunity for educational improvement. The room with a fireplace at one end can still be seen but is now in private hands, although during the Second World War it was used as the

Figure 8.7 *The Reading Room at Thornham Magna no longer provides a meeting place away from the temptations of the public houses.*

meeting place for the Home Guard. The long term tenant of the Hall and estate, Lt Col Hughes decided to leave in 1932 and John, the future 7th Lord Henniker, came to manage the estate as Land Agent for his older brother. He brought with him his son John, the future 8th Lord Henniker, who was then 16. The previous agent, Philip Palmer, died in 1932 leaving vacant the Red House, at the Model Farm. However the house needed renovation before they could move in so Rosie Douglas Hamilton, nee Kerrison, lent the family a house in Brome, enabling John to start work on the estate straight away. Due to the Depression it was very run down, although there were still seven gamekeepers on the staff, arranging regular shoots for the family and also for a group of London business men who leased the shoot, but whose aim always seemed to suffer after lunch. John and his brother Dick often went shooting with Harry Grass, the gamekeeper who had married a local girl from Stoke Ash. Later he left Thornham to join Lord Mountbatten's staff as Head Keeper at Broadlands where he gained national recognition. The estate yard still had three cowmen and the workshops and sawmill worked throughout the thirties.

At this time the Reverend the Honourable Victor Henniker Major returned to Thornham with his excellent cook, and moved into the Rectory at Magna, so once again the living was held by a member of the family who owned the estate. He was rector for 20 years and died in 1954. However for a short time the Hall itself was let to Lady Marr who held regular house parties to entertain her friends, including the family of Col Hughes the previous tenant. After Lady Marr left no further tenants could be found, and it was agreed that major changes should take place. The Hall then had ninety five rooms, most without heating, and there were no bathrooms. The house was reduced in size, leaving just one wing which was fully modernised by Guy Hake. This resulted in the sale of some of the contents of the house, with selected paintings, porcelain and furniture being auctioned. By 1938 the Hall was ready and at last Charles, 6th Lord Henniker could move in. However with the outbreak of the Second World War in the following year he had to vacate it almost immediately, because it was taken over as an Army Divisional Headquarters. During the Second War the estate became home to German and Italian prisoners of war. The footings of one of their living quarters can still be seen on the edge of the walled garden car park. The prisoners either worked on the estate or on other farms in the area, and the former tenant of Chandos Farm still remembers the prisoners going off to Eye at the weekend and has mementoes made by Italian soldiers. Charles did not move back into the Hall after the war and it was occupied by the Kerrison School for problem children. It was destroyed in 1954 by a fire, which started in a bedroom on the second floor. A similar fate had befallen the post mill that stood on the common. A new house was built two years later in a style which Norman Scarfe describes as having the 'agreeable simplicity of a pavilion', but one turret of the Smirke building remains (Plate 24). The Victorian stables, water tower and ice house also survive. John Henniker continued living at Red House and managing the estate until his brother's death in 1956 when he inherited the title as 7th Lord Henniker.

His son John, the future 8th Lord Henniker, was working in the Foreign Office until 1940 when he enlisted in the Essex Regiment as a 2nd Lieutenant of the 2nd Battalion, Rifle Brigade. He carried out his officer training on the Isle of Man where his uncle had been the Governor. He was wounded while serving with the 7th Armoured Division of the Eighth Army in Libya in 1942, the same year he was gazetted Lieutenant. Within a year John was promoted Captain and on 27 September 1943 he was parachuted into Bosnia to make contact with and support the Resistance Movement. He established contact with General Tito. This was a successful mission which resulted in him being dropped again the following year into Yugoslavia. After his return he was promoted Major and in 1945 he was awarded the Military Cross. Although his brother Dick was captured and held as a prisoner of war, both survived the war but Desmond Adair was killed and, as he was the last male heir, Flixton Hall was finally sold in 1950 and the family returned to their estates in Ireland. Memorials commemorate the fallen of the Second War, but not on the same scale as the losses of the First War, although Percy Lummis and Reginald Mayes from the Thornham area were sorely missed.

However the Second War made a considerable local impact. From 1942 onwards this part of the Suffolk landscape was being transformed into part of the military machine. Initially the Air Ministry was involved in the creation of airfields along the Waveney Valley and close to the Thornham Estate at Eye. Work was carried out at Flixton/ Bungay from June 1942 and completed by January 1943 when operations were commenced by the 29th Squadron who were flying to Germany on Intruder Flights to interrupt factory workers and generally upset civilian morale by causing air raid warnings. This project was abandoned by March 1943. Additional work was carried out to the airfield and by April 1944 it became fully operational under the control of the American 446 Bombardment Group, with their 2826 men including 363 officers. Just prior to this on 15 February 1944 an RAF Halifax bomber was forced to land at Flixton. The aircraft, nicknamed 'Pubwash', was piloted by Ted Grimwood and his crew, to whom the American base staff presented 200 cigarettes and a free shaving kit for each man. At breakfast the following day, to the amazement of the pilot, a plate of bacon and seven eggs was placed in front of him, which he immediately started to share with his fellow crew members. It transpired however that this was just for him and each crew member was about to receive the same! They stayed and enjoyed the hospitality of their American allies for three days, until a new engine was fitted. There were many losses from this airfield and on one occasion alone the 'Bungay Buckeroos' lost five Liberators over the Waveney, when their aircraft were attacked by enemy fighters on their return from a mission. Flixton played a major role in the D-Day landings and briefings for it were held at the airfield. The 446 Squadron was chosen to lead the bombing runs and at 1400 hours 'Fearless Freddie' took off to lead the attack on the Normandy beach area. In all 273 missions were flown from the airfield, which represented several thousand sorties, with a loss of 86 men. To commemorate these events there is a memorial book of the 446 Bomb Group listing all those who did not return. The gates to the churchyard at Flixton were given by the USAAF as an additional reminder of these events.

Metfield airfield, south west of Flixton, was built by 10 March 1942 and was home to a fighter group of Thunderbolts. On many occasions local residents witnessed one wheel landings by the returning aircraft. This squadron left early in April 1944, when additional work was carried out on the airfield, which was to house 51 Liberators. It now meant that Christmas Lane was closed to all local traffic and restrictions were imposed on the local farmers who lived and worked in and around the airfield. Mr and Mrs W Watts were issued with a special pass to enable them to get in and out of Common Farm, which was situated in the middle of the hospital block and living accommodation for personnel. The most dramatic event at Metfield during the war took place on 15 July 1944 when, at 1930 hours, 1200 tons of bombs blew up, wrecking the bomb dump and rocking the countryside for miles around. It would appear that a lorry containing 500 pound bombs was being unloaded when one of them, now thought to have been primed by mistake, exploded causing the first explosion, soon to be followed by another. Five ordnance men lost their lives and the axle of the lorry landed a mile away in Linstead. West End Farm, situated on the boundary of Metfield and St. James, was totally destroyed and a cottage on the St. James road lost its roof so that an elderly gentleman suddenly became exposed to the elements as he was in bed at the time! Fortunately he survived this indignity. The windows of buildings in the main street of Harleston were blown out, Bungay some eight miles away also sustained damage and the shock was felt fifteen miles away at Southwold. Five B24s were written off and a further six badly damaged. For three days the squadron went non-operational. Thorpe Abbots was home to the American 'Bloody Hundredth' from June 1943 to December 1945, when it was taken over by the RAF until the end of the war. This airfield sustained damage as a result of a mid-air collision on 5 January 1945, when debris falling from the aircraft caused the bomb dump to explode.

The closest airfield to the Thornham Estate was at Eye. This was built during 1943 and after it was commissioned a permanent guardhouse was established with gates across the A140 to halt traffic when aircraft taxied to and from the dispersal point on the west side of the road. Yaxley Hall was in direct line of the approach and take-off for the main runway. The firing butts were constructed beside the road and the fuel dump was situated west of the A140. In total 2894 personnel were based at the airfield to fly and maintain firstly Liberators and then Flying Fortresses. On 23 May 1944 two bombers collided on approach, with six crewmen being killed. Fragments of aircraft discovered close to Red House Farm might possibly have come from one of these bombers. Shells from the guns of the bombers flying out of Eye airfield have also been found throughout the estate. Similar finds have been made in the vicinity of the airfields in the Waveney Valley.

There were lighter sides to this local invasion of approximately 10,000 American airmen. With Norwich being a Liberty Town it is no surprise to hear that a Wild West Rodeo was held at Carrow Road Football Ground on 23 August 1944. Earlier that month Glen Miller and his Army Airforce Band had given a concert at Halesworth and the Band performed at Thorpe Abbots on 19 September. This was part of the final tour he made in England before his tragic death. After the 1960s these testaments to the Second World War were slowly taken back into agriculture or, as in the case of Eye airfield, provided ideal conditions for Industrial Estates.

At Middleton Hall in Mendham secret activities took place when a headquarters building was incorporated into the landscape. It was to be part of the Auxiliary Unit or Last Ditch Army that would have organised resistance to a German occupation of Britain. The headquarters was underground and had a lookout post constructed in an old oak tree. It was so well disguised that when a senior officer came to inspect he was not aware of the soldiers slowly disappearing into the underground network, and commended the Group for their cleverly designed entrance. Fortunately it was never needed, but still remains to this day as one component of a network that was spread throughout Britain. One wonders what future archaeologists might make of these structures!

After the war another major sale was held in 1948 to reduce the Thornham Estate as instructed 'by Lt Col The Right Honourable Charles Henry Chandos, Baron Henniker'. The land and properties were to be offered as a whole, but if there were no takers then they were to be sold off in 101 lots. This comprised 4553 acres, which included 37 farms, Yaxley Hall and grounds, small holdings, 64 cottages and village properties, freehold woodland and accommodation lands. All the dwellings were let and produced a rent roll of £5892 per year with outgoings paid by the landlord being some £1455. 14 shillings and fourpence. The timber for sale had been conservatively valued at the sum of £14,200 but would be included in the sale of the freehold without any additional payment. The cottages in Stoke Ash were sold mainly to the tenants for about £100 each. Many of the families of these estate tenants of 1948 can still be found in the area. The sale included properties at Yaxley, Braiseworth, Stoke Ash, Wickham Skeith, Finningham, Thornham Magna, Gislingham, Mellis, Burgate, Thorndon, Wetheringsett, Debenham, Winston, Ashfield and Worlingworth[4]. Thus the estate lost its last link with John Major's original property in Worlingworth. After the sale the estate had been reduced to approximately 3000 acres. In the post war years a few new houses were built in the adjoining parishes. When the houses were being built in Roman Way, Stoke Ash, the work revealed evidence of the occupation during the Roman period, hence the name given to the road. Other social housing was constructed in the 1960s. Some properties

Figure 8.8 *The Court House at Crows Hall in Debenham, where the Hennikers held their manorial courts in the seventeenth century. It was sold in 1948.*

were demolished as in the case of the cottage that stood near Swatsfield Hall.

Charles, the 6th Lord Henniker died in 1956 and a large block of stone near the Folly in the Park is carved with the honours of the Royal Green Jackets. It marks his military service and notes his interest in gun dog trials 'in which he became an expert'. It records that the Folly was restored and this gravestone erected 'in grateful memory of Uncle Charles'. He was succeeded by his brother John, who lived until 1980. The 8th Lord Henniker came back to Thornham in 1978 when his father, the 7th Lord Henniker, was 95. His first wife, Osla who died in 1974, is commemorated by a window of engraved glass by Lawrence Whistler installed in 1980 in Thornham Parva church. He married his second wife Julia in 1976 and they moved to Red House at Thornham two years later. He had retired after a successful career in the diplomatic service. After the war he spent two years as assistant private secretary to Ernest Bevin the foreign secretary in Clement Attlee's Labour Government. He loved working with Bevin. Then he spent seven years as the head of the personnel department at the Foreign Office, repairing the damage done to its morale by the defections of Burgess and Maclean, and creating a unified diplomatic service. During the 1960s he was Ambassador to Jordan and then to Denmark and held the post of Director General of the British Council (Plate 18).

As he and Julia had been involved in a number of charitable projects working with vulnerable people in London, they decided to use the buildings and open spaces of the Thornham Estate to support useful projects and to provide public access for walking, horse riding and fishing. Under their guidance many of the buildings on the estate which were no longer relevant to modern farming methods have been converted to new uses, and the public have been encouraged to use the estate for leisure pursuits. They developed the craft workshops in some of the redundant farm buildings of Red House Farm, starting in 1978 with workshops for a weaver and a concertina maker recommended by the Crafts Council, as well as a craft training centre in the Street Forge Workshop in the village which continues to support trainees with special needs. They turned the cowsheds into a Field Study Centre for environmental studies, which opened in 1985 and is used by large numbers of school groups and other organisations for educational purposes. They converted the blacksmith's forge into a tea room, as another way of finding new uses for buildings which were no longer suited to modern farming. In 1978 Lord Henniker gave 180 acres of Mellis Green to the Suffolk Wildlife Trust to preserve and manage it for wildlife. He opened the Thornham Walks to the public through a series of marked trails along footpaths and bridleways. The walled garden and its glasshouses have been restored and are again being used to produce plants as well as providing a base for horticultural courses (Plate 22). Some ponds are managed for fishing. There is a camp site for organised groups, originally set up in conjunction with Islington Social Services to provide a rural centre for young people from deprived urban areas. Cabin accommodation has been built for groups making longer visits to the Field Centre. The centre is administered by an independent charitable trust and the walks are managed by a warden for Mid-Suffolk District Council as part of the Upper Waveney Valley Project. Having set the estate on a sound footing and secured the future of his projects at Thornham John, 8th Lord Henniker died on 29th April 2004 aged 88. His son Mark becomes the 9th Baron Henniker.

In the 1980s the railway line between Norwich and London was electrified. Although

Figure 8.9 *Lord and Lady Henniker: the late John Henniker with his wife Julia.*

there is no longer a station at Mellis, all main line trains to and from London stop at Diss which is easily reached by car. This increased the attraction of local houses for commuters and so raised the prices. Several plans to upgrade the main A140 between Ipswich and Norwich by making it a dual carriageway throughout have been put forward but then shelved because of the costs involved. As changes in farming methods have reduced to an absolute minimum the numbers employed on the land and there is a lack of other employment in the immediate area there is only a small population working locally. There is also a shortage of houses for those with low incomes. Apart from the limited farming jobs that remain and a few specialist workshops most local employment is related to providing for leisure activities including catering for visitors to the countryside. In Thornham itself catering includes the Four Horseshoes, which like the Stoke Ash White Horse and other local public houses makes a serious business of serving food as well as drinks, the Forge Tearoom adjoining the Field Centre and a restaurant at Thornham Hall.

From a population in 1831 of 380 in Thornham Magna and 206 in Parva, by 1971 it had fallen to 120 in Magna and 65 in Parva according to the Decennial Census returns. The biggest single drop in the two parishes combined in a ten year period was 97 between 1891 (411) and 1901 (314), when the countryside was affected by serious agricultural depression influenced by the importation of cheap food from abroad. At a time when so few people make a living in the countryside it is difficult to imagine these two parishes in the middle of the nineteenth century when they supported over five hundred people.

In 1987, after the extent of the estate's property had been greatly reduced by sales

Figure 8.10 *The Greenhouse in the Walled Garden at Thornham after its restoration in the last decade of the 20th century.*

in 1919 and 1946–7, the family owned 2500 acres. About a quarter of the land was let and the remaining three quarters, including between 400 and 500 acres of woodland, was directly managed. The farm of some 1200 acres was almost entirely arable, growing mainly cereals, beans and oilseed rape. After a long period without much investment, the ten years from 1977 to 1987 had seen considerable expenditure including the provision of new grain driers and stores and a lot of drainage. Some sheep and cattle were kept on the grassland but most of the parkland was let to a neighbouring farmer for grazing. The woods needed much work, done in conjunction with the Forestry Commission, including the felling of mature trees and of elms killed by Dutch Elm Disease. Many of the trees were sawn and dried in the sawmill on the estate, with the better wood being sold for furniture, and the remainder going for gates and fencing or for pit props in coal mines. Some areas were replanted and new woods created to provide valuable timber, while at the same time providing an improved environment for the public and for wildlife. Some also shelters the more exposed areas of farmland from the force of strong winds. Much of the planting was oak and ash with some smaller more decorative trees, wild cherry, white beam and rowan, on the margins of the woods. A plantation of foreign trees, including Sitka Spruce a native of the west coast of America, was planted as a quick growing timber crop by the Economic Forestry Group. The best of the existing trees were retained in the woods and in the Park including native yew trees and ornamental species introduced from abroad such as the tall Wellingtonias which are natives of California. Trees and bushes near the Hall were cut back and managed to open up some of the avenues that had been planned as walks by previous generations. Some of the woodland was managed as cover for pheasants supporting shooting for

Figure 8.11 *A group of children using the Field Centre created from some of the buildings of the model farm at Red House, Thornham Magna.*

which many areas of planting had been designed. Although many hedges had been removed to make it easier to work the big arable fields with large modern machinery, some were being reinstated where they did not interfere with farming activities.

Now the amount of the estate's land that is farmed as arable is being reduced from 1200 acres to 600 acres and there is no longer a resident gamekeeper. This will have a significant effect on the management of the landscape. Many of the arable fields will be converted to pasture, creating more grassland than the estate has seen since the eighteenth century, but this will support store cattle being fattened for the beef market not dairy cattle producing milk. Efforts will be made to increase biodiversity with the greatest possible variety of wild plants supporting insects, newts in the ponds, birds and deer in the woodland and small mammals in their natural habitats. The present proportion of woodland on the estate will be maintained. Some organised shooting will continue but on a less intensive basis. The educational use of the trails and the field centre will be expanded with an emphasis on education for sustainable development, to encourage energy conservation and the maximum reuse of waste material. It will be interesting to see the impact of these changes which remind us that the landscape is not static and what we see today is the result of many changes that have taken place over the years.

Notes

1   SROI:FDA 257/A1/1a.
2   SROI:S1/2/300.68.
3   See Nesta Evans in Suffolk Review, New Series **25** (1995)
4   SROI:HA116/4676/Box40.

APPENDIX1

BURNT FLINT EXPERIMENTS

by Mike Hardy in 1984

Three experiments were carried out to observe the results of burning flints.

Experiment no. 1

A small enclosed hearth was built of old oak planks, upon which were placed twelve flints, ranging in size from 40 to 100mm: these had been collected from the surface of a field in Metfield. Adjacent to the hearth a small hollow was dug, producing a shallow basin 390mm in diameter. This was lined by pounding the loose soil to form a hard clay surface and filled with water to a depth of 110mm. The flints were heated in a steady fire for two hours and then removed and totally immersed in the water. The flints weighed 1.25kg before heating and 1.1kg afterwards and they raised the temperature of the water from 60°F (air temperature 68°F) to 104°F.

During the firing the flints cracked, some falling into several pieces, but none exploded violently (this was true for all the firings). After quenching, the surfaces of the flints were minutely crazed with small cracks, with some larger cracks going deep into the flints. In places the surface had flaked off, leaving a rough granular scar; in addition the flints were notably fragile and could easily be broken into several pieces. They also changed colour from a motley assortment of white, black and brown field flints to a fairly standard mixture of bluish-light grey and dark grey; each flint in fact showing a gradation from white (normally on the newly fractured surfaces) through various shades of grey to black (usually on the exterior surfaces).

Experiment no. 2

For the second firing twenty two flints were selected, ranging in size from 30 to 90mm. Two flints were extracted from the fire after 15 minutes; one was immersed in water and the other was allowed to cool naturally. This was repeated after 30 minutes with a slightly larger sample. After one hour the remainder of the flints were taken out and quenched in the water. The flints weighed 2.7kg before firing and 2.3kg afterwards.

The flints extracted after 15 minutes were noticeably redder in the cortex areas than those extracted after Experiment 1, but otherwise they were very similar; the different methods of cooling produced few differences although the naturally cooled flint was perhaps slightly more translucent and less crazed. Of those extracted after 30 minutes, the ones quenched in water were indistinguishable from those produced by Experiment

1, but the one allowed to cool naturally was atypical in that it was a rounded cobble shaped flint that split into several fragments revealing a rich rust-red interior without extensive crazing. Those quenched after one hour were very similar to those quenched after 30 minutes.

Experiment no. 3

Eighteen flints were fired and left in the fire for an 18 hour period, being removed from the ashes the following day after the fire had burned for at least eight hours and the ashes remained warm for at least another four hours. The physical state of the flints was very similar to those produced by Experiment 1, the only difference being the colour as in this case the flints were a whitish pale grey tinged with pale rust-red, the red being particularly marked on the areas of cortex.

These experiments showed that typical 'pot-boiler' burnt flints could be produced after thorough heating in a fire for as little as 15 to 30 minutes and that quenching in water made very little difference to the flints except for the colour: those quenched in water being blacker than the noticeably redder naturally cooled ones. The experiment also showed that flints could be safely heated in a hearth and that they could be used to heat water, although this did result in a certain amount of ash and charcoal in the water, in addition to shattered flint.

Finds of Concentrations of Burnt Flints

Recorded by Mike Hardy in certain parishes of the Waveney Valley:

Metfield	67 sites	with associated prehistoric activity in		2 cases
Mendham	30 sites	,,	,,	5 cases
St. James	8 sites	,,	,,	1 case
St. Cross	9 sites	,,	,,	1 case
St. Margaret	4 sites	,,	,,	2 cases
Homersfield	3 sites	,,	,,	all 3 cases

The very high number of sites in Mendham and Metfield without prehistoric activity show clear evidence of nineteenth century land improvement by 'clod-burning' (see Chapter one) in these parishes which may extend to some of the examples in neighbouring parishes. This is confirmed by finding that some examples were along the line of old boundaries where hedges had been burned along with the piles of clods, and others were associated with disused ponds which had become refuse pits suitable for clod-burning.

However in all parishes there are sites where the burnt flints were associated with prehistoric material and it is most likely that these examples were used as pot-boilers (see Chapter one).

Appendix 2

Family Trees

1   Briseworth to Killigrew

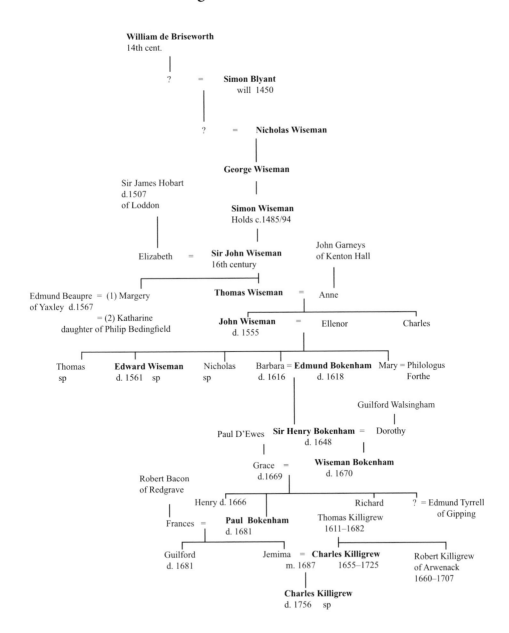

2   Major and Henniker

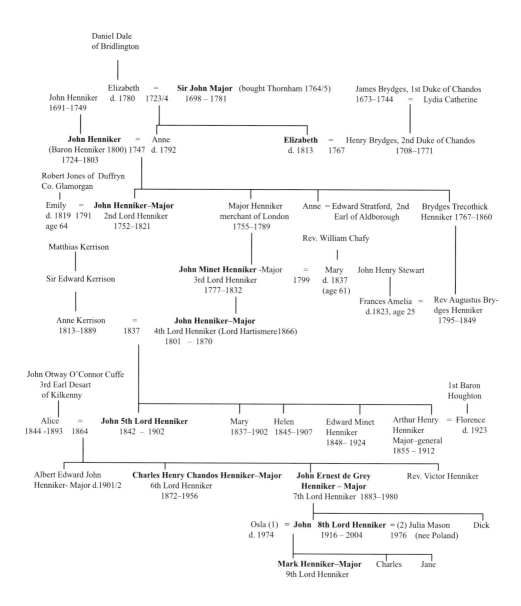

3   Hemenhale

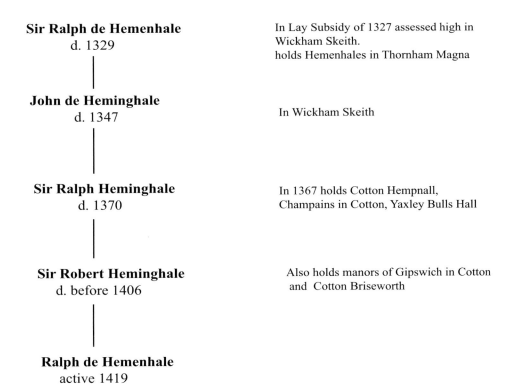

Sir Ralph de Hemenhale
d. 1329

In Lay Subsidy of 1327 assessed high in
Wickham Skeith.
holds Hemenhales in Thornham Magna

John de Heminghale
d. 1347

In Wickham Skeith

Sir Ralph Heminghale
d. 1370

In 1367 holds Cotton Hempnall,
Champains in Cotton, Yaxley Bulls Hall

Sir Robert Heminghale
d. before 1406

Also holds manors of Gipswich in Cotton
and Cotton Briseworth

Ralph de Hemenhale
active 1419

APPENDIX 3

Rental from Lady Day 1823 to Lady Day 1824 (extracts)

The Right Hon. Lord Henniker's Estates formerly those of Right Hon. Lord Henniker's

Tenant	Place	Size of farm a. r. p.	annual rent £	date of lease	term of lease	rent acc. to lease
Aldous, William	Worlingworth	33-1-35	43-10-0	1820	14	45-0-0
Brundly, Wm.	Bealings Gardens	387-1-14[1]	7-0-0	1818	14	411-0-0
Clarke, John	Ashfield		3-0-0			
East, James	Lavenham		65-0-0	not found the lease		
Estall, John	Ashfield		3-0-0			
Garrod, Robert	Stradbroke	197-2-0	220-0-0	1809	14	260-0-0
Grant, Frances	Worlingworth		4-0-0	1813	21	
Green, Mrs.	Fressingfield	147-0-0	175-2-4½	1809	14	190-0-0
Green, Thomas	Fressingfield	42-2-6	48-0-0	1818	14	56-0-0
Johnston, John	Bedingfield	224-0-3	225-0-0	1820	14	228-0-0
Jeffries, Daniel	Wetheringsett	22-3-39	29-0-0	1820	14	33-0-0
Moore, Edmd. Esq.	Bealings		11-0-0			
Oxborrow, James	Fressingfield	64-3-38	65-0-0	1809	14	81-0-0
Prior, Thomas	Bacton		15-0-0	no lease		
Quinton, Jeremiah	Ashfield	28-2-31	36-0-0	1818	14	39-0-0

The Right Hon. Lord Henniker's Estates formerly those of Her Grace the Duchess of Chandos's

Tenant	Place	Size of farm a. r. p.	annual rent £	date of lease	term of lease	rent acc. to lease
Berry, Richard	Stoke Ash	97-2-0	126-0-0	no map and no lease		
Button, George	Worlingworth	99-0-37	112-0-0	1820	14	125-0-0
Bull, John	Thornham		22-10-0	no lease		
Barker, Daniel	Rishangles	120-1-13	135-0-0	1814	14	160-0-0
Carter, William	Little Thornham		36-0-0	paid by cash for sheep		no lease, no map
Coe, Charles	Little Thornham	105-2-1	125-0-0	1813	14	146-0-0
Freeman, John	Little Thornham	106-1-1	112-0-0	1813	14	146-0-0
Frewer, Samuel	Bedfield	140-1-19	170-0-0	1820	14	190-0-0
Fairweather, William	Framsden		5-10-0			
Joy, Robert	Thornham	116-2-37	160-0-0	1813	14	215-0-0
Orford, James	Thornham	63-1-15	72-0-0	1818	14	85-10-0
Threadgell, William	Framsden		4-0-0			
Wilson, Samuel	Stradbrook	51-1-31	60-0-0	1820	14	67-0-0
Ward, Revd. John	Stoke Ash		25-0-0			

The Right Hon. Lord Henniker's Estates formerly those of Sir John Major's (Baronet)

Name	Place					
Aldous, John	Stradbrook	61-2-20	60-0-0	1818	14	79-15-0
Belman, John	Braisworth	65-0-0	65-0-0	1811	14	85-0-0 no map
Belman, Rainer	Earl Soham	5-1-0	10-0-0	1811	14	10-0-0 no map
Barrett, Thomas	Fressingfield	53-3-2	60-0-0	1818	14	65-0-0
Button, Samuel	Brundish	47-2-6	50-0-0	1818	14	58-0-0
Brundly, William	Bealings	382-2-7	348-0-0			
Barker, Charles	Monk Soham	111-1-36	110-0-0	1818	14	114-0-0
Brunning, Thomas	Debenham		3-0-0			
Barritt, Thomas	Debenham		3-0-0			
Craske, Edmund	Wickham Skeith	224-0-0	272-0-0	1823	14	(2)
Clarke, James	Worlingworth	79-1-13	90-0-0	1818	14	107-0-0
Churchyard, James	Earl Soham	90-1-9	80-0-0	1810	14	100-0-0 no map
Clouting, Tobias	Thornham	77-2-29	92-0-0	1818	14	112-0-0
Chandler, John	Tannington	48-0-28	58-0-0	1818	14	65-12-0
Dove, Lionel	Debenham	197-1-31	235-0-0	1820	14	290-0-0
Barker, William	Bealings		10-0-0			
Darby, James	Debenham	203-1-5	280-0-0	1810	14	300-0-0 no map
Eade, John	Framsden		10-0-0			
Farrer, William	Winston	96-0-27	125-0-0	1818	14	142-0-0
Green, Henry	Cratfield	53-0-13	60-0-0	1806	14	60-0-0
Green, William	Worlingworth	145-0-25	175-0-0	1818	14	200-0-0
Gooch, Thomas	Metfield	132-0-34	120-0-0	1818	14	146-0-0
Hayward, John	Stoke Ash	147-1-12	180-0-0	1810	14	200-0-0
Hayward, John	Thornham	174-2-0	180-0-0	1810	14	190-0-0 no map
Heard, Jeremiah	Little Bealings	88-2-32	100-0-0	1818	14	101-0-0 (3)
Hunt, Gilbert	Thornham	20-3-6 (4)	50-0-0	1818	14	52-0-0
Hammond, Thomas	Tannington	169-0-18	195-0-0	1818	14	208-0-0
Hammond, William	Ashfield	261-3-15	285-0-0	1823	14	290-0-0
Jessop, John	Worlingworth	84-0-0	85-0-0	1811	14	112-0-0 no map
Jessop, Joseph	Worlingworth	61-2-8	65-0-0	1818	14	82-0-0
Lacock, Samuel	Hasketon	109-3-25	67-10-0	1823 no lease		160-0-0 no map
Kersey, Pells	Winston	115-0-0	135-0-0			162-0-0 no map
Morgan, William	Thornham	110-0-0	140-0-0	1808	14	140-0-0 no map
Moore, William	Debenham	300-3-4	400-0-0	1818	14	475-0-0
Mullinger,	Wickham Skeith	about 20 acres	16-0-0	no lease, no map		
Noller, John	Ashfield		23-0-0	no lease		
Newson, Samuel	Worlingworth		6-0-0	no lease		
Pipe, John	Ashfield		7-0-0	no lease		
Plant, Robert	Worlingworth	39-3-3	42-0-0	1818	14	54-10-0
Potter, Zechariah	Stoke Ash	36-3-20	85-0-0	1818	14	95-0-0
Riches, Thomas	Worlingworth		7-0-0	1818		
Reeve, Richard	Starston	54-1-3	65-0-0	1818	14	82-0-0
Rogers, Sarah	Ashfield	42-1-30	50-0-0	1820	14	62-0-0
Steptoe, Nathaniel	Thorp	247-3-32	336-0-0	1820	14	370-0-0
Spurling, William	Worlingworth	186-3-39	210-0-0	1818	14	229-0-0
Spurling, John	Worlingworth		90-0-0	no lease		
Salter, Tessa	Thornham		18-0-0			
Turner, Richard	Tannington	81-3-0	85-0-0	1818	14	101-0-0
Warner, Edward	Ashfield	94-0-32	120-0-0	1818	14	149-10-0
Wharton, William	Stradbroke	82-0-0	105-0-0	1811	14	110-0-0 no map

New Purchases by the Rt. Hon. Lord Henniker in 1823

Name	Place				
Captn. Bolton	Bealings	27-0-0	63-0-0	1823	14
Barber's Kindred	Worlingworth		4-0-0		
Collins, Dinah	Worlingworth		1-18-0		
Newson, James	Worlingworth		3-14-0		
Stearn, John	Worlingworth		5-10-0		

New Purchases by the Trustees of the will of the late Rt. Hon. Lord Henniker in 1823

| Whitmore, Thomas | Mellis | 261-2-0 | 280-0-0 | 1823 | 15 |

Rental to Lady Day 1824

Total Rental £7,554-6-4½   Cash Recd. £5,795-6-5½   Disbursements £1,195-14-4   Arrears £563-5-7

Notes

The 2nd Lord Henniker died in 1821 and he and his wife Emily are recorded by a monument on the north wall of the chancel of Thornham Magna church. As they died without children, his nephew John Minet Henniker inherited the title.

(1)   note above the line 4-3-7
(2)   average price of 192 coombs Wheat. Average to be taken on first Market day in November & the last Market day in April
(3)   map not found
(4)   plus 10 acres late Craske

Index